Carbon Pages

CARBON PAGES

Three Plays by Daniel Gavilovski

/unreal/

Copyright © 2026 Daniel Gavilovski

FIRST EDITION

All rights reserved. No part of this book may be reproduced in any form without written permission from the publisher

This is a work of fiction. Names, characters, places and incidents either are products of the author's imagination or are used fictitiously. Any resemblance to actual events or locales or persons, living or dead, is entirely coincidental.

ISBN 979-8-9946101-0-7
ISBN 979-8-9946101-1-4

Unreal Press is an American independent publisher.

theunrealpress.com
unrealpress.substack.com

Illustrations by Luis Perez-Banus
Cover Design by Daniel Gavilovski
Cover Image: "A cast of the Berlin Archaeopteryx, from the American Museum of National History" by Jason Edwards
Back cover image of Eduard Limonov by Gérard Gastaud.

Table of Contents

A short preface 7

COGNITOHAZARD 9

No Weapon Formed Against You 67

Boring and Broke in Buenos Aires 289

This book is in dedication. To *les monstres sacrés*: sacred monsters.

A short preface

Since the stories that make up this book are so uniquely different from each other, in their subject matter, and in the feelings they're trying to evoke, my publisher has advised me to give the reader a bit of context. This is a collection of plays. There are three of them. I chose *Carbon Pages* as the title because of its connotations with Soviet-era samizdat (or self-published literature) which was printed on exceptionally thin, translucent and cheap carbon paper. *COGNITOHAZARD* is a horror comedy. I was inspired by the great tradition of Grand Guignol plays. These were popular in Paris at the turn of the century and they were fun and suspenseful and weren't afraid of blood, lewdness, and cheap thrills. *Boring and Broke in Buenos Aires* follows a group of digital nomad artists in the Latin capital. For the most part it's a comedy, or as I call it a *tableau vivant*, a painting of foreigners in a beautiful city. It was written over the course of 2023. The third play, *No Weapon Formed Against You* is by far the longest of the collection and is an attempt at an epic drama. It takes place mostly in Russia, following three political maximalists in the years preceding and following the collapse of the USSR and the construction of a new machine.

All three of these plays are 'closet plays' which just means that I intended for them to be just as readable as any short story or novel, rather than existing solely as blueprints for a theatrical production which is what almost all published plays are. *Carbon Pages* is different. My hope is that anyone who has ever read a short story will be able to jump into this collection without struggling to read it.

COGNITOHAZARD was previously staged in Munich under the title *Does No One Remember Vanilla? Boring and Broke in Buenos Aires* has been staged in Dublin, Ireland. The last play has eluded all attempts to be staged.

COGNITO HAZARD

COGNITOHAZARD, noun. an image, signal or idea that refuses to leave the mind and causes psychic harm upon being known.

COGNITOHAZARD

As plays Lo Strano Vizio Della Signora Wardh–Seq. 8

A sparsely decorated post-war Italian bordello. In the foyer there is a till stand and seats and a Cupid sculpture.

With his legs crossed is a customer. The customer is a man in his mid-60s, wearing a clean three-piece. He's waiting around, reading a newspaper. Playing faintly is Françoise Hardy's Italian cover of *J'suis D'accord*. Being frank, it's not very good.

A fat tabby cat brushes up sensuously against the client's legs. For a moment he puts down his paper and strokes the fat cat's spine.

Enters Madame Mandelstam. Mandelstam is in her 50s, tall, elegantly dressed and with class.

MANDELSTAM: Don't touch that thing, Rico.

CUSTOMER: Mandie!

MANDELSTAM: Who knows where it's been—it's Lola's stray.

CUSTOMER: Me and him have a lot in common.

MANDELSTAM: How are you, Rico?

CUSTOMER: My back's aching, and my left leg is stiff as a doorpost, I must've fallen asleep on it.

MANDELSTAM: You should take better care of yourself, or you'll end up like your brother.

CUSTOMER: You're telling me.

> Rico has a real bowler hat kind of accent.

MANDELSTAM: You're not getting any younger!

CUSTOMER: Don't I know it. You know what I read just now? Brother and sister beheaded by father in freak accident. They'd fallen asleep under a hay bale together. Then their father comes in with a pitchfork. A single fork ... and ...! (*pause*)... Think how they must've been lying for it to take *one* skewer.

Carbon Pages

MANDELSTAM: Lord, Rico.

CUSTOMER: In Abruzzo it happened!

MANDELSTAM: You really should cut down on reading the papers, you know that?

CUSTOMER: It would do *you* some good.

MANDELSTAM: Would it now?

CUSTOMER: (*joking*) You might be in them one of these days.

MANDELSTAM: (*catching his drift*) Really?

CUSTOMER: Have you heard about this business of shutting down the maisons?

MANDELSTAM: Have I heard of it? It's all the girls ever talk about.

CUSTOMER: That bloody bitch. Some minister. Hives of disease and degeneracy she's calling them.

MANDELSTAM: Oh stop it.

CUSTOMER: I'd like to show her some disease and degeneracy alright.

MANDELSTAM: Well ...

CUSTOMER: Not in that way.

MANDELSTAM: I worry about the girls, you know. Without this place, where will they go? Feels like forever they've been here—they're ... *family*. Will they be on the streets, pushing punts neath the railway bridge?

CUSTOMER: They could get proper jobs. Work at a toll booth?

MANDELSTAM: No, they're too dense for that.

> Our client smirks. Mandelstam doesn't surrender.

MANDELSTAM: (*dead serious*) They couldn't tie their shoes without me around.

CUSTOMER: (*moving in closer, sophisticated*) And what about you, my dear? What will you do if our dear minister gets her way? Will you move to Austria, or perhaps the sands of Argentina, where the oldest profession is given the respect it

COGNITOHAZARD

has so rightfully grown over the years like a gorgeous sunflower over the ash of a doomed Pompeii?

MANDELSTAM: I'd do what I always do, Rico. Add numbers and push pencils. I'd be in accounting.

CUSTOMER: (*closer*) Madame ...

> Madame reciprocates. Cautiously.

MANDELSTAM: You know how long it's been since I've had a night off, kicked off my shoes-watched the postman-had a glass of wine, how long since I've been caught in a thunderstorm and the warm rain soaking my clothes and sticking to my naked skin and me there not caring, how long since someone's breath sent goosebumps running down my spine and up and around my legs, to my gullet ...

CUSTOMER: Time makes fools of us all, if only one were to recall just how we drank and danced when we were young. Sometimes I think it is only that which we commit to stories and anecdotes that are true and remembered, only the moments which we whisper in ears are real. Memories borne from nights neath cotton thunder clouds, when we are all hidden from God who is distracted and impotent and we make sweet music and tell deep secrets and sing and tell and sing again in the steaming August hay.

MANDELSTAM: (*seductively*) ...

CUSTOMER: (*clueless*) Did you hear about the dead lawyer they found hanging in Gabralzzi's ...
The waiter didn't report it. He thought it was a movie prop from the horror shoot that week.

> Way to delete all sexual tension. Mandelstam puts some distance. Recalls why it didn't work out.

MANDELSTAM: No, can't say I did.

CUSTOMER: Oh I hope my Lola is ready for me, my dear.

MANDELSTAM: Go right ahead. (*yelling upstairs*) We have a gentleman!

Carbon Pages

CUSTOMER: Yes, thank you.

> Rico paces about waiting. Mandelstam scribbles at her till. Sounds of footsteps running down a stairs.

CUSTOMER: (*absent-mindedly*) Lola. Ell-Oh-Ell-Ayy: LO-LA. Fire of my loins, love of my groin. My ELL-OH-ELL ... Eh?

> Rico turns around and finds downstairs has come not his regular Lola, but some totally other prostitute.

CUSTOMER: You're not Lola.

MANDELSTAM: Lola's out. Meet Chichi.

CUSTOMER: (*looking her up and down*) Oh I can't complain, can't complain at all, yes. Have we really never met? But my dear is out is she? Is she feeling okay?

MANDELSTAM: She better not be.

CUSTOMER: Chichi is it?

> Chichi says nothing. Only nods.

CUSTOMER: And ... how long have you been here, Chichi?

> Silently she mimes SIX fingers.

CUSTOMER: What's the matter? You're not Siciliian are you?

MANDELSTAM: Save your breath, Rico, she's mute.

CUSTOMER: Mute?

MANDELSTAM: Yes she doesn't speak.

CUSTOMER: She doesn't or can't?

MANDELSTAM: I don't know. We don't talk much.

CUSTOMER: (*to Chichi*) Is that true, my dear?

> She nods.

CUSTOMER: (*to Mandelstam*) So. How did that happen? Some kind of accident or ...?

COGNITOHAZARD

MANDELSTAM: (*deadpan*) She got sick of silly questions. Now if you don't mind...

CUSTOMER: Oh yes, yes. Well, I dare say be as quiet as you want. It's not talking we'll be doing. And if you're as experienced as your friend was, it might even be a plus. Good chatting to you Mandie!

MANDELSTAM: Ciao, Rico.

>Rico and Chichi "go upstairs" arm in arm.

>Mandelstam is deflated, troubles herself with accounts. When the pair is gone, she crosses herself in jest.

>Enter Lola, wrapped in a ratty fur coat. She's frantic, runs in, glances over her shoulder.

MANDELSTAM: Lola! I have a question. Tell me what time it is.

LOLA: Miss—

MANDELSTAM: I've seen some things in my time. But THREE HOURS LATE? You know if you keep this up..!

LOLA: Miss, is Krystal in?

MANDELSTAM: Now hold on, young lady, and I don't want your excuses. And what are you wearing? Get that thing off, you think I'm running a chapel?

LOLA: I'm sorry, Miss, I was just...

MANDELSTAM: Why are you jittery? Have you been drinking? Is it the drugs again?

LOLA: Miss, something really important came up. But I'm here now. Is Krystal in?

MANDELSTAM: You *are* on something aren't you? Unlike you, Lola, Krystal has been working all day and filling in for you. We have Fabrizzio coming in today, so if you don't get your ass upstairs right now and get into shape I'll have you out on the streets faster than you can say hoopla. Now!

>Lola runs upstairs.

Just about to leave the bedroom are Krystal and a client with a red beard.

The bedroom includes a few stools, a bed stand, classical paintings on the wall of nude women and, naturally, a bed. To the left is a door leading out the hall and downstairs. To the right a door into the powder room.

The two have just done the deed, both are giggly but the belle de nuit is clearly pretending for her victim. As they are about to leave enters Lola, almost colliding with the pair.

KRYSTAL: Lola!

LOLA: Krystal!

RED BEARD: Hosea! Are you joining us?

KRYSTAL: (*cutesy-dutesy voice*) She's just leaving. Twelve, my sweet. Same time next week?

RED BEARD: You know I count the minutes. I have it marked on my calendar. Dentist appointment, it says. I've had thirty-two dentist appointments this year.

Money is exchanged and counted. Krystal's demeanor switches at the drop of a hat to stern and no-nonsense.

KRYSTAL: A girl comes for you and you don't tip?

RED BEARD: Oh, sorry. Um. Yes, sorry, Krystal.

He crumples out a note, all flustered, and hands it to her.

KRYSTAL: (*back to cutesy*) I'm missin' you, love!

She blows a kiss and the customer leaves. They're left alone.

KRYSTAL: What's up with you? You look tired.

Lola locks the door behind her.

COGNITOHAZARD

KRYSTAL: What are you doing that for, huh? You know I have another boy waiting. And where have you been all day? You know you really fucked over the other girls? You're shaking—

LOLA: Listen to me! I need to ask you something.

KRYSTAL: I'm listening.

LOLA: You say I fucked over the other girls. Can you tell me their names?

KRYSTAL: What?

LOLA: The other girls working here at the House. Can you name them to me? One by one.

KRYSTAL: (*realizing Lola is hopped up*) Okay. You. Me. Topaz. And Chichi.

LOLA: That's it?

KRYSTAL: That's it. Minus the Miss.

LOLA: So how many girls is that?

KRYSTAL: Are you on the stuff again?

LOLA: Just tell me.

KRYSTAL: One, Two, Three ... Four.

LOLA: But that don't make sense.

KRYSTAL: Why doesn't it make sense.

LOLA: I must be going crazy or something. But ... Did you stay over at my place last night?

KRYSTAL: Say again?

LOLA: After work, did you go to my place and spend the night there?

KRYSTAL: If you're asking whether we had a sleepover, then I'm telling you no.

LOLA: You're sure?

KRYSTAL: Yes.

LOLA: Are you sure you're sure? Maybe you're not remembering right?

KRYSTAL: (*insinuative...*) I remember where I end up each night.

Carbon Pages

LOLA: Well tell me.

KRYSTAL: Tell you? My last client of the night was a sailor cripple. His *cazzo* was blown off so he just wanted me to whisper his ear with the lights turned off. After an hour of it he refused to pay, before finally admitting he hasn't a penny.

I walked home. My left heel broke on the cobblestone on Via Mazzoni. At home I had some English gin and a vogue. Then I went to bed—alone. And in the morning I woke up—in my own bed—alone. Happy now?

LOLA: Then I don't understand.

KRYSTAL: What don't you understand? You hold us all up for three hours, barge in while I'm with a boy, you're sweaty, pink, look like you haven't slept all night. Then you start interrogating me.

Lola paces around the room. Heads in the bathroom.

LOLA: Maybe it was someone else. But why would I let anyone else in ... I can't think. Can I close this window? It's freezing.

KRYSTAL: (*asserting*) You think you slept with someone.

Lola closes the window.

LOLA: Not slept, exactly. But I just have a hunch ... that someone was in the place with me.

KRYSTAL: You probably took someone home. You drank too much. Wouldn't be the first time. Now look, Lola, I have a boy waiting for me—

LOLA: I didn't drink nothing. I didn't have a single drink.

KRYSTAL: Then you took a *digestif*. Now please ...

Lola blocks the exit.

LOLA: I don't take nothing. You know I don't. And you're wrong: I remember yesterday totally clearly. I remember some child stuck gum in the keyhole and when I put the key in it didn't turn at first and I was scared I had taken a wrong key.

COGNITOHAZARD

I remember the way my sink didn't drip drip when I turned the tap for a second and I was sure the pipes were clogged again but then it went.

> Lola has a tendency to speak in run-on sentences. One gets the impression she forgets her point halfway through any given sentence.

LOLA: I even remember that you *didn't* break your left heel last night. Because you didn't *wear* heels last night because Mandelstam gave you shit about your height so you've worn only flats since Tuesday.

KRYSTAL: (*flustered*) Okay ... No that's right. (*recalling*) So I didn't have heels. And your memory's twenty-twenty. So what's any of this to do with me?

LOLA: So I remember going to bed alone.

KRYSTAL: Okay and?

LOLA: So explain to me this:

> From her handbag Lola unearths a clump of newspaper. She unwraps it revealing ...

KRYSTAL: A toothbrush.

LOLA: I found it right next to mine this morning. In its little cup holder thingy. Right next to the brush I always use. Krys, why would I have two toothbrushes?

KRYSTAL: Okay. I admit that's weird.

LOLA: It's not just weird. It's creepy!

KRYSTAL: I know you're sober. I know. But maybe you bought it absent-mindedly. You forgot. You go shopping for eggs, leave with a toaster—it happens.

LOLA: It's not even new. Look at the bristles, it's older than my one. And this *isn't* mine.

KRYSTAL: I don't know what to tell you.

LOLA: Well I just thought... maybe I'm just having a moment.

KRYSTAL: Lola, it's fine. Here's what—

Carbon Pages

LOLA: I thought maybe you came over while I was sleeping to drop something off and forgot it then I thought maybe it was one of the other girls but they don't know me nearly as well. I don't know. I can't explain it. And I know it doesn't really matter. I mean so what. But I can't wrap my head around it and it makes me feel... (*Puts away toothbrush*) I don't know.

KNOCK KNOCK KNOCK!

KRYSTAL: Lola if *I* don't have *him*, *she'll* have my *head*.

LOLA: I'll take him.

> Lola goes and swings open the door for the client but at the door is no client at all. It's Topaz.

TOPAZ: (*singing*) *At the Copa ... Copacabana, the hottest spot north of Havana.* (*sycophantically*) Lola! Hi...

> Lola shuffles past her, saying nothing.

TOPAZ: What—a—day huh? Busy busy. I never knew so many men came to places like this. I guess they're not ones for telling though, right? Wow. Krystal...

KRYSTAL: Hm?

TOPAZ: I love your earrings.

KRYSTAL: Thanks, Topaz.

TOPAZ: Is Lola alright? She seemed upset. Is it okay if I say that?

> Krystal moves to the door.

TOPAZ: I didn't disturb you did I? Sorry if I did. It's just there's *so* many and I could use a break. But I can leave...

KRYSTAL: No, take the room. I'm done here anyway.

TOPAZ: Everything alright, Krystal?

KRYSTAL: I'm just thinking.

TOPAZ: Are you sure? I'm sorry if I did anything to—

Carbon Pages

KRYSTAL: Lola just spoke to me for the first time in three weeks. First time we talked in three weeks.

TOPAZ: Did you apologize to her?

KRYSTAL: Me? What would *I* have to apologize to *her* about? What do you mean, exactly?

TOPAZ: Nothing. I don't mean nothing.

KRYSTAL: She's all worked up.

TOPAZ: (*carefully*) She's on goofballs, is she?

KRYSTAL: ... No ... Maybe. Either way it's none of your business.

TOPAZ: Oh.

KRYSTAL: I didn't mean it that way. Just put it out of your head, is what I mean. Don't worry about it.

TOPAZ: I bet it's boy trouble. Everyone gets so obsessed—especially the men. Them with their favourites. *Is Krystal in?* they'll ask. *No, I don't want you I want Chichi, Lola. I want Vanilla.* Oh that Vanilla, especially. I've never met her and I hate her already!

KRYSTAL: Wait, say that again?

TOPAZ: What—they love Chichi, Vanilla...

KRYSTAL: Yeah? Vanilla be getting a lot of requests does she?

TOPAZ: *They kiss the floor she walks on.* And I tell them, she don't work here no more. She's moved to France with her boyfriend, see, so unless you want to chase her down you're stuck for the evening with *me*. That is unless you want to go home to your wife. That sets 'em straight.

KRYSTAL: Interesting.

TOPAZ: What is?

KRYSTAL: (*pause*) Nothing. Don't be dallying.

> Krystal exits. Topaz is alone by herself. She enters the little bathroom. Adjusts her hair in the mirror.

COGNITOHAZARD

Then, the CREAK of the door handle.

TOPAZ: (*from bathroom*) Occupied!

Creaking continues incessantly.

TOPAZ: (*leaving bathroom*) I said we're busy!

Creaking continues. She goes to the door.

TOPAZ: Listen you dense faggot, I said—

She OPENS the door. In strides Chichi. She says nothing.

TOPAZ: Oh, it's you! Come in. Hey. Oh I'm sorry, what's your name again? I'm still getting to know everyone. I'm such a fool, like. You're taking a breather too, are you?

Chichi plops down on the bed.

TOPAZ: Say, you don't have a zhoosher do you? My hair's a pig sty. Oh never mind there should be one here.

She finds a brush. Brushes her hair.

TOPAZ: Boy these boys are a handful aren't they? I'm like a hen in a fox den. I just had a chef, a short one. No manners. Unwashed as well. I hate it when you have to wash it for 'em.

Topaz goes and turns on the radio. At a volume which requires her to shout over the music plays *Ça Plane Pour Moi*.

TOPAZ: If you know you're making a night of punting why not give yourself a scrub beforehand. There I am being screwed and all I can think of is gorgonzola. Oh these boys! I hate them. They'll drive me crazy one of these days!

From her intonation we understand that she decidedly does *not* hate them.

> Suddenly, for seemingly no reason at all Topaz gets sullen and slouches on the bed. Even Chichi notices.

TOPAZ: Now I'm upset. Seeing Lola so sour is what did it. I'm sensitive to these things! I can't stand seeing people unhappy. (*affectedly*) *Negativity is infectious.* That's what Dr. Sphink told me at my checkup... Oh you know what?

CHICHI: ...

TOPAZ: I *love* your dress.

CHICHI: ...

TOPAZ: Where'dja get it? I'll get myself a dress like that. Once I leave this place, I mean. I just need to save up. I have it all figured out. I mean, how long have you been here? At the House I mean? I reckon I'll give it five weeks before me and Dino can make ends meet. That's more than enough time. Hey since you're there can you close that window? Freezing my willets. Thanks. Oh, I don't think I've told you about Dino. That's my boyfriend. I miss him so much. It was his idea, you know, me coming here....

> Topaz adjusts her hair in the pocket mirror...

TOPAZ: Hold this please.

> ...smacks down foundation, makes herself pretty while she talks.

Why? Well, we're fixing a boat. We be sailin' to the West Indies. Imagine that? The white sand... the palm trees... the little fishies that tickle your toes. Oh!

> With a devilish whisper:

It's all I think about.

> She takes a good look at Chichi for the first time, then turns down the radio.

TOPAZ: Hey. You're mute. I forgot. And this whole time ... I make such an eedjit of myself!

COGNITOHAZARD

CHICHI: (*shrugs*)

TOPAZ: How'd it happen? If you don't mind me asking?

CHICHI: (begins to open mouth)

TOPAZ: Okay, yes or no questions: Was it an accident?

CHICHI: (mimics no)

TOPAZ: Were you born with it?

CHICHI: (indicates yes)

TOPAZ: Hm ... it runs in your family?

CHICHI: (having fun) (*mimics yes*)

TOPAZ: Hold on. Say 'ahhh' for me. Ahhh. So you have a tongue! Well then. No problems there, is there? That explains why the boys love you so much. It's all they really care about! Chichi isn't it?

> Chichi takes out a cigarette.

TOPAZ: Oh, you want a light, Chichi? Here.

> Topaz lights Chichi's cigarette.

TOPAZ: But anyway, like I was saying about the boat. That costs money. Not so much even the boat itself. We got it from an oyster pirate for dirt. But it's all shabby, the boat. It needs painting. So we decided I'll move down here and make some money while he works on the thing in Genoa. The boat.

> Topaz goes and turns on the radio again—loud.

TOPAZ: (*yelling*) I mean I know what you're thinking: why would I agree to that? Any other man wouldn't even suggest it, but he loves me so hard, and he trusts me so much.

> She heads for the bathroom door.

Carbon Pages

He says to me, What's the big deal? We need the money, and *you'll always be my girl*. And ya know what? He's right!

> Topaz swings open the bathroom door and freezes in something that we can by minimal inspection describe as Terror. Her eyes are glued to a point high up, just out the door. She is totally silent, as if gazing at an erupting volcano.
>
> *Bertrand's* ballistico voice has turned to white static.
>
> Chichi hasn't been looking at Topaz, and so assumes she's mercifully shut up, until she turns around and sees the jabbermouth in shock.
>
> Her shriek shakes the rafters.
>
> Topaz SLAMS shut the door, scrambles to lock it, hugs it with her back. Her face is deformed by a traumatized expression. Behind that door could have been Satan himself.
>
> Chichi runs to catch her but not before Topaz collapses to her chest and buries her face in fear.

TOPAZ: (*deludedly*) Please ... no, please ...

> Chichi is understandably confused. She almost goes to open the door, then decides against it.
>
> Radio's dead.

TOPAZ: Oh don't ... don't ... don't ... (*as if waking from a nightmare*) I'm sorry. That is embarrassing. (*distancing*) I'm always making such a fool of myself. Look at this. I drooled all over your pretty dress, Chichi. I'm sorry. Oh God, I bet I messed up my hair too. I just did it!

> Chichi mimes her utter bewilderment. Then, seeing that Topaz refuses to acknowledge the last minute, she gestures at the door.

TOPAZ: (*perky as a daisy*) Yeah. You're right that's enough nattering. Here talking your head off bout my Dino. You're probably sick of me! I put people

COGNITOHAZARD

through the wringer, I know. You need some peace and quiet and I need to get back to it.

>Topaz goes to the hall door but Chichi grabs her arm, stopping her.

TOPAZ: What is it, Chichi?

>Chichi positions herself between Topaz and the door.

TOPAZ: You're freaking me out a little.

>Before Topaz can leave, Chichi makes one more attempt at recalling her memory. She mimes a hand on throat, yelling, points.

TOPAZ: I really don't know what you're trying to say. Soz, I've always been bad at charades.

>Enter Krystal, exasperated.

KRYSTAL: What the hell's going on? Chichi, you're in here too?

TOPAZ: Nothing, Krystal. I'm just leaving!

KRYSTAL: Did you scream?

TOPAZ: No? Well depends what you mean by scream...

KRYSTAL: It's like herding cats with you all.

TOPAZ: (*confused*) Herding what?

KRYSTAL: I need a mirror. Some idiot just finished in my hair. You have one?

TOPAZ: I don't. Just the one in the powder room.

KRYSTAL: Alright. What are you two still doing here anyway? It's not enough that *Lola's* three hours late...

>This whole time Krystal moving across the room to open the powder room door.

Carbon Pages

KRYSTAL: You okay Chichi?

>Chichi mutely indicates at the door. To stay away from it. That it's dangerous. It's weird.

KRYSTAL: Yeah. It's in the powder room. Gotcha.

>She goes ahead.

>Chichi grabs her by the wrist and kind of re-diverts her into a 180.

KRYSTAL: Chichi, what's the matter? The powder room? What's in there? You know, Topaz?

TOPAZ: No idea.

>Chichi rushes over to her handbag on the other side of the room and pulls out a hand held looking glass. Hands it to Krystal.

KRYSTAL: Thanks. But now I'm curious. (*knock knocks on the door*) Hello? Anyone in there? Is it a client in there Chichi?

>A way out!

CHICHI: (*Nods vigorously*)

TOPAZ: There's no one inside, Krystal. Place is empty. I was just there.

KRYSTAL: Well then I'm going ins—

>Chichi once again yanks Krystal's sleeve from the door. Harder this time. Immediately she uses a key to lock the door.

KRYSTAL: I'm so sick of this...

>Chichi backs away still holding it. She tries to hide it but it's too late.

KRYSTAL: Topaz, help me get that key will you.

COGNITOHAZARD

That initiates a game where the two girls chase Chichi all over the room. She jumps over the bed, dodges all moves.

Without her noticing enters Lola...

...who instantly snags the key from Chichi who's holding it behind her back.

LOLA: What's going on here? (*throws keys over to Topaz*)

KRYSTAL: Chichi's hiding something in the powder room!

TOPAZ: Gonna open it now find a pair of boots and a ladder out the window! (*throws keys to Krystal*)

KRYSTAL: I swear if it's a client...

TOPAZ: Open it, Krystal!

Krystal hunches over the powder room keyhole.

LOLA: Girls ... the Miss ... Miss Mandelstam is dead.

Just as the key was meant to be turned, all eyes fall on Lola.

KRYSTAL: Hush. What'd you say?

LOLA: (*cold*) I was coming down the stairs. Thought there might be clients. Didn't want to keep them waiting cause you know how the Miss gets when you mug her. Then I hear this 'THUD' ... and next thing I see is her lying there on the ground. I got out of there fast as I could.

TOPAZ: Oh my God. How do you know she's dead? Maybe—

LOLA: She's dead.

KRYSTAL: What is it, a heart attack?

LOLA: (*lost*) A heart attack?

KRYSTAL: Yeah?

Carbon Pages

LOLA: No. I don't think so. There's blood getting in all the floor cracks. It's leaking out the gash that's in her throat. To be honest, girls, there's not much left of her neck at all.

TOPAZ: Oh my God.

    Chichi and Topaz run out to see the incident.

KRYSTAL: You're telling the truth?

LOLA: Course I am. Go see for yourself.

KRYSTAL: There's a gash in her throat you said?

LOLA: That's right.

KRYSTAL: That sounds like she was killed.

LOLA: Killed? Sorry. That makes sense. She must've been.

KRYSTAL: Well you're awful calm for someone whose Miss just got murdered.

LOLA: I'm *just* as *terrified* as you are. Know what I'm realizing? We're in danger. Shooed out all the boys and luckily no one saw nothing but—

KRYSTAL: You shooed out the boys? I thought you said you came here fast as you could.

LOLA: Yeah—well, yeah I mean. That's what I meant. You're confusing me is all. We're in serious danger, Krys. I'm confused.

KRYSTAL: Yeah? Why do I feel more in danger than you are?

LOLA: What's that supposed to mean?

KRYSTAL: Nothing. So you saw who did it?

LOLA: Did what?

KRYSTAL: Whoever killed the Miss, Lola.

LOLA: No I didn't see who killed the Miss.

KRYSTAL: But you said you heard the 'THUD'.

COGNITOHAZARD

LOLA: I *did* hear the 'THUD'.

KRYSTAL: And right after you saw the Miss ... the Miss's body.

LOLA: Right.

KRYSTAL: So you must've seen the killer. Him running away at least.

LOLA: I didn't look. I don't know. And I don't like your tone.

>In a bit of a scuffle, Krystal grabs a pill bottle from Lola's pocket.

KRYSTAL: So ... you *are* back on the stuff.

LOLA: That's nothing. I just took a bit this morning. To take the edge off. I told you I was freaked out.

>Enter back in Chichi and Topaz.

>Topaz is wailing, hysterical. She keels over the bed and buries her head in a pillow, sobbing.

>Krystal goes out the hall.

TOPAZ: (*sobbing*) Her head ... her head ... hanging...

>Krystal comes back, brandishing a pair of scissors

KRYSTAL: Chichi will you stay here with her [Topaz]. I'm taking Lola to the station.

LOLA: What station?

KRYSTAL: What do you think?

LOLA: To the *polizia?* Are you out of your mind?!

TOPAZ: The blood ... all the blood...

KRYSTAL: (*to girls*) Keep away from her. *She's* the only one who was down there... *She* killed the Miss.

Carbon Pages

LOLA: You're really out of your mind, you know that. No way I'd ever KILL Miss Mandelstam. Right? I mean yes she wasn't the nicest but...

KRYSTAL: (*brandishing scissors*) Grab whatever you need and get dressed.

LOLA: Girls, won't you say something? You know I did nothing. Topaz? Look. Chichi wants to say something.

> In fact, Chichi is fairly convinced.

KRYSTAL: Let me illuminate ye. For three weeks Lola hasn't spoken to me. After three weeks of silence, she opens her mouth and what's the first thing she has to say?
Rambling about her toothbrush. That she can't remember things.

> Chichi takes notice. She's connecting the dots.

KRYSTAL: I'm sorry, Lola, but you've finally fried any last brains you had left in there.

> Chichi tugs on Krystal's sleeve.

LOLA: I really did kill her didn't I?

KRYSTAL: It's for your own good. This is ... no life. At least behind bars you'll harm no one.

> Chichi keeps trying at Krys' attention.

LOLA: You're right. I've been forgetting things... I'm losing my mind... I'm sorry.

KRYSTAL: What is it Chich? Yeah, I don't have paper on me. Fine, go get a pen and paper.

> Chichi leaves.

> Lola gets dressed, puts things in her handbag.

LOLA: I really didn't mean for this to happen. I'm sorry.

COGNITOHAZARD

TOPAZ: I saw her just this morning...

KRYSTAL: Don't be hard on her. She's turned her brain into leftover sewage.

LOLA: Give it a break.

KRYSTAL: Don't make it difficult on me...

LOLA: (*compliant but indignant*) It *isn't* difficult. You just wanna feel like you're doing a good deed like while locking up your friend.

KRYSTAL: You think I'm happy, that it?

There was a time I'd do anything for you. But the way you've gotten...

> Enter back in Chichi, holding a ballpoint pen and a box of Kleenex tissues.
>
> She removes a tissue and starts scribbling.

TOPAZ: What's she drawing?

KRYSTAL: She's writing.

LOLA: Okay let's go.

KRYSTAL: You first (pointing with scissors)

> Lola leaves the room, Krystal goes to follow but...:

CHICHI: (hands Krystal the tissue)

KRYSTAL: I can't be leaving Lola. Topaz see what she has to say won't you? (*hands back tissue*)

(*leaves*)

TOPAZ: Sure, one sec.

> Chichi hurries over, relieved.

TOPAZ: What is it?

> Chichi hands the note. Topaz reads over it. Then again. Then again.

Carbon Pages

TOPAZ: God this ... this is silly. I really make such a retard out myself. Sorry, Chich. I ... (*laughs nervously*) ... I can't read. (*hands back note*)

> In any other sex comedy which our characters would ordinarily inhabit, this would be the punchline. But for Chichi, it's the end of the line. Her last hope has been dashed, and she's condemned herself to an eternal Tartarus.

TOPAZ: I never learnt.

> A wave of terror washes over Chichi's face, as if Topaz is some demon. She backs away.

> She hesitates by the Powder Room door. Then she opens the Hall door and sees no one outside.

> She takes a pot of flowers and SMASHES it against the floor.

TOPAZ: What'd you do *that* for?

> Enter Krystal. Lola is in the doorway.

KRYSTAL: I ... forgot my vogues.

> She strides over, as a stern Italian mother might with a son, not breaking eye contact with Chichi and

> GRABS the tissue out of Chichi's hand.

KRYSTAL: (*reading*) Topaz ... it's about you.

TOPAZ: Me?

KRYSTAL: Come read this.

TOPAZ: I can't read.

KRYSTAL: (*to Lola*) You. Read this.

> Lola takes the tissue and:

COGNITOHAZARD

LOLA: (*reads it to herself, then asks*) Did you see anything before Mandelstam was killed?

TOPAZ: (*glances at Krystal*) Me? No. Well, depends. Me and Chichi were talking and then you ... and the Miss...

LOLA: Well this says...
"Topaz and I were *alone* in *this* room right before Mandelstam was killed.

Topaz was talking a lot. About her boyfriend. About work. It was exhausting, no offense Topaz.
Just before leaving she opened the powder room door"...
(*improvising*) She says you saw something that scared the wits off you. She never saw someone more terrified. "You screamed and screamed."

TOPAZ: I did not.

LOLA: I'm just reading what she's saying.

TOPAZ: Well, what happened after?

> Jackrabbit-quick Chichi scribbles another note and hands it to Lola:

LOLA: (*briskly*) "You couldn't remember a thing. It was as if nothing happened."

TOPAZ: If it was so scary why can't I remember it?

LOLA: (*to Chichi*) Why can't she remember it?

> Chichi writes and hands:

LOLA: "I don't know."

TOPAZ: Ask her If *she* saw it.

LOLA: (*to Chichi*) Did you see it?

> Chichi writes and hands:

LOLA: No.

TOPAZ: Ask her—

Carbon Pages

KRYSTAL: For Shit's sake she's mute not deaf. What are you translating for?

TOPAZ: (*offended*) TransLATIng? I'm transLATIng now, am I?

KRYSTAL: It's a word not a jab, calm yourself, woman.

LOLA: But how's that possible. Don't you remember before and after...

TOPAZ: That's if she's not lying.

KRYSTAL: Chichi don't know *how* to lie.

TOPAZ: I recall everything. I did open this door. I guess it's a bit fuzzy ... but everything after is clear as day.

LOLA: So what's it to do with anything? The Miss is still dead, and I still killed her. Take me away, what are we wasting time for.

KRYSTAL: Now hold on. Everyone just ... wait. *There's something seriously off in this bordello.*

All eyes on Krystal, everyone listens.

KRYSTAL: This morning, *you* came to me saying someone you can't remember left a toothbrush at your place.

Then Topaz can't remember something she saw five minutes ago...

And now the Miss is lying on the floor downstairs.

Now, maybe I'm crazy. But something's making us forget things.

LOLA: Making us forget things...

KRYSTAL: I don't know how, but I bet whoever's scary enough to make Topaz scream, is also who murdered our Miss.

LOLA: Sure.

TOPAZ: Why can't I remember...

KRYSTAL: I don't know. But here's what I *do* know. If we're not careful, I'd say we could be forgotten too.

LOLA: Where'd you pull that from?

COGNITOHAZARD

TOPAZ: I'm not following.

KRYSTAL: I'll tell you. You all wanna know something *really* fucked? It's something ... *you* ... told me this morning—I didn't think much of it until now. Apparently someone came in asking to do Vanilla. Misses her like all hell, he does.

TOPAZ: Well, it's not a "he" exactly, Krys. Can I call you Krys by the way? Three different boys have asked for her just this week, wondering if she'll be back.

What?

> At this point the three experienced girls—Krystal, Lola, and Chichi—are looking at each other as if to say *"this is majorly weird"*.

> But why?

KRYSTAL: (*to Lola*) Djuanna tell her?

LOLA: Topaz ... no one's ever worked here with that name.

TOPAZ: How do you mean?

LOLA: Just that. They must be thinking of a different brothel.

TOPAZ: There in't one for *miles*, you told me yourself.

LOLA: Right. So are you sure you've not been mishearing them?

TOPAZ: But I thought this was the girl that was here before me. That's what I've been telling everyone... I'm sure.

LOLA: What girl?

TOPAZ: Y'know. That one who moved to France with her boyfriend you were telling me about.

KRYSTAL: (*to Lola*) She's thinking of Genova. (*back to Topaz*) She left a month before you came.

Carbon Pages

LOLA: She had that thing ... always with the cleaning ...

KRYSTAL: A germaphobe, is what she's called. Sweet girl she was, but not so popular with the boys was she? Always with the takeyershoesoff and the changingthesheets. Trust me, no one's coming in asking her.

TOPAZ: So how come people are begging for this other girl?

KRYSTAL: I don't know. Fact is, *there never was no Vanilla.*

LOLA: Or we don't remember her.

KRYSTAL: That's what I'm thinking. In't it weird? You come to me saying someone left a toothbrush at your place. And now there's a girl who apparently worked here, fucked here, and, I think, had to sleep somewhere too.

LOLA: So what was she—my roomie? Vanilla lived with me?

KRYSTAL: Say she did.

TOPAZ: This is crazy. So, some girl exists who we can't remember. Same with the killer. So then there's only one answer left: Vanilla was who I saw.

LOLA: Vanilla is the killer?

KRYSTAL: Hold on. Just because we forgot Vanilla don't mean she's the killer. She disappeared all total like. Where'd she go?

TOPAZ: Left her toothbrush. Must've been in a hurry.

KRYSTAL: Such a hurry that I think she got killed. Just like the Miss.

TOPAZ: So why can't we remember her?

KRYSTAL: Maybe if you get murdered you get forgotten too.

TOPAZ: Well none of us have forgotten Miss Mandelstam have we? (*to Chichi*) Have you?

LOLA: None of us saw her get killed either.

A pause...

KRYSTAL: So make a note. You think not only is the killer un-rememberable, but also whoever you see *with* him...?

COGNITOHAZARD

TOPAZ: Now you're just making things up. How do you know that? How do you know the killer makes you forget things? Doesn't make sense!

KRYSTAL: Well none of this makes sense, really. I mean *you're* the one who saw him. You mind just telling us what he was doing?

TOPAZ: I ... can't remember.

KRYSTAL: Thought as much.

TOPAZ: Can I be honest? I'm totally confused-like.

LOLA: Here's what I'm thinking. Whoever killed this Vanilla girl, whoever made it as if she never existed, is also the same person that did Mandelstam ten minutes ago. And the same person that scared *you*, Topaz, like hell in the Powder Room.

TOPAZ: Wouldn't that mean he's still...

> Chichi indicates head towards door.

KRYSTAL: ...behind that door.

> Girls give each other a look, and back away from the powder room door.

LOLA: (*to Krystal*) Djou still have the key?

KRYSTAL: Topaz. I gave it to you!

TOPAZ: Yeah it's right here...

LOLA: It's a serial killer I'd say. They always be going for ladies of the night.

TOPAZ: Ask him if he's a serial killer.

LOLA: Why me?

KRYSTAL: I'm going nowhere near it.

LOLA: (*inching closer*) Hello? We know you're in there. Who are you? (*to girls*) He's saying nothing.

TOPAZ: Say if he tells us what he wants we'll let him leave. Obviously we won't *actually*...

Carbon Pages

Lola inches right up to the door and gives a *knock knock*.

In answer the door goes SLAM! SLAM!

The girls give a shriek, Lola jumps back.

TOPAZ: That door'll stay, yeah?

KRYSTAL: I seen a man bust through a door once. Broke his shoulder, but he did it.

SLAM! SLAM!

LOLA: No way he's getting through that.

KRYSTAL: I think we're safe.

TOPAZ: That's it. I'm leaving!

KRYSTAL: Where are you going?

TOPAZ: (*hysterics*) To the *polizia*! Miss Mandelstam is still lying there downstairs in a mess. I'm telling them everything that happened. They'll help us. They'll sort everything out!

KRYSTAL: Look at us. Four whores. You're gonna tell them about the killer that can't be remembered?

TOPAZ: I'm not listening to you!

KRYSTAL: Or about the girl who found her who's hopped up on pills. Or that you're the only one who saw him and don't remember what he looks like?

TOPAZ: (*wailing*) Who gives a fuck??! You're talking about it! Like this is a normal situation. This—isn't normal, Krystal! I mean—hopped up, drugs, who gives a shit? Words mean nothing. We get the fuck out of here. I mean—you're thinking about it—You can't think about it—You're going to die! I say just scram! Who's with me? Chichi?

Chichi writes something down. Lola reads.

LOLA: Yeah. I don't want to be put in a nuthouse either.

COGNITOHAZARD

TOPAZ: (*succumbing*) Oh my God! You people are crazy! We're going to die! Just like Mandelstam! I'll never see the West Indies!

KRYSTAL: Fine. We'll go the *polizia*. Just give us a minute will you? I still don't understand how he can make us forget things.

LOLA: Why "he"? Maybe it's a lady behind that door.

KRYSTAL: I've never seen a lady do *that* to someone.

LOLA: I've not seen no man do it neither.

TOPAZ: Communists.

LOLA: What?

TOPAZ: It's one of those, oh what do you call em ... operations.

KRYSTAL: Operations?

TOPAZ: That's right, like in the movies. They use all these kinds of gizmos for secret operations and stuff. Maybe one of 'em was in here. That's why we can't remember them, they wipe our minds so we don't blow their cover. They do this kinda stuff you know.

LOLA: That's right, my cousin is a communist.

TOPAZ: They use drugs even. I hear they inject people with drugs without them knowing and it makes them forget things.

LOLA: I have a friend who works at Pasolini's and she has a regular who said men in suits kidnapped him while sleeping.

TOPAZ: When was this?

LOLA: Two weeks ago, not even.

KRYSTAL: And what exactly does Mandelstam have to do with it. What, was she an agent?

LOLA: You're laughing but that happened in Germany. Didn't they be taking Hitler's favourite *brothel* and replacing the girls with Nazi *hookers* and spying on the officers like.

KRYSTAL: Gimme a break.

TOPAZ: Wait a minute. Where's my lighter? I left it right here, I swear. Did one of ye take it?

LOLA: I didn't.

KRYSTAL: Not me.

TOPAZ: Well wait just a minute. Someone must've ... otherwise ... where is it ... I could've sworn—Oh. It's here. That's right I left it here.

LOLA: I heard a story once about this one lad. A friend of a client.

One day he finds this handwritten note, telling him to turn off the lights when he leaves the room. It's weird yeah? But he forgets about it. The next morning he finds a note telling him to close the toilet seat. He's confused right, because the guy lives all alone, no wife, no kids—nothin'. He's a fairly big salesman. Pretty rich, very brainy. But he never made the time to start a family.

Day after day he finds notes. So when he leaves for work he locks the doors, shuts the windows. Still when he comes home he finds a sea of 'em. There's no sign of breaking in so he figures, the only person with a key is his landlady. She's really old. We're talking like almost one hundred or something. So he's fumin' yeah? He's all pissed that she keeps breaking in and leaving these notes for him. He's gonna show her a piece of his mind so he makes his way up to her apartment and finds her place filled with doctors. She died from a stroke days ago. He's all confused, and back home he finds his whole KITCHEN has been plastered with notes like *turn off the lights* and *clean up after yourself* and that kinda stuff and *change the bins*.

TOPAZ: Then what?

LOLA: Well listen. He keeps living like that, trying to ignore it. But eventually he goes loony. He's convinced he's being haunted. Finally he hangs himself. They do an autopsy on him afterwards, right. They cut him open to check if he was killed or whatever and the doctors find that his head's muzzy from poison gas. Turns out his home had a gas leak and he was breathing that stuff all day.

He was writing the notes to himself, leaving them around the house and forgetting, again and again.

TOPAZ: (*revelation!*) So the House has a gas leak.

COGNITOHAZARD

LOLA: I *have* been getting headaches lately.

TOPAZ: Me too!

LOLA: That's why we're forgetting things.

TOPAZ: And you know, come to think of it. Three nights ago I forgot my lighter at home. I never forget my lighter!

LOLA: We must've been breathing it for *days* then!

TOPAZ: So someone's doing it on purpose.

LOLA: That's right. Hoaxers probably, to get out of paying.

TOPAZ: Hoaxers, and it would only make sense that they're communists.

KRYSTAL: Jayzusmaryandjoseph Toe wouldja ever shut the fuck up about communists? It might not be a gas leak even. I've had no headaches, (to Chichi) have you? And how would that explain Mandelstam being killed?

God you get these ideas in your heads, they're like molerats making a nest up there, and then you just run with them.

TOPAZ: I was gonna say something. But now I'm not sure you want to hear it.

LOLA: Just say it.

TOPAZ: Well it's something I noticed. About ... the Miss ... her body. This is gonna sound crazy.

KRYSTAL: Can't get much crazier than this.

TOPAZ: Well I thought nothing of it at first. But she's just stuck in my mind, and something keeps jumping out at me. There's this ... stuff all over the floor where she was lying.

LOLA: Blood?

TOPAZ: Not blood. It reminded me of something. I stepped in it by accident. Right in the middle. It's sticky—like glue, I was scared my shoe was ruined. I had to slip my foot out then yank it out by hand, and it pulled this long rope of the stuff. Stuck to the heel, it was. Smells rotten too. Then it hit me. It reminds me of ... you know how some stranger's dog might come up and starts licking you all over, and you'll try to get it off but it keeps smacking its filthy lips all over your fingers or your feet or whatever. Slobberin' over you something nasty. That's kind of what's in a puddle all over the floor where the Miss be lying.

LOLA: Slobber?

TOPAZ: Like, drool.

LOLA: Ew.

TOPAZ: And it's a lot, see. I mean a bucket's worth.

KRYSTAL: You're right. I didn't think of it at first, but now that you mention it...

LOLA: I saw it too. You know, you think she was stabbed? Like with a knife? I mean, to me it looks like a big bite taken out of her. Like whoever killed her was *eating* her and didn't finish the job.

KRYSTAL: Oh Lord...

TOPAZ: Eating her ... as in...

LOLA: I mean I don't know. Maybe he's a killer cannibal.

TOPAZ: Maybe he's not a cannibal. Or a person at all. I mean think *how big* you'd have to be to try eat a whole lady.

KRYSTAL: What, an animal?

TOPAZ: It would have to be massive. Like *The Blob*. It's about this big ugly monster yeah and it slimes about the town killing all these American teenagers with their cars. It's like a big lump of jelly. The more people it eats the bigger it gets.

LOLA: Maybe it's a vampire? That's why we haven't seen him? They love skimpy women, vampires. Like Dracula. And then he turns into a bat and hides away. That's why we haven't seen him before.

TOPAZ: You think Dracula is behind that door?

LOLA: Not Dracula. There are other vampires, you spaz.

TOPAZ: I am not a spaz. And vampires aren't real!

LOLA: They are so!

COGNITOHAZARD

TOPAZ: (mocking) They are so!

LOLA: Alright sheesh, I'm sorry.

TOPAZ: Look through the keyhole!

KRYSTAL: There's an idea.

LOLA: How did we not think of that!

LOLA: (*struggling*) No, I'm seeing nothing.

TOPAZ: Let me look! (*peeking*) It's just the powder room. Whole place is a mess—all smashed up like. Looks like a hurricane tore through.

KRYSTAL: Don't tell me it's gone...

LOLA: You see the window, yeah?

TOPAZ: Nah, no way it gets through that.

KRYSTAL: Well, how do you know? We don't even know what it looks like.

LOLA: Come to think of it, we haven't heard from it in a while. You think it's still in there?

TOPAZ: It's just out of sight I bet—keeping quiet.

LOLA: Maybe it's invisible.

TOPAZ: What's that mean?

KRYSTAL: Means you can't see it, like. Like a ghost.

TOPAZ: Ah yeah invisible! So that means ... he could be in this room right now...

KRYSTAL: ...

CHICHI: ...

>   The girls check their surroundings.

>   Lola goes to the Hall door, checks the handle, creeps it open, before locking it good.

LOLA: How long has this door been unlocked?

Carbon Pages

(It's been a while).

KRYSTAL: Well what are you all looking at me for? What am I, the only one here? Anyway, it can't be invisible. Topaz saw it clear as day. (*looking through keyhole*) What makes it weird is that there's no way to remember it. Wait ... I see it... There's my stuff. Making a mess of everything ... It's gone.

LOLA: What'd it look like?

> Krystal shrugs. Chichi smokes.

TOPAZ: Chichi, can you use an ashtray — Puh-Lease! You spill that ash and whaddya know it ends on my feet and all over the floor and my shoes which I *just* bought!

LOLA: Hold on, you realize we haven't seen anything left behind by this thing this whole time?

KRYSTAL: As in?

LOLA: Even if we can't remember it, wouldn't it leave prints?

TOPAZ: Prince?

LOLA: Fingerprints, like. There weren't even a stain.

KRYSTAL: Lola's right. Like in the Maigret films.

> Lola scouring the room, under the bed, behind cupboards etc.

TOPAZ: I don't— What are you staring at? (*breaks off*)

> Chichi stares at the ceiling. Something's caught her eye. Topaz looks, then the rest.

LOLA: One, two, three...

KRYSTAL: That's a lot.

> Their eyes follow the ceiling to the door.

TOPAZ: They're all over the ceiling.

COGNITOHAZARD

KRYSTAL: Looks a bit like a painting I saw once.

LOLA: They lead to the door ... and back ... and—all around the place.

TOPAZ: Fuck!

KRYSTAL: Did you lock the downstairs?

TOPAZ: I don't know ... maybe ... no. Did you, Chichi?

LOLA: It was in here...

> Chichi shakes head. They're all dead terrified.

KRYSTAL: So if it got out the window, whatever killed Mandelstam could waltz right back inside the House. And then what's our plan.

TOPAZ: I just... didn't think ... I was scared...

LOLA: You notice how the door makes a squeaking sound?

KRYSTAL: Which door, this one?

LOLA: No. The one downstairs.

KRYSTAL: Not really.

LOLA: Well I have. Maybe you didn't notice it but I did, once. It only takes the once. When I was on the stuff. It zooms your senses like. So that a pin dropping makes you jump or drawing a cigarette makes you cough up your lung juice like you're twelve again and it's the same with the squeaky door cause when it squeaks—it's a CANNON. Makes a noise each time a client walks in. It BLARED that day. Was all I could focus on. Even when mollying. It freaked me out. And that freaks boys out that you're freaked out so they can't get it on with you. They'd be all thrusting like and all I could do was think about the person swinging open that door causing it to squeak and I could see him in the ceiling flakes with his bowler hat and his buttons and the grease stain on his sleeve.

Even when I stopped taking pills it was there. It's drilled in forever, I guess. I work fine now, it doesn't bother me. But I'm just saying.

KRYSTAL: What are you saying?

LOLA: So, that door didn't squeak. Not a single time we were talking. Which means *whatever killed Mandelstam is still in that room*. Or at least not downstairs.

Carbon Pages

KRYSTAL: Well it's being awful quiet...

You have to remember *something*, surely?

TOPAZ: I'm telling you, no.

KRYSTAL: You're the first who saw it. Maybe if you really think *hard*? Give us something?

TOPAZ: I opened the door to check my hair, next thing I know I'm crying over Chichi. It's like the *worst* hangover! If you hadn't told me about it, I wouldn't know anything's off at all. I'm thinking, you know maybe we've all seen it before and can't remember. Who knows. Who knows how long that thing's been here.

LOLA: Maybe it's been picking off girls and eating them for years and we keep on forgetting and we're the last ones left until it gets us. Maybe it lives here and we be guesting.

KRYSTAL: For the love of...

> This is as depressing as it is likely. Krystal sits down on the floor at the foot of the bed. She needs a cigarette.
>
> Topaz puts her ear to the door.

TOPAZ: I think I can hear it stumbling. Or maybe not.

> Lola—who throws off her shoes to the corner—and Topaz have cigarettes with Krystal.

LOLA: Is it morning, Chich? Maybe it's almost morning. Feels like a bad dream. I just want to see the sun.

KRYSTAL: (*singing tune*) *Her name was Lola. She was a showgirl... yellow feathers in her hair, and a dress cut down to there*

LOLA: Cut it out will you.

KRYSTAL: I got it from *her* [Topaz]

TOPAZ: I got it from the radio.

KRYSTAL: It's stuck in my head now.

COGNITOHAZARD

TOPAZ: Earworm.

    Chichi writes down a note. Krystal reads.

KRYSTAL: It's dark. Look she even drew a little moon and stars and everything.

LOLA: Damn.

KRYSTAL: Well I think it's nice.

LOLA: Do you three think maybe it's a demon behind there?

KRYSTAL: Demon? Where'd you get that idea?

LOLA: Well, the Bible. I was reading it the other day—

KRYSTAL: You reading The Bible!

LOLA: Just thought it might be interesting.

KRYSTAL: (*sardonic*) Sure won't we all be reading Bibles soon...

LOLA: I might apply for a dairy license I thought. Open a gelato shop.

KRYSTAL: You and Vanilla. What about you Chichi? Where are you going once it's axed?

    Chichi writes.

KRYSTAL: (*reads*) A vineyard, yeah?

> As the girls kill time, stands up Topaz and walks to the center of the room, and it's like a spotlight blankets her and everyone else disappears. To *Don't Believe* by Vashti Bunyan Topaz dances. She has on a pair of tap shoes and a lot like Christina Ricci's scene in *Buffalo '66* for that minute or so and with flourish they do be tapping upon the floor.
>
> Then the spotlight shares with the other girls again and Topaz returns to her position as if nothing happened and it did not.

LOLA: What about you, Krystal?

Carbon Pages

KRYSTAL: Me? Ah, I'll think of something...
Know who else would keep going as if nothing happened? The clients. Oh Mandelstam? She must've retired ... well good for her ... now back to business ... Where's that Lola of mine ... how's Topaz doing.

TOPAZ: Oh no one asks about me.

LOLA: Oh they do. Now me, I'm no one's favourite.

TOPAZ: That's not true!!!

LOLA: Oh no one likes me.

TOPAZ: They do!!

KRYSTAL: Hun they ask for Lola all the time.

LOLA: Really?

KRYSTAL: Just this morning some fit bloke wanted to see you.

LOLA: Was he tall?

KRYSTAL: He was.

LOLA: I think I know who it is. That makes me feel good.

KRYSTAL: Yeah, you're the most requested girl after Chichi.

TOPAZ: Idea! You only forget about it once you stop looking at it, right?

LOLA: Yeah.

TOPAZ: How about this. One of us gets in there real quick and yells out to the others what they see.

KRYSTAL: You'd get killed doing that. Yelling will scare it like a pound dog.

TOPAZ: Then how about one of us draws what it looks like?

KRYSTAL: It'll take too long. You wanna be in and out.

LOLA: Doesn't have to be a masterpiece or nothing. Just a—what do you call it—a sketch.

TOPAZ: Yeah. Just so we know what we're dealing with.

LOLA: Well, say we try it.

COGNITOHAZARD

TOPAZ: So who here's best at drawing?

> Eyes look each other before everyone's gaze arrives at quiet Chichi, the foremost artist of the group.
>
> Krystal steps in between Chichi and the girls, as if saying "you'll have to go through me".

TOPAZ: Well then we'll never know!

> Chichi steps up. She's gonna go in.

KRYSTAL: (*sympathetic*) Don't do it...

TOPAZ: Are you sure, Chichi?

> Chichi nods.

LOLA: (*looking through the hole*) It's quiet. I think if we're quiet as well... if we don't startle it... We're gonna lock that door behind you.

TOPAZ: That'll take too long. You'll have to *un*lock it.

LOLA: Fine, let's not lock it. We'll hold it shut. Give you ten seconds to screeve it down. Don't have to be fancy—

KRYSTAL: Five seconds.

CHICHI: (*puts up 6 fingers.*)

TOPAZ: Six seconds.

LOLA: If you need to get out early, knock. If you're in danger, knock. If we hear *nothing* and I mean *nothing* from you, then...

KRYSTAL: Then that door is *getting* locked. I won't have that thing prancing about the Miss's House again. Take the scissors.

> Scissors are handed.

LOLA: Ready?

CHICHI: (*nods*)

Carbon Pages

>Lola unlocks the door... and flings it open before Chichi steps in with pen and paper.

>Lola holds the door shut. Hard.

>Topaz counts.

TOPAZ: (*slow as can be*) One...Two...Three...Four...Five...Six...

>*She looks at the others before continuing.*

KRYSTAL: Chichi!

TOPAZ: Seven...Eight...

>Each digit is sapped with less and less hope.

TOPAZ: Nine...Ten...Elev—

>KNOCK KNOCK!

TOPAZ: Open it! Quick!

>Lola THROWS the door open and out stumbles down to the floor Chichi covered in a viscous black goop.

KRYSTAL: Oh shit!

TOPAZ: You okay?

LOLA: What's that all over you?

TOPAZ: Look, it's on the scissors too.

LOLA: Fuck off, you chibbed it?

KRYSTAL: Fucking hell, she chibbed it.

LOLA: It must've tried some funny business.

TOPAZ: Did you get a drawing at least?

CHICHI: (*nods*) (and takes the paper and pen from out of a pocket)

COGNITOHAZARD

She got the drawing. And it's not half bad either.

All the girls gather round the kleenex sketch Krystal's holding while Chichi wipes herself off with a towel.

Silence...

...then...

LOLA: Ah you're shittin me.

KRYSTAL: No way.

TOPAZ: Oh God.

Krystal, enraged, crumples up the kleenex and throws it as far as she can.

KRYSTAL: No matter what we do! For nothing!

TOPAZ: It's blank. How is it blank!

Chichi, confused, uncrumples the Kleenex, examines it. Her drawing has disappeared.

She tries to "explain herself"

KRYSTAL: Yeah, I know you sketched it. I know.

TOPAZ: Well it's went west. Why?

KRYSTAL: My memories, drawings. It's all the same to that fuckin vampire son of a bitch. Erases it like a blackboard.

SLAM! SLAM!

KRYSTAL: Was a stupid idea.

TOPAZ: It's for nothing.

KRYSTAL: Quit your whinging... My fault for thinking four hookers could come up with a half decent idea between 'em!

TOPAZ: I'm not one!

Carbon Pages

KRYSTAL: Whatcha mean you're not one?

TOPAZ: I mean I'm not really a hooker.

LOLA: What are you on about?

TOPAZ: I mean I'm just here to earn a bittabob. Only for a few weeks, you know? I'm not really like you all. Really in the business like.

KRYSTAL: You're no different from us. You sleep around for money.

TOPAZ: I'm not a hooker just cause I work in a bordello.

KRYSTAL: Look at her! This in't no *bordello* ... it's a *whorehouse*. And YOU'RE the whore.

TOPAZ: Unlike you Krystal, I actually have a life outside of this. I have a home, see. I have a boat. I have a boat, see and I have a boyfriend!

KRYSTAL: Oh you mean your pimp?

TOPAZ: My what!?

LOLA: Alright, ladies.

KRYSTAL: Your pimp!

TOPAZ: He's not a pimp. We're gettin' married.

KRYSTAL: Oh he's not a pimp, I forgot. You just send him cash while he fucks a new Genoan girl every week but he's not a pimp.

TOPAZ: You take that back, Krystal! I ... He loves me!

LOLA: Lay off her, will ya Krystal?

KRYSTAL: And what are you yammering on about? Whole reason we're in this mess is 'cause of you!

LOLA: How's it my fault?

KRYSTAL: You and your fucking toothbrush. I don't know how but I'd bet everything I own it's your fault.

LOLA: Excuse me, you tried to have *me* booked the second the Miss got killed.

COGNITOHAZARD

TOPAZ: Ladies! Why are you two always at each other? I swear you're like... peas and beans. What happened between you?

KRYSTAL: It's none of your business.

LOLA: It's just the way *she is*.

TOPAZ: Why don't you talk it out?

LOLA: There's nothing to talk out. Keep your nose out of it.

TOPAZ: Fine, don't tell me. Do *you* know? (Chichi)

CHICHI: (*shrug*)

TOPAZ: Your eye shadow's messed up, Krystal. I don't mean nothing by it. You want me to do your eyeshadow for you?

KRYSTAL: What's it matter? We're not on the job.

TOPAZ: It'll make you feel better.

KRYSTAL: Sure. No, wait. All my stuff is...

TOPAZ: ...in the powder room.

KRYSTAL: In the powder room. Under the mirror I have this dear bottle of... hm—see, I can't recall what it is even—

TOPAZ: Revlon Rouge?

KRYSTAL: No, not Revlon Rouge. I remember it's not that—

TOPAZ: Luminescence Elegance?

> That Topaz can pronounce a word I can't even spell stumps Krystal.

KRYSTAL: No... Not that either—

TOPAZ: (*no doubt*) Then it must be Golden Glamour!

KRYSTAL: (*thinks for a moment*) Yeah... I guess it must be.

LOLA: That's right you have a Golden Glamour.

LOLA: If you can't recall it, then it must be it.

COGNITOHAZARD

KRYSTAL: That's right isn't it.

TOPAZ: I don't follow.

LOLA: It's only Golden Glamour she's forgotten, so that's what must be on the shelf.

KRYSTAL: Well, was. All smashed up I bet. And I'm the one paying for them I bet—

LOLA: You don't recall them smashing?

KRYSTAL: I don't.

LOLA: Well then they must've smashed.

>Moment of silence where all absorb this information. It's seemingly obvious, but reveals a deeper truth:

KRYSTAL: That's a good point. Come to think of it I've never heard of Golden Glamour in my life.

TOPAZ: You've never heard of it?!! Impossible. It's the only thing worth getting this year. Dino went all the way to Rome to—

KRYSTAL: I'm just saying that... Here's the deal yeah. Listen. We don't know what that thing *is*. But you wanna know what I think? I think we can narrow down what it's *not*.

LOLA: (*giddy*) *At the Copa ... Copacabana, the hottest spot north of Havana ...* In't that a deadly fuckin idea! So it's like by process of...

KRYSTAL: ...emanation.

>SLAM! SLAM! ... an alien SCREECH!

LOLA: Right so by process of emanation let's do that.

KRYSTAL: Alright so who's seen it?

LOLA: Everyone but me.

TOPAZ: Right. So, where do we begin?

Carbon Pages

KRYSTAL: Lola, ask us about it. Something. Anything you want to know about the thing behind that door.

LOLA: I'll make it a Yes or No question. Let's start simple. "Is it a square?"

KRYSTAL: No, I dunno what it is, but I know it's NOT a square.

LOLA: Okay, it's not a square.

TOPAZ: How does that help us?

KRYSTAL: Well that means we know it's something that's not a square. Look that's already something—one step closer, no? Okay next...

LOLA: Is it a circle?

KRYSTAL: It's not a circle—

> Topaz has had enough of this theoretical mumbo jumbo. Let's get to the point, she thinks.

TOPAZ: (*interrupting*) —Does it walk on six legs?

CHICHI: (shakes head)

KRYSTAL: No.

TOPAZ: Yeah, I know it don't walk on six legs... Does it walk on four legs?

> Girls ponder for a moment.

KRYSTAL: Nope.

TOPAZ: Then it must walk on 2 legs!

KRYSTAL: Well hold on. Maybe it walks on a hundred.

LOLA: Or one or three or maybe it's a big jelly with no legs.

KRYSTAL: It'll take ages to narrow it down.

TOPAZ: Oh my God, we'll be here all night!

> Just then a MEOWING SOUND by the hall door.

TOPAZ: (*SHRIEK*) ARGH! What is that!!

COGNITOHAZARD

She runs and hides behind Chichi.

Lola goes to look.

KRYSTAL: It's just Lola's cat.

TOPAZ: A what?!

LOLA: Ohh ... come here sweetie-kins. Shoo hunny—shoo, shoo. (*to girls*) It's so cute!

TOPAZ: It's like a ... tiger ... but small.

LOLA: You never seen a cat before?

TOPAZ: Obviously not! I've never seen one of those ... things before!

LOLA: How'd she forget cats?

KRYSTAL: Must've seen one along with the thing 'hind the door.

LOLA: It's okay, Tope, it's harmless.

KRYSTAL: Or maybe the creature looks like a cat. Does that make sense?

TOPAZ: (*bemused*) It's weird!

LOLA: (*slams door shut*) So what, the creature is like, cat-like?

KRYSTAL: Okay! I got it! Everyone think of what you can't remember! That's how we narrow it down.

TOPAZ: How are we meant to know what we can't remember? *We can't remember!*

LOLA: Well... (*to Krystal*) It's a small thing. But when we were fighting, you didn't know what a tie was. I thought that was strange.

KRYSTAL: There's no such thing.

LOLA: You know. A tie. Men put it around their necks.

KRYSTAL: Okay.

LOLA: ...What kind of a monster wears a tie?

TOPAZ: Who do you see every day that would wear a tie?

Carbon Pages

LOLA: Clients.

TOPAZ: So maybe it's not exactly a monster, but someone we've all been with.

KRYSTAL: You think what's behind that door is a regular?

SLAM! SLAM!

LOLA: Would explain why we all remember different things. Or *don't* remember different things.

KRYSTAL: Okay, what else, what else.

LOLA: Horns! You didn't know what horns were last week! [To Chichi]

KRYSTAL: Who, her?

LOLA: Yeah. I called her goat-headed.

A giggle runs through the cohort.

KRYSTAL: (*giddy*) Alright, I don't know what horns are!

TOPAZ: We don't know so many things!

LOLA: Chichi, you got anything?

CHICHI: (*scribbles*)

LOLA: She says she didn't think of it before, but she doesn't remember the whole evening of Friday the seventh.

KRYSTAL: Jayzus. What'd you do, spend all day in bed with this thing?

Scribbles.

LOLA: So it was gnawing at her. So she went around town asking about what happened that night. No one at Antonioni's remembers that evening either. None of the waiters or the staff.

KRYSTAL: Antonioni's. That's that seedy club three streets down init? You're telling me no one who works there remembers that evening either?

COGNITOHAZARD

LOLA: Almost no one. Right, Chichi? What's stranger... (*reads and stops for a moment.*) What's stranger is that ... the only people who *did* remember her there all remembered her from one thing. (*stops reading*) You're not making this up, Chich?

TOPAZ: What's she saying?

LOLA: They remember her from one thing—

>   She looks up from the note.

LOLA: Friday the seventh at Antonioni's is karaoke night.

TOPAZ: So, what's that mean?

LOLA: Look. She knows.

KRYSTAL: It's a kip of a place, Antonioni's. But I tell you one thing: You go to Antonioni's on karaoke night—you sing karaoke.

LOLA: ...She's forgotten her voice.

TOPAZ: You're telling me just a week ago you were able to talk? How could that happen?!

KRYSTAL: Who knows.

>   Lola sits and comforts Chichi.

KRYSTAL: It's alright, Chich.

LOLA: How many times have we been played for fools? We've been sleeping around with this fucking thing this whole time, while it picks off girls one by one and we can't remember it. (*yelling at door*) And I bet it's just waiting to get out to try it all again!

KRYSTAL: Quit your yelling will you.

LOLA: What...

KRYSTAL: Your yelling isn't helping.

LOLA: Oh here we go. I'll tell you what's not helping. All your stupid ideas! It's gotten us nowhere. All it's done is almost get us killed. And who's gonna care?

Carbon Pages

Girls get killed all the time. On the street, at the whorehouse—who cares? We won't even be in the evening paper I bet. *Loada tramps drop dead.* You know what, I know *you* don't care 'bout living or dying no more, but *we* do!

KRYSTAL: You think anyone's gonna remember you when you're gone? Give me a break. I wouldn't touch you with a ten foot pole.

LOLA: You're just old and bitter is your problem. No wonder no one wants you. Look at yourself. You turn everyone off!

KRYSTAL: I turn everyone off. Remember when I said you're the most asked about girl in the House. That was a lie! I just said it to make you feel better cause I know you'll go try and kill yourself otherwise!

LOLA: If you had to look at you everyday you'd wanna kill yourself too.

KRYSTAL: Ah shut up you busted up whore.

LOLA: I'm a whore. At least I'm not a *bitch.*

>   Cries of indignation from all sides.
>
>   Krystal leaps up and chases Lola around the room, up and over the bed until— The POWDER ROOM door starts slamming again.
>
>   SLAM! SLAM!

TOPAZ: Enough out of you two! I'm sick and tired of you fighting. And I'm even more sick of trying to figure out what happened to make you like this. Tell me once and for all, what is it that happened, so you can settle it. Lola?

LOLA: She knows. I want to hear her side.

KRYSTAL: Butt out.

>   Suddenly Topaz rushes to the other side of the room and grabs the still gunky SCISSORS.

TOPAZ: (wildly feigning scissors) Tell me!

>   No real response.

COGNITOHAZARD

SLAM! SLAM!

KRYSTAL: (*to Chichi*) Let's say hi at the station.

> Topaz drops them and grabs the box of kleenex tissues Chichi's been writing on.
>
> Now Chichi and others rush after her. Topaz dodges them, holding the tissues high over her head like some cash prize.
>
> Finally she gets up on the bed stand, holding the box in one hand, and snaps open her lighter. She holds the flame under the box threateningly. This whole time the door is close to breaking open, but no one seems to care.

TOPAZ: Krystal, tell me your issues or I'm burning the tissues!

LOLA: Will you get down!

TOPAZ: (*holding flame*) No! Start yammering!

KRYSTAL: Fine. Look. Okay. Fine.

TOPAZ: Why do you hate each other?

LOLA: It's because...

KRYSTAL: It's complicated. I'd have to... Can't really put it into words—you caught me off-guard okay?

LOLA: If I could write it down, maybe...

TOPAZ: Oh my God (*flicks off lighter*) I see what's going on. I've seen this a million times. You've been feudin' so long you don't even know what started it.

> The POWDER ROOM door FLINGS open.
>
> An uncanny insectoid din...
>
> The girls give the thing in the powder room a courtesy head turn before continuing:

KRYSTAL: Course I do. She rumped a taken man.

Carbon Pages

LOLA: (*indignant*) That was BEFORE you broke it off with him. You broke my stuff.

KRYSTAL: That was only because you started going through my belongings once a week.

LOLA: That wasn't even me!

KRYSTAL: Okay ... well look I don't really remember. But it don't matter.

TOPAZ: You don't even remember what you're feuding over, and you know what? My guess is it's not cuz of anything *it's* done. (*pointing at creature*)

LOLA: (*to Krys*) Shut that door! It's creeping me out.

KRYSTAL: Go do it yourself.

TOPAZ: You've gotten such a liking for this aul song that you've tossed out the actual *reason* for feudin'. An earworm is what it is! I just wish you'd do the same for how you *feel* 'bout each other.

KRYSTAL: I wish I'd never known her!

LOLA: (*moving to powder room door*) Me too! She's an eyesore. You make me sad just lookin atcha! (*at creature*) And what are you staring at?!

TOPAZ: So that's what it looks like.

KRYSTAL: (*increasingly worried*) Lola, shut that door fast.

LOLA: It's not budging.

>The door won't shut.

>Lola moves away but before she can, the LIGHTS go OUT.

>Strange alien noises. Scuttering. Broken glass. A shriek or two.

>Finally...

>...Lights return...

>The girls are all lying where once they were standing.

COGNITOHAZARD

Slowly,

One by one,

They wake up as if from a dream, look around. The creature is gone.

One by one the girls exit. Lola looks back.

LOLA: (*to Krystal*) Who are you?

    Unforgettable by Nat King Cole plays.

The End.

No Weapon Formed Against You

"My daughter was my treasure. But when was that... What am I saying? My daughter is alive. Inside this box! ... my box ... my daughter ... "

Baroque

1980
"YOUNG PIONEERS"

> I say unto thee it was the summer of plump behinds and florets in the sun on the air of titanium railways. It was the summer of tanktops. It was the summer of water rills shining in the sand under the volleyball nets. It was the summer of detours and tag. It was the summer of pretty girls who crossed their legs on the curb. In those days I'd run with them on the sand and when I'd get tired I'd lay and stringy grass would print gravings on my skin.

BLUE SUIT: Would you prefer we speak en vi or skip straight to ti? It's your choice.

YOUNG MAN: I don't speak ti with strangers.

BLUE SUIT: Too right.

> The man in the blue suit unfurls some files and papers on his desk. He almost looks as if he's about to ask a question, looks up, and then decides against it, and pretends to autograph a page. Finally he looks up:

BLUE SUIT: Do you know where you are?

YOUNG MAN: Yes.

BLUE SUIT: Where do you think you are?

YOUNG MAN: In the KGB.

BLUE SUIT: What is your name?

YOUNG MAN: Igor.

BLUE SUIT: Patronymic?

YOUNG MAN: Fyodorvich.

BLUE SUIT: Okay, Igor Fyodorvich. My name is Aleksei. Now that we're no longer strangers would it be preferable on your part that we skip to ti?

YOUNG MAN: No.

Carbon Pages

BLUE SUIT: Do you think you have reason to be in *the KGB*, as you say?

YOUNG MAN: No.

BLUE SUIT: Well you're almost correct, Igor Fyodorvich Letov. Almost, in that *the KGB* as such does not exist. What exists is the State Security Committee. Correct, in that you are *in it*.

   The officer in the blue suit takes a look at his file.

BLUE SUIT: So you're from Omsk originally. What are you doing in Moscow?

YOUNG MAN: Studying.

BLUE SUIT: Yet you've been occupying your time otherwise, haven't you?

YOUNG MAN: I don't know.

BLUE SUIT: I get the impression you're a clever young man, Igor. You wouldn't want to lose your spot in the Young Leninist League would you?

YOUNG MAN: I'm not in the komsomol. I was kicked out a year ago.

BLUE SUIT: But you're a Soviet Man aren't you?

YOUNG MAN: Yes.

BLUE SUIT: Then you want to help your fellow citizen?

YOUNG MAN: I want to get out of here. My mother will be worried.

BLUE SUIT: That's alright—your mother knows you're with us. Are you engaged in the smuggling of contraband into Soviet territory?

YOUNG MAN: No.

BLUE SUIT: Did you willfuly intercept a cache of audio devices on April the 28th?

YOUNG MAN: No, I—

BLUE SUIT: You run this outfit.

YOUNG MAN: No I...don't.

No Weapon Formed Against You

BLUE SUIT: Who runs this outfit? And before you answer I must say that I already know absolutely everything in detail. Your statement is only needed for my paperwork.

YOUNG MAN: Just fake it.

BLUE SUIT: The State Security Committee fakes nothing.

YOUNG MAN: I don't know who runs it. I don't know a single thing, you filth.

BLUE SUIT: If the only thing differentiating your statement is namecalling that won't reflect so well on you, Igor!

> Igor locks eyes with the officer and disengages his bladder as the warm smell of urine fills the interrogation room. That night he's taken underground, where four soldiers lock him in a cell and beat him half way to ischemia.
>
> Before he knows it, the young man Igor is in a psychiatric hospital on the outskirts of Moscow, being led down a white corridor by a lanky four-eyed doctor behind and a middle aged pudgy babushka in front. Some years ago she was a thin starlet.

PUDGY NURSE: This is where you and your comrades can watch the television. They're watching *Fanfan la Tulipe*. Have a seat.

> *Fanfan La Tulipe* followed a swashbuckling swordsman in his romances and fights with duplicitous monarchs. It was an old adventure film, imported from France.

IGOR LETOV: Lady—

PUDGY NURSE: —Who, me?

IGOR LETOV: When will I be able to—

PUDGY NURSE: I wouldn't consider myself *lady* exactly, Igor. I may be old but I'm not *that* old.

IGOR LETOV: I didn't mean—

PUDGY NURSE: Do you always call young women *lady*? Do you call your sister *lady*?

Carbon Pages

IGOR LETOV: I'm sorry.

PUDGY NURSE: Have a seat.

IGOR LETOV: Please. When will I get out of here?

PUDGY NURSE: You'll *get out* when you're feeling better. It's *prisons* that have sentences.

IGOR LETOV: But I think I'm all well now. I just had a lapse of reason. My mother will be worried about me.

PUDGY NURSE: If you're well then I'm sure the doctor will share the same prognosis next week.

> It's a spacious room with windows barred in the shape of sunrays, and in one corner there's a caged television watched by patients. I'm watching too but personally I always prefer the spectacle of people. Igor has a seat next to a lardass in the centre row. Letov must be the youngest man in the building.
>
> There's some sort of public service announcement playing:

TELLY: Parents! Expert research tells us that to limit mental fatigue and to ensure the proper intellectual development of the mind one must limit a child's exposure to advertising media. You wouldn't let your child smoke! A day of commercials does to your child's brain what a cigarette does to their body!

> There is no ward for juveniles, nor is there separation between the delinquents from the truly deranged. Suddenly a voice beckons the kid from way behind.

VOICE: Hey.

IGOR LETOV: What?

VOICE: Can you lend a smoke?

IGOR LETOV: Me?

VOICE: You. What room are you in?

IGOR LETOV: Down there on the left.

No Weapon Formed Against You

VOICE: You're with the chronic masturbator?

IGOR LETOV: I don't know.

VOICE: What's your name?

IGOR LETOV: Igor.

VOICE: I'm Alexander. Good to meet you.

> He's a skinny young boy, maybe the same age as him, with a shaved head. They shake hands.

ALEXANDER: Let's go over here. I can't hear myself think.

> They sit by the windows.

ALEXANDER: Every day they beam some shit. But they won't allow a single book request.

IGOR LETOV: They have a library.

ALEXANDER: Not those kinds of books... You really have to wonder how stupid someone has to be to enjoy the rot they put on. But y'know, in a way, I sympathize—our neighbours are subhuman. The realities of the world as-is would make them cross-eyed so they have to distract themselves with shadows on the wall.

IGOR LETOV: How long have you been here?

ALEXANDER: I don't count anymore.

IGOR LETOV: Why are you in?

ALEXANDER: On account of my insanity.

IGOR LETOV: I got nabbed for 8-tracks.

ALEXANDER: Don't confess to me. I could be KGB.

IGOR LETOV: Fuck them.

> Alexander hoists up to sit on the windowsill.

Carbon Pages

ALEXANDER: What is an 8-track?

IGOR LETOV: It plays songs. Like cassettes. The westerners are so much more advanced in this stuff.

ALEXANDER: They always are.

IGOR LETOV: Yeah?

ALEXANDER: They always will be.

IGOR LETOV: For sure.

ALEXANDER: It's all our guys do is chase fads like a dog with a tail. Who knows *what* we'll adopt in a hundred years.

IGOR LETOV: Maybe loafers that aren't shit.

ALEXANDER: Right yes. Ha, maybe loafers that aren't shit. Exactly. Or music. Personally I've always found The Beatles quite evocative.

IGOR LETOV: Everyone likes The Beatles. It's old news. Ever hear of The Rolling Stones?

> Alexander is a bit taken aback that Letov effectively called his taste old, but he doesn't show it and, anyway, he quite likes that this kid has brains of his own.

ALEXANDER: Yes, I've read their magazine.

IGOR LETOV: Want to hear a song?

ALEXANDER: From The Rolling Stones?

IGOR LETOV: No from me.

ALEXANDER: Okay.

IGOR LETOV: It's a *romance*.

ALEXANDER: I'm sorry to say you need a guitar to play a *romance*, and here guitars are considered demagogic.

IGOR LETOV: Don't need no guitar.

No Weapon Formed Against You

>He picks up a violin and places it on his lap like you'd do a guitar and then he starts plucking it like a six-string.

IGOR LETOV: Okay. Let's see...one two three...

>And he belts this ballad with a puffed chest:

IGOR LETOV: *I see her rise from her knees—my Motherland!*
I see her rise from her ashes—oh my Motherland!
I hear her sing—oh my splendid Motherland!

My holy Motherland straightens her back
Our wrathful power moves mountains

The sun's tattoo
In this deadliest cold, in this nadir of night.

>Both the young boys are grinning ear to ear at each other and Igor continues:

IGOR LETOV: *I see her rise from her knees—my Motherland!*
I see her rise from her ashes—my Motherland!
Scolding does she burn in me—my Motherland!
I hear her sing—oh my wonderful beautiful Soviet Motherland!

>Alexander laughs and applauds the bard, and there's even some claps from the other patients who turned their head to see.

NURSE: Boys—quit making fools of yourself. Give that instrument the respect it deserves or put it down.

ALEXANDER: The guards here are no fun.

IGOR LETOV: Are you scared?

ALEXANDER: Of what—this place?

IGOR LETOV: Yeah, of this place.

ALEXANDER: I think of it as a sanatorium.

> Igor considers this for a moment. Then he considers if Alexander is really insane like he says, and decides that he's not. So he says:

IGOR LETOV: Listen. I've been eyeing the bars on my window. They're steel but the sill is chipped.

ALEXANDER: Right.

IGOR LETOV: I think we can break it but I need your help. We need to find something steel and sharp. Are you with me?

ALEXANDER: Sure.

IGOR LETOV: First step is we start collecting towels. We have to figure out how often the laundry—

> The nurse calls out for the boy:

NURSE: Alexander Dugin? Your father is here.

> A towering grey man enters the psychiatric room. Dugin's father wears a pristine navy suit with war medals adorning the lapels. Uttering no words and wearing an expression of grief and pity, he takes his son away and out the door of the psychiatric hospital. But before he does this, the boy turns and says to his ex-cellmate:

ALEXANDER: Listen. Once you're out of here why don't we share a drink? I live on Nevskaya Street. Third podyest, third floor.

> A platoon of the Crown's para-regiment comes through the scriptorium of a majestic German castle. They're all soaking tired. They make their way through the chapel house and the spiral stairs. Captain Mosbey has not eaten in two days. There's some stink coming from his gash. The crew take shelter under the thronsaal's leaky roof. Shorty cracks open a kachelofen at the foot of a bed. Shorty's not seen a woman in eight months and he's never seen a kachelofen and he's so very very sleepy. Back home he used to cut fox tails. They don't wait for the sun to set—the men place their damp boots on the

No Weapon Formed Against You

> window and curl up in beds and ottomans. Red shaves in the marble.

IGOR LETOV: Okay.

> The men doze off in the bed of the kaizer's daughter and Red is shaving in the marble. I was here.

OLIVIER: Well friend what's the matter?

GEORGES: I don't know, Olivier. I think I'm tired of parties.

> And there was not a ray of sunshine in Paris, where the trees that summer of nineteen-eighty were bare and birdless.
>
> In a snazzy electrically-heated pied-a-terre, the walls of which are reamed with bookshelves, a party is in its early throes. Couples graze on crackers and refreshments, flute glasses in hand. New guests are entering all the time.

OLIVIER: Close your eyes and pretend you're in an Ecuadorian jail then, or school, or whatever it is you find pleasant.

GEORGES: I had a chat with Hallier. We agreed I write an article on the kids of Cambodia. Maybe it'll dissolve this rut.

OLIVIER: You take things too seriously. Hey, you know I have a countess coming over? Why don't you try chatting her up. If you're lucky she might bust out *prima nocta*.

> A frantic woman spills drink on Olivier:

FABIENNE: Olivier, Olivier! On a scale of one to five am I an assertive person who doesn't take no for an answer?

OLIVIER: Yes. Five. Why do you want to know?

Carbon Pages

FABIENNE: Hi, Georges.

GEORGES: Hello, Fay.

FABIENNE: That kid is taking a survey or something. What's this I hear about a Countess?

OLIVIER: Nothing, *ma lapin*. I hear someone's invited Lady De Lisse.

FABIENNE: You hear. It's your home, you should know.

OLIVIER: I don't give it much thought.

FABIENNE: I know de Lisse. Do you know de Lisse, Georges?

GEORGES: I—

FABIENNE: I saw her in a play as a child. Something about a family. That's the most beautiful woman I've ever seen in my life is what I told my grandmother. Of course that was yeeears ago. Olivier, I think I'll be an actress when I grow up.

OLIVIER: You *were* one.

FABIENNE: That was then. I wanna try again.

> A bespectacled voyeur interrupts the group holding a pen and paper.

MANNIE: You rarely worry about whether you make a good impression on people you meet.

OLIVIER: I've never liked a man I didn't meet.

FABIENNE: Two!

> And at that moment enters through the front door the Countess de Lisse, dressed in an elegant white dress.
>
> She had dark hair tied up with wisps falling down, and her face was delicate and kind, though aged. In everything she did there was a sincere gratitude and a gentleness, as if she was owed nothing and it was all she could do to live up to life's everyday blessings by standing straight with perfect poise.

No Weapon Formed Against You

Immediately her hand is clutched by a little old man with elbow patches:

OLDER GUEST: *Cheri*! What a nice surprise!

LADY DE LISSE: Dominique!

OLDER GUEST: Lady De Lisse, you are beautiful like the rings of Saturn!

LADY DE LISSE: What a little flatterer you are...

OLDER GUEST: What I say is truth and nothing but. Any resemblance to flattery is pure coincidence!

In a corner the hosts observe the radiant newcomers.

OLIVIER: There they are.

GEORGES: He seems to be trying too hard doesn't he.

OLIVIER: Who—Dominique?

GEORGES: No, *her friend*. The man in purple.

OLIVIER: You think he's her son? Or maybe a concubine? Place your bets.

The Countess's escort is a boyish gentleman, short in stature, dressed in splendid purple velveteen with a white bow-tie, and high-heeled ankle boots, all too splendid in fact for a party where the dress code is almost exclusively dull turtle-necks, blazers, loose ties and grey scarfs—a competition of indifference. Among them the man is like a Madagascarian parrot among crows. He has thick square glasses and flowing hair. A somewhat baby-like face. Were he to smile one would see that his teeth are brutally yellow.

The sound of Vivaldi fills the apartment.

LADY DE LISSE: May I introduce to you my friend. This, Dominique, is Eduard Limonov.

LIMONOV: How do you do. Where is the food?

OLDER GUEST: Over there.

Carbon Pages

LIMONOV: Thank you.

Eduard scurries.

LADY DE LISSE: He's a writer.

At the snack table the voyeur approaches Eduard.

MANNIE: Bon Soir. Mannie.

LIMONOV: Eduard.

MANNIE: On a scale of one to five: *When you meet a person you cannot help but compare yourself, ranking them below or above you, and drawing from this either satisfaction or mortification.*

LIMONOV: ...One. I don't care what others think. Aren't there any grapes?

OLIVIER: Are you speaking to me?

LIMONOV: Yes.

OLIVIER: That's an interesting accent.

LIMONOV: It's Russian.

OLIVIER: A real life Russian?

Fabienne pipes in.

FABIENNE: I've been very *into* the Russians. What a mysterious people. I *adore* Tolstoy's *War and Peace*. He gets at the core of emotion.

LIMONOV: Tolstoy is a charlatan.

FABIENNE: I didn't think so...

LIMONOV: Nor is he Russian.

FABIENNE: Yes he is!

LIMONOV: No book whose foremost chapter is in French can be Russian.

GEORGES: Absurd.

No Weapon Formed Against You

OLIVIER: (*earnestly*) Well I'd like to read a true Russian author, if you have recommendations.

LIMONOV: Jean Ganet.

OLIVIER: But...he's French.

LIMONOV: But he writes like a Russian.

OLIVIER: I've been enthralled recently by whatshisname. Oh what's the name of the New York poet making the rounds. You know, they kicked him out of Moscow on account of dissent.

GEORGES: Brodsky.

OLIVIER: Yes, it must be nice seeing Brodsky getting such praise considering he's, uh, a comrade. And excuse me what *is* your name?

LIMONOV: Limonov. Eduard Limonov.

GEORGES: That's just what we need—another Eduard.

OLIVIER: I'm Olivier. This is Georges, and Fabienne. And Brodsky...?

LIMONOV: I loathe that prick.

OLIVIER: Really?

LIMONOV: Joseph was a sub-rate poet in Moscow. We used to laugh at him behind his back.

OLIVIER: You're not a fan.

LIMONOV: He got an all-expenses pleasure cruise across the Iron Curtain. I had a bag put over my head.

OLIVIER: Oh—you were exiled?

LIMONOV: I have to throw off their trail every morning in the Marais.

OLIVIER: Whose?

LIMONOV: The KGB's, of course.

OLIVIER: (*astonished*) Even here?!

Carbon Pages

LIMONOV: I'm still picking glass out of my head after a minor ambush. They'd cornered me in New York, see. I was a bum. Where are the plates?

GEORGES: I'm sorry—did you just say you were a bum?

LIMONOV: It's hard to lose a tail when you spend your days picking up cigarette butts. I thought it was time for a change of pace. Is this your glass?

> He brushes his expensive tie. The hosts don't know exactly how to take all this, or whether he's for real or not. And before anyone can formulate a reply again the surveyor interjects:

MANNIE: *When you meet a person you cannot help but compare yourself, ranking them below or above you, and drawing from this either satisfaction or mortification.*

FABIENNE: Four.

OLIVIER: Really, Emmanuel. Uh, let's see well, um. A three. After all I think every person does social arithmetic to some degree—

LIMONOV: Five. Every person is either worth my time or not.

GEORGES: You must miss the motherland, Eduard.

> They look at the strange man expecting something wistful. Instead, he wrinkles his nose:

LIMONOV: It's a nation of drunks and potato farmers. I hate mediocrity. Their slavers deserve each other. And in Moscow and Petersburg, all the aristocrats and intellectuals exiled to stoke the brilliance of The West. Thank God for it. I *kiss* Paris. Piaf, George Washington Bridge, porno films. When I die, I want my grave here under my feet, and for it to say *here lived the bastard son of a great mother who did all he could to please her.*

> Olivier looks at the carpeting.

OLIVIER: Well the neighbours might object, but we can arrange it.

GEORGES: We were just discussing Southeast Asia.

OLIVIER: It's a nuanced situation.

No Weapon Formed Against You

LIMONOV: Starve the fuckers and shoot the rest. What's nuanced about it? The west is the future. The rest is death. It's like those fat-fingered peasants I knew back home. All they wanted was to have everyone as satisfied as them. An officer came up to me once and said why don't you do something productive instead of reading your little stories? Well I robbed his home and made love to his wife.

> Olivier laughs. Georges looks at Fabienne's expression and smiles into his glass.

OLIVIER: Did you hear about that woman, Eduard?

> He points.

OLIVIER: Her husband passed away. Sad thing, seeing a widow.

LIMONOV: We should execute widows. Jesus, they're worse than Communists.

> Everyone laughs. No one can quite decipher if the strange man in velveteen is serious or not, which somehow makes him funnier. Olivier takes him aside.

OLIVIER: Eduard what do you occupy yourself with?

LIMONOV: I'm a writer.

OLIVIER: I could've guessed...

> He puts his arm on his shoulder, leading him to the bar...

OLIVIER: ...Now tell me—have you ever been to *La Procope* on the Seine?

> ...leaving Georges and Fabienne alone.

GEORGES: I quite like him.

> Fabienne looks over at the countess.

FABIENNE: What a clever arrangement they have.

GEORGES: How do you mean?

Carbon Pages

FABIENNE: He gets to mingle with the city's literati, and she gets to be seen with an exciting young lover.

GEORGES: I believe they call that love.

>The Countess in the corner now talking to another octogenarian:

OCTOGENARIAN: Why don't we ever see you in anything anymore, darling? We so loved you in that one picture. Oh what was it called? Something of the something?

LADY DE LISSE: I'm just focusing on myself for now. But I want to do something new.

>But her eyes keep shifting. To her lover, who entertains a whole orbit of admirers.

>The River Seine holds a constant odour of a warm, dank, bathhouse. The Moskva, on the other hand, has never had any smell, pleasant, not-so-pleasant — it does not exist. Many years ago all the earth was Moskva, and wherever it spilled was retained forevermore the universal odour.

>We were all gathered at Vasya's dacha around a campfire. Sitting on stumps and tabourets passing around a bottle of samagon.

KOST: There really is a pecking order of banned literature don't you think?

VASYA: Whaddayamean?

KOST: If you read Guenon, that means you're on the dregs and probably schizophrenic. Second on the rung is Solzhenetsyn. Means you're a baby boomer who wants to seem hip to the girls by the photoprinter. Elvis Presley? Then you're a skank who sucks Uzbek cock while her boyfriend's off on duty.

No Weapon Formed Against You

SPEER: Just one night I'd like to spend without hearing about this girl.

VASYA: I know.

SPEER: And what's it mean, Kost, that you haven't returned me *Crisis of the Modern World*?

KOST: I will. Remind me, I will.

SPEER: I *am* reminding you, idiot.

VASYA: You have a girl, Letov?

IGOR LETOV: On and off.

VASYA: Speer, what about you? Which bird you like?

SPEER: I can't say.

VASYA: Fuck not?

SPEER: I'm not at liberty.

KOST: Speer is going steady.

VASYA: Who with?

KOST: The canvasser. Georgian girl.

VASYA: I didn't know Georgians had girls.

SPEER: It's not her—

KOST: —Katherine!—

SPEER: I wouldn't go with her anyway. She has night classes. She looks at me like a bug.

VASYA: Ah, don't get upset.

SPEER: I'm not.

VASYA: I'm kidding—I know you're not.

KOST: These komsomol bitches are all the same. Same birds be sucking off gestapos for bread scraps under occupation.

VASYA: Only we could round em up and shave their heads like the French did do.

Carbon Pages

SPEER: Yeah so we couldn't tell them apart from Dugin. Right, Dugin?

> Alexander Dugin is on his knees lighting a kazbek cigarette with the bonfire.

KOST: You know who I like? Glenn Miller.

VASYA: Look. Letov's lookin at you like whoever the fuck still listens to him. Baby, you're a philistine. What kinda songs your boys get you from out west?

KOST: Yeah, what are the droogs of kapital-in-decline making now?

IGOR LETOV: The Who.

VASYA: I never did hear of "the hoo".

SPEER: What's it mean?

IGOR LETOV: I don't know. But they've a great sound.

> Dugin breathes tar.

ALEXANDER: The who. The what. The where. These are interrogatives. "Who" denotes questionable personhood. Aka nobody knows "who" they are.

SPEER: No shit.

ALEXANDER: It's a joke, see?

SPEER: I didn't know they had jokes over there.

KOST: That's the one advantage of undeveloped social systems. The Vandals were ribaldrous.

VASYA: Hey Igor, Dugin's a real brainiac. He learned Italian just to translate *Ride the Tiger*.

SPEER: Our circle would lose half its greymatter if something happened to him.

VASYA: Dugin speaks American, don't you Dugin? And German too.

ALEXANDER: Sprechen.

SPEER: Vas, hand me the bottle, baby.

No Weapon Formed Against You

> He spritzes it over the campfire and resurrects it with a burst.

KOST: Not only that but he's psychic.

SPEER: So am I.

KOST: Speer, if you're a psychic then I'm Wolf Messing. Dugin is—well, Dugin is certifiably clairvoyant.

SPEER: Whatever.

KOST: Remember the day after New Year's? The train tracks. What he made Vasya do?

SPEER: Gyp, baby.

VASYA: Roll me a cig will you?

SPEER: Hand the bottle.

ALEXANDER: I have something a bit stronger.

VASYA: That's right. Bring it out.

IGOR LETOV: What's that?

VASYA: Thinner.

KOST: I hate this shit.

> Vasya swigs. Then he passes it around. Speer coughs up a lung.

SPEER: Wait wait wait. Ok but seriously Dugin spill it.

VASYA: Letov, you know about this?

IGOR LETOV: (*enthralled*) No.

VASYA: Teach Letov how to hypnotize someone.

SPEER: You can't teach it.

ALEXANDER: You can teach anything, baby. All ability is a matter of study and conscious application of technique.

Carbon Pages

Dugin's soft green eyes observed Letov, and he decided that he should hear his secret. He tells as if he wrote the book on it.

ALEXANDER: The basis of hypnosis is the stealing of your slave's will and replacing with thine own. You must trap their vitality in your gaze, give no reprieve to their Earthly anchor, lose them in your eyes. You must know every inch of your slave's fear and weakness. Now think of your command, what you want more than anything in the world. Convince yourself—fulfilment is life, denial is death. There can be no room for vagueness. You must conceive of your order with the ardent turning of a thousand indivinities to the single purpose of your golem's command. Hardly believe that it's not a memory rather than a prediction. Conceive the precise wording. And just when it seems too much, keeping eyes locked all the while, and you're about to utter your command in words—you say nothing at all. Your sight has done the work.

VASYA: Wild.

KOST: Easier said than done.

ALEXANDER: Keep at it.

KOST: Letov. Weren't you interrogated?

ALEXANDER: He was—by the KGB.

KOST: No shit.

SPEER: Did they beat you? They tortured you, right?

ALEXANDER: Yes—

IGOR LETOV: I—

KOST: —Intimidation is against Soviet law.

IGOR LETOV: I'll be sure to mention that next time they have me in for ansov, baby.

KOST: (*amused*) King! Fucking KING! How old did you say you were again?

IGOR LETOV: Fifteen.

No Weapon Formed Against You

KOST: Christ, man. At fifteen I was a tree marker. In the summer...I marked trees in the oblast with chalk and they cut them down the next day.

They swig on thinner.

VASYA: Castro—now he has the right idea. He's fervorous. Stylish. Our guys won't even torture no more. He reminds me of Adolf, Castro.

ALEXANDER: We live in the midst of a terrible infestation. Everything he said turned out to be right, and everything our parents fought for was wrong.

KOST: Careful, Dugin. My uncle died in Stalingrad.

ALEXANDER: Your uncle's a patsy.

Kost is genuinely taken aback by the riposte.

KOST: I like you baby, but sometimes you take things too far.

VASYA: It's a colony of bugs.

ALEXANDER: A great pillar of light was extinguished and replaced by a cabal of geriatrics. Comrade Brezhnev is a termite. Suslov is a termite. And every professor, butcher lady, every komsomol girl is a termite. I shit on the accursed Sovdep. In one thousand years it too will fall.

Alexander is very drunk.

VASYA: Now Adolf...

ALEXANDER: —He's out of it too. What's to love about someone who through his own pompousness led the greatest empire on Earth into the hands of a hoard of mongoloids.

SPEER: Me personally, I always err on the side of Blok: *Ahem....!*

...he stands on a stump and clears his throat...

Carbon Pages

SPEER: *And yet, my Russia,*
I love you still.

        Applause all around for Speer's display of poetry.

KOST: (*swigs thinner*) Jesus. Did nobody bring *zakuski*? Not even some pickles? You people are degenerates.

VASYA: I was waiting for the right moment and thank you Kost for the pretext.

        Vasya digs into a suitcase and unearths a glass jar like the ones used for pickling vegetables. But rather than tomatoes, inside the jar are black communion wafers.

IGOR LETOV: What are those?

VASYA: These a—

ALEXANDER: Light Cakes.

IGOR LETOV: Light Cakes…

ALEXANDER: Yes, Igor.

VASYA: (*standing up*) You want *zakuski*, gentlemen? HERE are *zakuski*. Dugin has been so kind as to provide the recipe.

IGOR LETOV: What's in em?

ALEXANDER: Flour, honey, sweat, semen, and mooncalf blood.

        Everyone shuts up… And then:

SPEER: Give me one.

KOST: Alright pass one over.

ALEXANDER: Where's the drink? Who has the drink?

SPEER: Here.

VASYA: Hey, Give me it!

        Igor examines the wafer, flipping it between his fingers. Then Dugin makes a speech:

No Weapon Formed Against You

ALEXANDER: Gentlemen, it's an honour to partake in the eucharist, the true eucharist, with luminaries of such distinguished taste. A communion of the Human, of... give me the bottle ... the irrational. With this I take eat of the undivine and become one with the Antigod.

> And he swallows the wafer and he doesn't even wince. He waits an appropriate amount and only then does he swig down some rotgut. Kost does the same. Then comes Igor's turn. Without missing a beat he lays the wafer on his tongue, not breaking eye contact with Dugin. Chews it. Slowly. Savours it. And he sticks out his tongue like a toddler at the table.
>
> Everyone claps and cheers.

VASYA: How's that for young blood!

KOST: Right on!

> Only Speer is left.

SPEER: I can't do it.

KOST: Pussy, baby.

SPEER: I'm having a reflex...

IGOR LETOV: I'll have it.

KOST: Hardcore. Letov's going for a second helping.

> If you could see Dugin the way I did see him that night by the fire, you could see the immense pride harboured in his eyes when he looked at the young man with moppy hair who was like of his own blood.

SPEER: I'll do it. I'll do it. Fine.

> And with difficulty Speer choked it down and then choked on the swill too, but by then some of his reputation had been flushed.

KOST: Not for nothin' but it's not menstrual blood in there.

Carbon Pages

SPEER: Oh thank God.

ALEXANDER: Why the hell not?

KOST: Artyom pussied out and now his sister's on retreat.

ALEXANDER: So whose blood is it?!

KOST: Blood's mine, baby.

No Weapon Formed Against You

Eduard liked the old districts the most, seeing the old monuments which to him breathed with life and liberty. He even loved seeing the occasional advertisement, if for no other reason than you wouldn't find them in a Soviet village, the bigger the better. He admired their colours and designs.

What he'd return to was a grimy chambre de bonne at the top of a walk-up in the Marais district where the only view was from a tiny window which received twenty-two minutes of direct sunlight a day, and the mattress on which the Russian slept had to be flipped regularly for bedbugs. That is where Limonov lived. Cold and damp. An American flag hung over the bed next to posters of Charles Manson and Oscar Wilde, and an orange telephone sat on the desk next to a typewriter. Dumbbells ranging from two to five kilos lay underneath.

The Countess de Lisse spent a lot of time here with her lover. As I found her, she was straining her feet into heels. As always, she was dressed white as a ghost. Limonov flounced around in a strawberry parabola dinner jacket, a tight thong, and nothing else.

LIMONOV: ...and then he suggested we have lunch at Lipp and we met a publicist and then he invited us for drinks at *La Palace*.

LADY DE LISSE: I see.

LIMONOV: Are you almost ready? *Palace* is okay but the lighting in *Bain-Douches* is unbeatable. Marc-Nabe turned me onto it.

LADY DE LISSE: When will they turn on the heating, Eduard. It's close to freezing.

LIMONOV: Sit on me.

LADY DE LISSE: What?

LIMONOV: Perch on my back. I need to do some push-ups.

LADY DE LISSE: That's nice velvet.

LIMONOV: On my back.

LADY DE LISSE: Like this?

Carbon Pages

LIMONOV: The steam...ONE...is on. It takes...TWO...three days to arrive. If he could just lose that girlfriend he could make a fine writer...THREE... But she's constantly on his ass about his mother-in-law. Last night he almost fainted. FOUR.

LADY DE LISSE: He *is* perspicacious. Maybe we can see Mozart's home the two of us.

LIMONOV: SEVEN... EIGHT! Jackie, we've *seen* his home. NINE.

LADY DE LISSE: We could go see Combescot in the country. I hear they're having an auction.

LIMONOV: TEN! Combescot's got the most rubbish sayings.

    Eduard looks in the mirror and buttons up his jacket.

LIMONOV: Yeah, that'll hold.

LADY DE LISSE: What?

LIMONOV: This pump. Want some cabbage soup? You know as well as I do you'll get nothing from Olivier or Stefan.

LADY DE LISSE: Who's Stefan?

LIMONOV: Olivier's friend. He wants me to come on a radio show with Mannie. Some pygmy thing. Do you think he'll appreciate it? Do you think he's nervous around me? Ever since that Herald Tribune piece, he's developed a stutter.

LADY DE LISSE: Mannie's quite promising and actually Eddie I think you'd be a great role mod—ARGHH!!

LIMONOV: Say hello!

LADY DE LISSE: EDDIE!

LIMONOV: He's a new arrival!

LADY DE LISSE: What is even that?!

LIMONOV: Cockroach! It's a sign of civilization.

LADY DE LISSE: Get it out of here.

No Weapon Formed Against You

LIMONOV: Did I tell you about the saxophonist? I met a saxophonist. Steve something.

LADY DE LISSE: Via Olivier too and as well I suppose?

LIMONOV: Huh? No, just on the street. I tell you, Jackie. There's something in the air. The whole Earth spins in my favour. I was reading Baudelaire's biography. He submitted Flowers of Evil on November the sixth. THAT'S THE DAY I PAID MY FIRST MONTH OF RENT.

> Harsh, oxygenated rain did pelt the chambre window. In those days the door was never closed, and all the time I let myself in.

LADY DE LISSE: How's progress going on the novel?

LIMONOV: What?

LADY DE LISSE: How's progress on the novel is what I said.

LIMONOV: Fine, Jackie.

> They dress themselves in silence. The Countess tries on her earrings, and Limonov puts on trousers.

LADY DE LISSE: I read an excellent piece on Ethiopia in *L'Idiot*. I think you'd like it. The author has a brilliant way of chaining these rich images.

LIMONOV: I'll check it out.

LADY DE LISSE: Maybe you could write a story for them?

LIMONOV: What—in Russian?

LADY DE LISSE: Your French is very good!

LIMONOV: Damn it!

LADY DE LISSE: What?

LIMONOV: Look at me.

LADY DE LISSE: What's the problem?

LIMONOV: Poplin with silk? It's uncanny.

Carbon Pages

LADY DE LISSE: Oh, Eddie.

LIMONOV: I can't wear this—it's heinous. It's provincial. I look like a muzhik.

LADY DE LISSE: Eddie, you can wear anything you like. They don't love you because of what you wear. They love you because of how genius you are and brave and handsome...

LIMONOV: It's not about them. Poplin?! Am I insane?!

LADY DE LISSE: Come here, darling.

LIMONOV: And what's this about the novel? It's going. Ca Va. Jesus, it's going. You know that writing is like fishing. Jesus.

LADY DE LISSE: I know, Eddie.

LIMONOV: What about your Opera House?

LADY DE LISSE: Eddie, I want you to win.

LIMONOV: Remember that story about my childhood? In the middle of the night I climbed the belfry, I clasped my hands and prayed to whoever was listening. When I grow up, make it so that my fate is not like those of others. Make me succeed and my enemies tremble. Let them remember my name. Well look at me. I'm there. I'm in Paris. I know people. Less than a year ago I had holes in my shoes. I'm hard for you. We're conning these people. I don't give a shit about them.

LADY DE LISSE: Okay, Eddie.

LIMONOV: Jesus. Fuck.

LADY DE LISSE: Darling? Are you crying?

LIMONOV: I...

LADY DE LISSE: Tell me.

LIMONOV: I can't believe they levelled Penn Station! Everything in this world is rotten and ugly and falling apart. No beauty remains unraped. Just do the Sainte-Chapelle next — replace it with a fucking izba.

> Eduard Limonov looks outside the chambre window, then back at his lover.

No Weapon Formed Against You

LIMONOV: And... YOU! You're worst of all!

LADY DE LISSE: What is it you think I said, Eduard?

LIMONOV: You baptized whore! I work my ass off all day welding uranium! And I come home and find you squandered it on some guy? You—

LADY DE LISSE: —I don't understand. Eduard, what's gotten into you?!

LIMONOV: Get your ASS in that BATHROOM!

LADY DE LISSE: Eduard? Eduard!

LIMONOV: SHUT UP! SHUT UP SHUT UP SHUT UP SHUT UP! And don't take one step out this bathroom! HEAR YE HEAR YE you skank. I'll eat you alive. I already nibbled on a piece of that *vendeur*. Remember how you cried? Remember how you said NO NO DON'T EAT THE NICE VEGETABLE MAN—

LADY DE LISSE: (*wailing*) Let me out!

LIMONOV: I DON'T WANT TO HEAR A SINGLE WORD. I'M SICK. I'VE GOT WORMS IN MY GUT—

> KNOCK KNOCK KNOCK.

LIMONOV: You hear that? He's come for you. You've set me OFF and now the TSAR is here—

> The apartment door smashes Eduard's nose and he topples over.

LIMONOV: OW OW!

> Two stonefaced men make themselves at home. One short, one tall. They aren't KGB. They're wearing leather jackets and scarred physiognomies.

LIMONOV: *Messieurs*, you'll have to make an appointment with my doctor—

INTRUDER 1: —I can show you lunatic. I can show you real lunatic.

INTRUDER 2: Where's the money, Eduard?

Carbon Pages

INTRUDER 1: Look at this shithole.

>He pulls Eduard by the collar.

INTRUDER 2: This what you're putting it towards?

INTRUDER 1: You look like a flamingo.

>The other one upturns his writing desk.

INTRUDER 2: The crazyman act only works so many times, Eduard.

INTRUDER 1: Where's the money?

LIMONOV: I don't have it.

INTRUDER 1: Don't make me hurt you!

INTRUDER 2: (*chewing*) What's this—Russian soup?

LIMONOV: You can break this whole apartment—see for yourself.

>The creditor bitch slaps Eduard, throwing him against the bathroom door.

INTRUDER 1: I'll be back Tuesday morning. That time I'll be alone. Don't pay your dues you'll be legless.

INTRUDER 2: Don't borrow what you can't pay back Eduard!

>The shorter man rips down the US flag as they leave.

>Limonov's huddled on the floor.

LADY DE LISSE: (*gently*) Eduard. Unlock the door.

>He does so and then sits on the edge of the bed. The countess silently sits next to him. Her tears are already drying. She strokes Eddie-baby's head and lays him on her lap which is soft like an eiderdown and caresses his hair as he weeps.

LADY DE LISSE: Oh Eddie-baby. Shh.

No Weapon Formed Against You

It's okay.

>The chief pastime of the boy called Igor Letov was masturbation. At night, sometimes, Igor would get dressed and walk the streets of Moscow. He might smoke a papiross. The city would be fast asleep, the trolleybus wires waving in the breeze, the giant faces of cosmonauts illumined by traffic lights glowing amber, fading, glowing again, he'd see the posters for new comedy films, incandescent arrow-signs reading *crosswalk*, translucent dark gazette stands, apartment complexes mid-construction, soon to be identical to countless apartments of the same kind, housing people identical to countless other people, living fragile lives, some not so fragile, some leaving early this life, some not. The boy felt like no one understood him, and that no one could. But, he supposed, things could be worse. At least there is no war.
>
>And just like that, as if no time had passed at all, it was a hot summer afternoon again, and everyone was buying wafer cups of fat-cream ice cream or beer and wore their short-sleeve button-ups, because today was the day of a big parade.

ALEXANDER: Well did they at least tell you if they'd be at the front of the parade or the back?!

IGOR LETOV: What?!

ALEXANDER: I said—

IGOR LETOV: I can't hear you over the noise...the trombone. *Hey...guy with the trombone!*

ALEXANDER: How do we find them?!

IGOR LETOV: Just stick to me, we'll run into them eventually!!

No Weapon Formed Against You

On the roadside was a big barrel on wheels with a tap attached and the barrel read KVASS and underneath in hand-painted lettering, 20 kopecks. The minor folly of a thousand customers in the early afternoon had made already a dark puddle and rill on the porous concrete which rose in sugary humid. A man in a van had given out signs and placards. Through the mainstreet went a jormugandr of students and youths all carrying flowers and picket signs and portraits and ribbons. There were banners adorned with slogans like GLORY TO PEACE and FORWARD TO THE CONSTRUCTION OF COMMUNISM and GREETINGS OLYMPIANS. And though ostensibly it was a celebration, Dugin and Letov, and Dugin especially, could not help but feel in the air the strange omen that the celebration was in fact a protest, a protest against what he could not put his finger on. Chauvinism, Nazism, Minolta Weathermatics. These were all good guesses. Certainly the marchers did not know, and maybe there was no answer. What could you possibly be protesting? thought Dugin. Don't you understand you own it all?

A giant papier mache globus of the Earth was lettered in red with WORLD PEACE NOW. A smiling anthropomorphic corn boy which at that time was already fifteen years old with a sash reading Wonder Corn. After the parade the people would line up at the same delivery van and return the signs one by one to wherever they came from.

IGOR LETOV: Maybe...maybe if we start at the front and make our way back...?

The crowd was like thicket. Suddenly a voice yelled in his ear and he felt a hand on his shoulder.

BRAT TEVANIAN: LETOV! What's cookin!

IGOR LETOV: Jesus. Hey. We were looking for you.

BRAT RYMIAN: Smelled you from afar, weasel. Where's your tuba?

IGOR LETOV: You couldn't think of a better spot? I almost got trampled.

BRAT RYMIAN: You needa build some muscle, weasel. Experts now know exercise five times a week is essential to warding off dystrophy. I hope you're eating—

Carbon Pages

BRAT TEVANIAN: —Look here's the deal—

Dugin interrupted:

ALEXANDER: —If you're the marketeers you guys get to business or what?

BRAT TEVANIAN: Letov who's this kid. I'm quivering! Listen yeah uh, *hey watch where you're stepping!*

...Callin me a marketeer in broad daylight like this...me and my brother be businessmen.

BRAT RYMIAN: We're businessmen.

BRAT TEVANIAN: How old are you?

ALEXANDER: Seventeen.

BRAT TEVANIAN: Then shut up and let the businessmen talk, birdshit.

BRAT RYMIAN: Yeah.

BRAT TEVANIAN: Nah I'm kidding with you. Like, dig it, you're right in that we got business. Me and my brother we get so far, but we need someone with a Moscow residency. Brat can't get picked up again. Does your buddy have a Moscow residency, weasel?

IGOR LETOV: Yeah.

BRAT TEVANIAN: Brat, tell him about the merchandise.

BRAT RYMIAN: We have these Finns bringing us some knickers. Crêpe. Says Made in Finland and all. They meet us near the border, we book a room, have a few drinks and change hands right? I got a guy in Leningrad—shit, you would not BELIEVE the *babki* he'd doll for these things. We've got a thing in Tomsk with these fur trappers. You would. not. BELIEVE what they give for a few jars of grandad's samagon. Anyway, he's coming down only late next month right? We can't stay that long—Tevanian has re-sits. *Hey comrade take my eye out why not!* Anyway all you have to do is sit on the cargo till our friend gets there, deal?

IGOR LETOV: What do we get? And my friend—

ALEXANDER: I'm taking a risk. It's my residency.

No Weapon Formed Against You

BRAT RYMIAN: Plenty to go around, Stierlitz. Yknow, I had these Polacks exchange us some records. It didn't end well. Apparently they were covers or something. All I know is whole thing cost me an arm and a leg. Yes, weasel, fact of the matter is the kapitalist nations are as unique to each other as Kursk is to Chelyabinsk.

BRAT TEVANIAN: How's that sound for a deal?

IGOR LETOV: Colossal.

BRAT TEVANIAN: Look enjoy the parade. We're meeting some girls at my place. Mam's a vegetable she don't know what's going on. Join?

IGOR LETOV: (*looks at Dugin*) Eh. Some other time.

BRAT RYMIAN: Oh yeah one more thing.

> The brother sticks a pistol barrel to Letov's temple.

> Dugin's heart skips a beat. The other brother just laughs.

BRAT RYMIAN: Relaaax. It's welded shut, see?

IGOR LETOV: Comrades don't know that do they?

> He smacks it down.

BRAT TEVANIAN: It's a sports pistol. Same thing they use in the Olympics.

BRAT RYMIAN: Take it as a souvenir. Just don't pull the trigger unless you never wanna do shadow puppets.

BRAT TEVANIAN: Never know where life'll take you.

BRAT RYMIAN: If an officer comes knocking just tell 'im you're an Olympian.

> Limonov is shopping at a corner shop. He stands at the counter in a brilliant wool coat. He buys bouillon cubes, dishrags, tinned pork, and baking chocolate.

LIMONOV: And this.

SHOPKEEPER: Four francs forty.

Carbon Pages

He turns out his pockets.

LIMONOV: I think I don't have enough.

SHOPKEEPER: Four francs forty.

LIMONOV: I'm five cents short.

SHOPKEEPER: ...

LIMONOV: It's only five cents. Can you let me off?

Waiting behind him is a line of impatient customers.

SHOPKEEPER: If you don't have enough, you don't have enough.

LIMONOV: I'll be right back. Can you wait?

The lady, annoyed, simply looks back at the long line behind him.

But he knows his apartment is too far. So Eduard reaches for the dishrags, yet it's the pork which he clanks back down on the shelf.

In his cozy Moscow apartment Igor watches a documentary on life abroad which plays in grainy black and white. A staccato montage barfs a melange, all set to ugly jazz, of long-hair hippies, rioting negroes, titty mags, obese millionaires, skydiving, papal processions, cabaret, Dali, girls slobbering for Paul McCartney, the bombing of Nagasaki, May '68, Alain Delon smoking a Marlboro, high speed Italian racecars, Dachau, African boys with swollen bellies.

Later he'll watch the lead of this detective show kiss the main girl and he's seen the episode before but she's drop-dead, and that's all he'll think about.

The night after the parade, the two boys sit at the waterfront, taking turns swigging a bottle.

ALEXANDER: So on my birthday, the old bastard, my father, gives me a book. Something about the Whites. Anyway I don't usually read *apparatuschina* like

No Weapon Formed Against You

this, but I'm at the dacha all week and have nothing to do so I might as well. And to my surprise, it's good. Not great and maybe not good in the way the author intended, but it touches me. The hero is this cold-blooded grenadier on the Caucasus who lays down squads of revolutionaries. Obviously at the end he bawls his eyes out, but for the meat of the book he's just this...man. He's a degenerate and keeps his cool under pressure. I almost start believing that he's some sort of a secret code. That the author is trying to whisper in my ear. *This is a true hero, he says, and though I sneak it under the nose of the censors the little touches can't evade the most thoughtful and erudite among you.* I'm talking about his long hair or like the way he rests his hands in his pockets. So ok he gets reformed in the end.

But maybe what the author is *really* saying is that all the world is the Caucasus, and to grow your hair and to make watermelon wine is what it means to be a real hero. Does that make sense? The point is I was feeling some mystical tether to this trash. For a summer and a half that paperback was my bible. No matter how awful the world got, Ferin was the angel on my shoulder. That's the author. I knew that he was *on my side*. Not even Vasya and Kost and the others got it. One day, and this is amazing, I find out he lives three floors above me, the author. Imagine that? My whole life. What are the odds? I mean really what are the odds? Long story short I make his acquaintance and one evening he invites me for tea.

He's ancient. In fact he fought in the Civil War. He shows me his badges, his patches. He's proud. *We're lucky to be passing the torch to your excellent generation. Every day I watch the TV and I see how heroic you are. Everything begins with the youth. Everything, everything, everything. You remind me of Steel Arms Burlov,* he says. *But you probably wouldn't know who that is—he's before your time.* And that's another thing I hate. Don't you hate this; when one of these geriatrics says that? Does no one else realize that in the seventeen years I've been alive nothing has been invented. Nothing has been achieved. And nothing has changed. He probably thinks we have our own Steel Arms Burlov. Anyway, what was I saying?

IGOR LETOV: You met him for tea?

ALEXANDER: So... I tell him how much I love the book and he's actually surprised. I think most of 'em end up in libraries. Eventually I say something like how much I relate to Saberov, the hero. He corrects me; the amoral human centre. Okay well I like the amoral human centre. In fact I like him before he joins the Reds, and I end up implying, probably, that he does too. At some point for no reason at all I bring up high rim-and-trims. He looks at me like I fed him a frog... Look at the couple over there by the front. They're smooching.

IGOR LETOV: What happened then?

ALEXANDER: He says... *The truth is, I wanted to kill Saberov at the end. Brutally. But the* gosizdat *wanted something edgier that summer. In truth I despise that character. And I can't understand how anyone couldn't. If you actually view Saberov as some sort of figure to be emulated then you haven't understood a damn word I've written and I want you to leave my home. Everything you're telling me is wrong. All these hints, they are your fabrications.*

Well okay so they're fabrications is it such a crime if I use my imagination? And finally he stands up and says *you are the evil which I wished to expose in my book. You are everything wrong with the common weal of the Earth, whose perversions and avarice are stoked by a minority of Earthly cretins.*

> There is some leviathan of resentment submerged in his unsteady tone, swiftly washed away by the amnesiac tide of drunkenness.

I remember his exact words. At least I think I do. Thinking's fuzzy and...over time...the order of it... But anyway...that must be exactly what he said...what did I do with that paperback? I don't remember.

> He looks over the water. Alexander becomes quiet and sad and for the first time Letov sees him not as the older kid but as a good friend.

ALEXANDER: All I want is for what I say to have some effect. If I can just get this manifesto printed in a foreign paper—I can die happy.

> Letov toys with the gun. It's a funny looking weapon. The barrel is like a German Luger but three times as long, and the handle is carved from wood.

IGOR LETOV: I've got an idea.

ALEXANDER: What?

No Weapon Formed Against You

IGOR LETOV: Let's rob the Pioneers' camp.

ALEXANDER: The Pioneers' camp?

IGOR LETOV: That's right—let's rob em.

ALEXANDER: Why?

IGOR LETOV: They lock up all sorts of stuff. Confiscated gold, *hic*—jewellery, from all over the district. Cause it's the last place anyone'll look.

ALEXANDER: That's—*hic*—genius.

IGOR LETOV: With that kinda money we can get you in a million papers.

> The Young Pioneers were a youth organization in those days, a bit like the Scouts. They hiked and sang songs. Their camp grounds were on a lakeside.
>
> Alexander and Letov staggered over the fence bordering the camp grounds and reached the living quarters.

IGOR LETOV: All these places are built the exact same. I know them through and through—*hic*.

ALEXANDER: Here are the wash basins.

IGOR LETOV: Alright then the Quartermaster office is over here.

> They open a window and climb in, totally hammered, but once they look around they find they've made a huge mistake:

ALEXANDER: Get up. Up. This isn't an office. This is the sleeping quarters.

IGOR LETOV: Shh. It's the sleeping quarters.

ALEXANDER: That's what I said.

IGOR LETOV: I know!

ALEXANDER: Heh.

IGOR LETOV: Shh. Hehe.

ALEXANDER: Quit giggling. What now?

Carbon Pages

IGOR LETOV: Go through. Canteen is behind us. So office must be straight through.

ALEXANDER: If one of these anklebiters sees us they'll wake up the whole board.

IGOR LETOV: Follow me. Through here. Quiet. Here we go. Office.

ALEXANDER: Let's try the drawers.

> Inside the administrative office stands a bust of Lenin who eyes them with disappointment.

IGOR LETOV: Wouldja look at that stash?

ALEXANDER: Slingshot. Magazine.

IGOR LETOV: Any money?

ALEXANDER: Basketball cards? American.

IGOR LETOV: Records.

ALEXANDER: Records?

IGOR LETOV: I mean, like, documents.

ALEXANDER: What a gyp. Hey did you lose the pistol?

IGOR LETOV: No, I have it.

ALEXANDER: Is it loaded?

IGOR LETOV: Yeah.

ALEXANDER: Just don't pull that trigger.

IGOR LETOV: Whatever. Take what you can and let's—*hic*—scram.

> Again, they tiptoe past the long rows of bunk beds full of sleeping children.

IGOR LETOV: Alright I'm out.

ALEXANDER: Hold on.

IGOR LETOV: Hurry up.

No Weapon Formed Against You

ALEXANDER: Quiet.

IGOR LETOV: What's taking you?

ALEXANDER: Be quiet.

IGOR LETOV: Shit. Al?

> In Alexander's way stands a child rubbing his eyes under his glasses. He stares in disbelief right at the hairless creature of the night in front of him.

CHILD: I don't know you...

IGOR LETOV: Al! C'mon!

ALEXANDER: Wait.

IGOR LETOV: Let's for the gate!

> But Alexander doesn't move. No one moves.

IGOR LETOV: Al, he'll wake the councillors. Just make a break!

> His vision hurtles the child's features up and up like a spacecraft launching a hundred times a minute.
>
> He tries to fasten his gaze on the ginger boy's eyes, but they're like one of those targets on a swivel in a shooting range. Who is this man standing in front of me thinks the boy.
>
> Alexander says nothing. He takes a deep breath, raises his hand and summons all his energy to command, mutely, go to sleep. *Turn around, walk to your bed, and forget my presence as you forget a nightmare. Return to your bed, and pull the cover over your ears.*
>
> Out by the lake the camp dog has spotted Igor.
>
> Mutely too the pioneer seems to respond. He thinks he's having a nightmare, that maybe it would be better to retrace his steps and invent a new dream, one more pleasant, one not involving a stinking hairless man in a dark coat passing his verdict. Is this because he wet the bed? It wasn't his fault. Is

the man here to pass judgement? Has the councillor sent him as punishment?

Return to your sleep and forget my presence. Return to your... And just like his instructions, Dugin conjures in his mind's eye the image of the bed and the ginger's head on his pillow, still not breaking his gaze.

No that can't be it! The councillor would never let ANYONE stay up after hours. Not even the canteen lady!

And just like that the boy bolts to tell on the burglars.

IGOR LETOV: Hurry! It sounds rabid.

For a moment Dugin is so depressed that he doesn't want to go, but the noise of the barking mutt running ever closer sobers him up.

ALEXANDER: I can't see anything in this dark.

IGOR LETOV: Just keep going, just keep going.

DOG: BARK BARK!

IGOR LETOV: Hold on.

ALEXANDER: What?

IGOR LETOV: Stop!

ALEXANDER: I can't! The dog!

IGOR LETOV: Where are you going?! My foot's stuck. Help me!

But Alexander has leapt over the fence already.

And the dog is getting closer...

ALEXANDER: Scare it, Igor!

...closer

IGOR LETOV: BOO! BOO MUTT! It's not stopping!

No Weapon Formed Against You

Now Igor removes his sports pistol.

The dog is drooling at the mouth. It's a fierce doberman and he can almost see himself in its black eyes. Its bone canines are three inches long.

IGOR LETOV: SHOO YOU MUTT!

He aims the barrel in the air.

The whole camp is awake and they're staring at the commotion out the windows. Igor aims the barrel between the dog's eyes, then back in the air.

As the mutt strains its legs into a leap Igor hides his face in the nook of his elbow as far as possible from the blast which will liberate his digits from the bone. He clenches his eyes shut. The mutt leaps, he pulls the trigger and

KABOOM!

The dog scampers in fright.

There are screams from the living cabins. Igor frees himself and scrambles over the gate and into the night, never to be seen again. As he runs, he sees his hand.

IGOR LETOV: Thank you God.

The bullet had warped the barrel, which sent the bullet backward, narrowly scratching the nail of his picking thumb and leaving a white mark.

No Weapon Formed Against You

FABIENNE: So, Olivier, what's this—the fourth glass this week? You keep dropping them and they'll have to start importing sand from Dover.

OLIVIER: It's alright. Anyway, Eduard, as I was saying. Where *is* your Jacqueline?

LIMONOV: She's not feeling well.

OLIVIER: Don't let her get you down. She can be a real recluse.

LIMONOV: Is that...?

OLIVIER: Who are we looking for?

LIMONOV: Thought I saw creditors. I have money troubles.

OLIVIER: I see.

LIMONOV: I keep thinking about this idea for a short story. For L'Idiot maybe. But I've to invent a way to convince them to take a Russian-language story.

OLIVIER: You should write it in French.

LIMONOV: You think so?

OLIVIER: *L'Idiot*'s been wanting you for weeks.

LIMONOV: That's true?

OLIVIER: It's what I hear.

LIMONOV: Okay, then I'll write it.

SPEER: Ciao Al. And where's Vasya?

ALEXANDER: He'll be here. He's on Bo's farm.

SPEER: The hell is he doing on Bo's farm?

ALEXANDER: It's a surprise!

Carbon Pages

KOST: Speer get with the program.

SPEER: What?

KOST: Try this. Just swallow.

SPEER: What's it.

KOST: Periciazine.

SPEER: Isn't that the stuff they use on mental cases?

KOST: Where do you think we got it.

>Igor's picking away at the six-string and for a while the night swims past.

SPEER: Who's that in the shadows?

KOST: It's Iron Felix!

SPEER: Kost you're doped.

IGOR LETOV: It's Vasya. Vasya who's your friend?

KOST: It's a goat!

IGOR LETOV: Why'd he bring a goat? Dugin, this your doing?

ALEXANDER: Well since you ask, yes. Vasya stole this goat on my recommendation.

VASYA: You, this is the lads. The lads, this is...well I don't know what his name is. I didn't exactly ask.

ALEXANDER: Today is a very special day.

VASYA: Kost, help Speer tie it up...

ALEXANDER: I've made your dreams a reality.

VASYA: ...and get me a drink.

KOST: (*sarcastically*) Yes, Fuhrer.

SPEER: Oy Vasya if you're my Fuhrer how come I didn't vote for you?

>They all laugh and string up the goat.

No Weapon Formed Against You

> Goat lets out a noncommittal bleeh as he plops onto his ass.

VASYA: Food for thought, Dugin.

ALEXANDER: What?

VASYA: I never figured how much they look like a big baby.

> The goat masticates, with its pot belly hanging out. Its slit eyes stare off into space.

VASYA: Like a...giant hairy baby.

ALEXANDER: Now you see why the Greeks invented Pan.

VASYA: Is he to your satisfaction? Does he fulfill the requirements?

ALEXANDER: He's perfect.

> Alexander Dugin takes the guitar on the tree stump and plucks strings at random. Loud. And he recites words all the while:

ALEXANDER: Devil or beast, to me, to me,

My man! my man!

Come with trumpets sounding shrill!

VASYA: Igor, here. Take this end of the rope and knot his horns together. Yeah. Knot them. I'll tie his front hooves. Got it?

IGOR LETOV: I think so.

VASYA: Alright let's hoist him up. Ready? Kost.

KOST: Me?

VASYA: You've got a big day coming up. You do the honours?

KOST: Of course.

ALEXANDER: Over the hill!

Come with drums low muttering

KOST: Hold that rope.

Carbon Pages

SPEER: Now, pull!

ALEXANDER: From the spring!

Come with flute and come with pipe!

Am I not ripe?

VASYA: Pull Igor! For god's sake pull up—he's saggin'!

KOST: Nearly...

ALEXANDER: I, who wait and writhe and wrestle

With air that hath no boughs to nestle

My body, weary of empty clasp,

Strong as a lion and sharp as an asp —

SPEER: I can't smell so good lads. It's too bright.

ALEXANDER: Come, O come!

VASYA: Sig Heil!

IGOR LETOV: My arms are getting tired!

ALEXANDER: Wish for something everyone! Everyone make a wish!

SPEER: KEEP CUTTING.

KOST: Hold it!

VASYA: SIG HEIL. SIG HEIL.

ALEXANDER: I-am numb
With the lon-ely lust of devil-dom!

KOST: There!

ALEXANDER: ...

IGOR LETOV: ...

SPEER: ...It's done...

The crickets chirp.

No Weapon Formed Against You

IGOR LETOV: Now what?

ALEXANDER: ...

KOST: ...My step-father is taking me to the physician's tomorrow. I might have jogger's foot.

>Speer lunges for the acoustic and explodes into a chorus of nonsense-chords:

SPEER: BAHBAHBAHBAHBAHBAH BAH bah BAHHHH!

>As he looks around, for the first time in a long time, Igor Letov feels truly at home and laughs at everything in the world. In all the chaos, everyone starts showing off their cool moves. Kost is howling and they're kicking and laughing and twirling and whooping in the noise while the red soaks through their coffee-cream tweed. While the red saturates their corduroy coats. The music went chaos and they're howling and he's on all fours in the puddle barking naked—now THAT'S what I call a dog's life! And Dugin is jiggin' his bum like Bob Dylan. I am watching you go! My rosy-cheeked babies. My little centurions. Look how you've grown. Look how you're jiving! I'll never forget—I've taken the snapshot. I'll cry it forever and ever this moment no matter what mistakes my Alexander makes, no matter what path he goes down in years hence, no matter the crowd, to me he'll always be this little kid with a heart of gold. I will. Never. Let. You. Be. An. Orphan: one day again I'll squeeze your cheek under the cover of gigantic cyatheles and we'll watch it together.

>Because look at your jigging the red soaking the same earth baptized by the Euphrates and I'm almost crying remembering these little moments. This is my late nights. This is my walks on the promenade. This is my youth, my wooings and goings. This is my alchemic designs, my cadavers of fortune. This is how we lived and breathed. On the porch went nineteen-hundred-eighty.

* * * * * * * * *
* * * * * * *
* * * * * * * * *

Carbon Pages

LIMONOV: You smell like a lilac on fire. You smell like a petal pressed for years between the pages of a Teutonic tome.

LADY DE LISSE: Mm. My strong bard. Kiss me.

LIMONOV: Your wrinkles are like the rills of the glittering Volga on the noble Kievan steppe.

LADY DE LISSE: Kiss me.

LIMONOV: There's something I can't stop thinking about.

LADY DE LISSE: What?

LIMONOV: That story I wrote for *L'Idiot*. They still haven't paid me.

LADY DE LISSE: Still? You said that a week ago.

LIMONOV: That was a week ago and now it's now and I haven't heard a word.

LADY DE LISSE: Try calling.

LIMONOV: I've been calling. They say he's not there—the guy.

LADY DE LISSE: Hallier?

LIMONOV: Hallier. Yeah. It's fine living like Van Gogh but even he sold a painting once in a while.

LADY DE LISSE: You need to get some answers.

LIMONOV: I know.

LADY DE LISSE: You should march right up to *L'Idiot* and ask him in person.

LIMONOV: I've been thinking the same.

LADY DE LISSE: Now come. Kiss me, muscular man.

LIMONOV: I think I'll go right this second.

LADY DE LISSE: But... we wanted to stay in, didn't we?

LIMONOV: I can't let them get away with this, Jackie—they remember everything.

No Weapon Formed Against You

LADY DE LISSE: Okay.

> Before Eduard closes the door behind him:

LADY DE LISSE: Eddie...

LIMONOV: Yes?

LADY DE LISSE: Nothing...

> The writer rushes off towards *L'Idiot's* HQ.
>
> Left alone, the Countess weeps silently into her palms as rain clouds gather outside.

LIMONOV: Is this Jean-Edern Hallier's office?

SECRETARY: Yes.

LIMONOV: Well I'd like to see him. I printed a story with you two weeks ago and I haven't seen a cent.

SECRETARY: That's alright but I'm afraid Monsieur Hallier is on a vacation.

LIMONOV: Oh really?

SECRETARY: Yes.

LIMONOV: So if I walk into that office I won't find him at his desk?

SECRETARY: Monsieur, I would not advise—

> The writer does not wait for an answer and barges into the editor-in-chief's office.

LIMONOV: There's no one here.

SECRETARY: It's like I told you!

LIMONOV: Right, right. Whatever you say. Then I'll tell you what. I'm not leaving this building until I get my money.

SECRETARY: It will be a long time before he is back.

LIMONOV: I have all the time in the world.

Carbon Pages

> Hour after hour passes, with no sign of the editor. Limonov drifts in and out of dreams on the waiting room couch. He dreams of being a little boy, and the little boy dreams of being a knight.

JEAN-EDERN: Morning, cheri. Who's this? A circus performer?

SECRETARY: It's an Eduard Limonov, monsieur. He's complaining about a payment for a short story.

JEAN-EDERN: Did you tell him I'm on vacation?

SECRETARY: Yes, but—

JEAN-EDERN: How long has he been here?

SECRETARY: Since yesterday morning, monsieur.

JEAN-EDERN: Hey? Hello. Rise and shine. Let's step into my office.

> In his office:

JEAN-EDERN: Sorry to keep you like this uh what's the name again?

LIMONOV: Eduard Limonov.

JEAN-EDERN: I was in the Sologne. No business—you know how it is. So what brings you?

LIMONOV: My money.

JEAN-EDERN: Yes?

LIMONOV: Where is it, you bovine cock.

JEAN-EDERN: I don't understand.

LIMONOV: You printed my story. Where is my two hundred and fifty francs?

JEAN-EDERN: Why, it should be in your piggy bank, monsieur Eduard.

LIMONOV: Is that your story? If I don't leave this room with what I'm owed I'm going to tear apart this room and pawn the remainder.

JEAN-EDERN: Just one second. (*on phone*) Allô? Marie? Can you check Eduard's billing address. Yes? Right? Ok. God bless you goddamit, Marie.

No Weapon Formed Against You

LIMONOV: What.

JEAN-EDERN: You're rue des archives, aren't you? In the Marais?

LIMONOV: That's right.

JEAN-EDERN: Well that's where we sent your cheque.

LIMONOV: You sent it.

JEAN-EDERN: Well Eduard, the closest I can guess is that one of these assholes screwed up somewhere along the line. It can't be a pretty hole can it?

LIMONOV: It's not.

JEAN-EDERN: I don't blame you for being angry. The systems they have in the Marais are draconic. Goddamn incomprehensible. Look here's what I'll do, I'll issue you a new cheque and sticky on another forty for your sorrow. This time you'll take it in person, no? Last one's probably in Frankfurt.

LIMONOV: I, uh. Thank you.

JEAN-EDERN: Don't worry about it. It's an unnavigable system. Especially for a foreigner such as yourself.

LIMONOV: I appreciate it, Jean-Edern.

JEAN-EDERN: You wrote the story about the millionaire's butler in Manhattan, yes?

LIMONOV: That's right.

JEAN-EDERN: And him fucking the master's maid on his own bed and pissing pow pow in his sink.

LIMONOV: Yes, Jean-Edern, that's mine.

JEAN-EDERN: Well, Eduard I liked it. You know that? I really like it! I had my jaw open reading it like in the Disney cartoons.

LIMONOV: Thanks.

JEAN-EDERN: Can I ask you a question? Is it, you know, semi-autobiographical?

LIMONOV: It's documentary.

Carbon Pages

JEAN-EDERN: I knew it. Ha! I knew it! When he was left alone while the master went to a party and the hero took aim from a bolt-action at his master's head. I was hoping he'd pull the trigger. It'd be like that *Taxi Driver*. Goddamn if I didn't want to do that to some of the assholes I've met.

LIMONOV: There's a whole lot more I could write about that parasite.

JEAN-EDERN: And what about the part with the African in the sandpit. Did you really...well, yknow...?

LIMONOV: Didn't I just say it's all true?

JEAN-EDERN: Excellent!

LIMONOV: I could probably write fiction that wasn't about me but I just don't feel like it.

JEAN-EDERN: Well monsieur Eduard, it's been a pleasure meeting you. Now look, when you finish this book of yours and uh I assume it regards the same subject, meaning yourself?

LIMONOV: Myself.

JEAN-EDERN: And this book following the subject of myself do you have a publisher for it yes, no, maybe so?

LIMONOV: I have some bites but I'm fishing.

JEAN-EDERN: Well when you finish this book with the subject of myself and the publishers for whom you are fishing let's *put our heads together* as the Americans say. I have a friend who specializes in emigre authors. I make no promises. But I'll tell him that you're the best Russian writer I know. Marie will give you my personals.

LIMONOV: Out of curiosity what exactly do you mean by that—the best Russian writer. The story's in French.

JEAN-EDERN: Naturally. But it shines through that you are a man out of time and out of place. You're a rogue.

LIMONOV: Yes, yes but what does that mean *best Russian author*.

No Weapon Formed Against You

JEAN-EDERN: Don't be offended. We have quite a few brilliant Russians in Paris.

LIMONOV: If the story is so good, then under what auspices do you neglect calling me simply—and I tell you Hallier, there's a million publishers that were clawing for this story by the way—so under what auspices do you neglect to call me the *best author*.

JEAN-EDERN: Eduard. Let's not get off on the wrong foot. Paris is filled with talented artists.

LIMONOV: Anyone could have taken that story. It's better than any of the slop you're putting out.

JEAN-EDERN: Have a seat again.

LIMONOV: What — Marc-Nabe? That troglodyte?

JEAN-EDERN: It's not on the level.

LIMONOV: You wanted me to pull the trigger, is that it? You people have no imagination!

JEAN-EDERN: If you MUST know—sit down. Sit down! If you must know, it's—look let me get the issue. It's lacking.

LIMONOV: How?

JEAN-EDERN: Well, the grammar, for one thing.

LIMONOV: What about it?

JEAN-EDERN: It's how a child speaks.

LIMONOV: Yes?

JEAN-EDERN: There's spelling mistakes every second word, the punctuation is lousy, you substitute English and Russian all over the place, and half the sentences are just incoherent. What do you want me to say? That it's Henry Miller? You know how long it took *L'Idiot* to edit this?

LIMONOV: So it's the language after all...

JEAN-EDERN: Oh c'mon.

Carbon Pages

LIMONOV: I knew it.

JEAN-EDERN: Don't be offended. It's a fine romp.

LIMONOV: I appreciate you taking the time to see me, Monsieur Hallier.

JEAN-EDERN: Now hold on. You're offended. Tell me about this new novel. Sit down. Are you very far along?

LIMONOV: It's taking the time it deserves. Writing is like fishing: you can't rush it. You must throw in your hook and wait.

> Later that morning, Limonov in the chic pied-a-terre of his friend Olivier:

OLIVIER: So what's the problem, comintern?

LIMONOV: I feel awful. I don't know. I guess...I feel like I've made a clown of myself. It was a half-baked story.

OLIVIER: What are you talking about? It was an excellent piece. Didn't Hallier say so?

LIMONOV: He said it was good.

OLIVIER: Coming from him good is great.

LIMONOV: I feel like a...a bear on a unicycle.

OLIVIER: Because of the grammar?

LIMONOV: I disgraced myself.

OLIVIER: Don't be ridiculous.

LIMONOV: And don't laugh, I disgraced this city.

OLIVIER: Paris?

LIMONOV: Paris.

OLIVIER: Oh please—Paris!

LIMONOV: What.

OLIVIER: It's a village!

No Weapon Formed Against You

LIMONOV: You don't like Paris?

OLIVIER: Of course I like Paris, don't get me wrong. I grew up here and I have fond memories. But, for me, the joy of life is constant reanimation. I'd like to visit Cambodia. Next month I'm being escorted to Tibet. I want to visit New York for God's sake!—it's the greatest city on Earth. You know they have a statue of the Fonz?

LIMONOV: So what—you don't care about it?

OLIVIER: It's a bore, this country. It's so blase.

LIMONOV: It's yours.

OLIVIER: Any place can be yours!

LIMONOV: I don't think I feel that way. And I don't understand why you don't feel a little insulted. I think you should be angry at Hallier that he didn't have higher standards and at me that I permitted it.

OLIVIER: Gosh don't take it so seriously! Look, that butler was on everybody's lips. Character. Shock. That's what people want. Before you came along I had no meaning of the word adventure. You opened my eyes! I don't just mean the story but in general. Yes. So WHAT if the story has some mistakes and some punctuation. It broke the rules. Fuck the rules! There's a MILLION fluent French writers with perfect prose and grammar. The same Flaubert, Balzac blah blah blah. Who cares about them. There's a million of them.

But there is only ONE Eduard Limonov!

Eduard fights an overwhelming urge to coldcock this weasel.

The Russian dandy goes to his Countess De Lisse. He enters her opulent but bare dwelling, where she is packing her bags.

LADY DE LISSE: Eduard, I—

Carbon Pages

In a paroxysmal fit, he hugs the countess, pressing his face into her breasts and weeping.

LIMONOV: I love you Jackie.

I love you.

I love you Jackie.

I'm sorry.

I'll never leave you again...

Into the office came in an older officer, ten badges for each one of the other's, and a sickly pallor.

BLUE SUIT: Hello, Igor. (*to KGB Ive*) Psst Ive. I got some...uh, stomach bug. Don't worry though all's well. (*to Igor*) Now Igor. What should I write in my report? Are you cooperating?

KGB IVE: Sir, citizen Igor Fyodorvich Letov is in suspicion of the proliferation of anti-Soviet propaganda with intent of defaming the Soviet state and social system, as per Article One Ninety dash One of the Criminal Codex.

BLUE SUIT: Tell us about these crimes you've committed. And before you say anything, just know we're already well aware of everything

IGOR LETOV: I've done nothing.

KGB IVE: Article seventy: participation in an anti-Soviet organization.

BLUE SUIT: Yes Ive. One moment Ive. Igor, if you provide us with the names of your accomplices, and recount the details of this organization with total honesty, then we'll formalize your story as a confession.

IGOR LETOV: ...

No Weapon Formed Against You

The officer in the blue suit has basically a kind and grieved face. Many years ago he was very handsome. Now, he wrinkles his brow in trying to understand what the need is in sticking your head out like this. Why do this to yourself, he seems to say. It's a nice sunny day: there's a concert on, and people are enjoying themselves.

BLUE SUIT: Are you a Soviet man?

IGOR LETOV: Yes.

BLUE SUIT: So you wish to help your fellow citizen.

IGOR LETOV: Yes.

BLUE SUIT: Then confess to that of which you are guilty.

KGB IVE: Or maybe you'd prefer 3 years of correctional labour?!

BLUE SUIT: Ive—!

KGB IVE: Or worse—execution!

IGOR LETOV: As a matter of fact, intimidation during interrogation is illegal as per Soviet law!

KGB IVE: And who's intimidating you? I don't see anyone intimidating you.

BLUE SUIT: Ive can you bring me some charcoal tablets. No. Nevermind. It's passed. Igor, why don't you tell us about your manifestos. We know all about them, so just confess where you're hiding them.

IGOR LETOV: I've no clue where they are.

BLUE SUIT: Why do you continue, despite a lengthy psychological evaluation, to meet with your criminal accomplices.

IGOR LETOV: They're my friends.

BLUE SUIT: Why are all your friends either anti-Soviet or mentally unwell?

This is a question that stumps Igor.

IGOR LETOV: I don't know.

BLUE SUIT: It's a sick sort of political party.

Carbon Pages

IGOR LETOV: No.

BLUE SUIT: Then why do you advocate for the liquidation of the Soviet system and the enslavement of its people?

IGOR LETOV: I don't advocate for their enslavement.

BLUE SUIT: So you advocate for the liquidation of the USSR?

KGB IVE: You're after a coup aren't you?

BLUE SUIT: You collude with kapitalist elements, and via this collusion hope to bring about some sort of a violent revolution in our country?

IGOR LETOV: No and that's an impossibility anyway. Don't they teach Marx at the KGB?

BLUE SUIT: Don't they *what*?

IGOR LETOV: Marx himself mocked those—as early as *The Communist Manifesto*—he mocked those who think a Revolution can be enacted by the will of individual actors. A revolution can't be forced but rather arises organically from conditions that fulfil its material prerequisites.

BLUE SUIT: Yes, but that has nothing to do with the crimes for which you are under suspicion.

IGOR LETOV: What—of being a politically active proletarian? Why are you, the world's sole socialist vanguard hounding me—a working class minor, rather than pursuing bourgeois elements?

BLUE SUIT: There are no bourgeois elements in the USSR.

IGOR LETOV: Like hell there aren't! Corruption? Bribery?

KGB IVE: There is NO corruption in the USSR.

The officer in the blue suit begs to differ:

BLUE SUIT: Hold on now of COURSE there are individual cases of corruption. But this doesn't constitute a systemic uh...hold on I won't be pulled into an ideological debate! You are under serious suspicion!

No Weapon Formed Against You

IGOR LETOV: And if you are the vanguard of the party of Marx and Engels how do you explain seizing me with a whole group illegally?! And without an arrest warrant? Is that your idea of class solidarity?

BLUE SUIT: It was not illegal. You were never arrested but detained on reasons of suspicion. Detainment does not require a warrant. If you are unsatisfied, you have the right to appeal to the supervising authority – the prosecutor's office.

KGB IVE: And how about, young man, I include in my statements these very examples of attempted anti-Soviet indoctrination!

IGOR LETOV: Who is it I'm indoctrinating?

KGB IVE: Us! Are we not men?

IGOR LETOV: What—is it illegal to be a Marxist in the USSR? I'm more Soviet than you! I'm in the midst of a clandestine takeover by bourgeois forces over the organs of power, and here I am being lectured on revolution and the Soviet Man. Ha! And you don't even know the basics of dialectical materialism! What a laugh!
You are the bourgeois elements, and I promise in the name of Marx, Engels, and Plekhanov to fight corruption wherever it persists or die trying!

    The officers exchange a look that asks—uh what's the protocol for this?

IGOR LETOV: Excuse me. I'm here to see a friend.

NURSE: Their name?

IGOR LETOV: Alexander Dugin.

NURSE: Dugin's in the isolation ward.

IGOR LETOV: How is he?

Carbon Pages

NURSE: Your friend suffers from sluggish schizophrenia.

IGOR LETOV: Well I'd like to see him.

NURSE: That's not possible. He's highly disoriented, has little spatial awareness. I'm afraid his memory has deteriorated too.

IGOR LETOV: Maybe that's just how he is? Have you considered that?

NURSE: He's showing signs of improvement. He's learnt how to swing the tests. But ultimately the boy's as sick as ever.

IGOR LETOV: You made him sick. It's you.

NURSE: Young man, don't make me call the director.

IGOR LETOV: He's a great guy, and he shouldn't be here.

NURSE: The patient is an antisocial malcontent. He's become radicalized into a dehumanizing extremism.

IGOR LETOV: *You* think it's dehumanizing.

NURSE: It's not a question of what I believe. It's medically substantiated. *He is a danger to you.*

IGOR LETOV: You're sick, and he's gonna outlive you. He's better than you. He's smarter than you. And the moment he gets of age he'll get a propiska to America or Japan and he's gonna live there and make a hundred times more money than you, and he'll drive a red corvette, with terracotta t-tops and a cigar tray and rottweiler at his side and he'll make all the money in the world and we'll bust our asses to smuggle his books into Omsk.

NURSE: Young man. In your little *America*, they wouldn't treat your friend half as well. They lobotomize patients.

IGOR LETOV: You're a fat hag.

NURSE: That's it. I'm calling the director.

IGOR LETOV: Do what you want—I'm seeing my friend.

> In a spacious room Dugin sat under an open window smoking a cigarette.

No Weapon Formed Against You

ALEXANDER: Hello.

IGOR LETOV: Ciao. Got your own billet?

ALEXANDER: I've been getting treatment. So... yeah...

IGOR LETOV: You're alright.

ALEXANDER: I've gotten this limp. It's starting to worry me...

IGOR LETOV: Don't start moping. Look, feds nabbed me again.

ALEXANDER: Was it serious?

IGOR LETOV: Nah. They don't know shit.

ALEXANDER: Got some sweets or something? Something sweet?

IGOR LETOV: Here. I fed them some shit about Marx. You'd be proud. They didn't know *what* was going on.

ALEXANDER: Cool. Kost?

IGOR LETOV: I don't think so. He's busy with his chess thing.

ALEXANDER: Still I should move my luggage once I'm back. Better safe than sorry.

IGOR LETOV: Easy, they don't have a clue. That's what they were grilling me about but I said I've no clue where they are.

ALEXANDER: You said that?

IGOR LETOV: That's right.

ALEXANDER: Wait. So they asked you if you have contraband, and you said no.

IGOR LETOV: They say *tell us where you're hiding these manifestos*. I say *I don't know where they are*.

ALEXANDER: You said that? I can't believe you said that! Fuck, Igor.

IGOR LETOV: I didn't say nothing!

ALEXANDER: They didn't have shit and you told them it exists. They baited you.

Carbon Pages

IGOR LETOV: Shit.

ALEXANDER: You imbecile.
(terrified)
They're on their way to ransack my home right now.

IGOR LETOV: I have a Kharms collection at home!

ALEXANDER: Who gives a *fuck* about your Kharms?! You have *any* idea what they'll do to me if they find a syndicated treatise under my bed?

> Two senior doctors entered the ward.

DOCTOR: Alexander, you're not meant to have visitors. Time to go, kid.

> The boys both on their knees, his mentor pulls Igor close:

ALEXANDER: Ok listen close. Take the thirty-two from Tbirskaya street (the one on the corner not by the newsstand) what time is it ok if you run you can make the three-oh-five, step off on Victory not Lenin, then take the three oh eight trolleybus to Burdenko and under the crossover, turn left, then left again and take the oh-two with the shifty door, turn left then right and cut through the grass to my square.

Burn the revisions. They're in the top-right shkaff in the entry behind a winter coat.

> Letov enters a wallpapered family apartment.

IGOR LETOV: Ma? Ma, you home?

> The apartment is eerily empty, and dead quiet except for the television playing opera. Igor investigates the living room.

> Nothing but the drapes fluttering in the breeze.

No Weapon Formed Against You

Now he's sweating and investigates the kitchen and then his bedroom, both empty.

Suddenly the front door creaks open and a figure enters:

IGOR LETOV: Ma!

MOTHER: Oh, you're home.

IGOR LETOV: I was at Dugin's. Was anyone here?

MOTHER: I don't know, Miss Shoskowitz lost her ring.

IGOR LETOV: Where's my suitcase Ma?

MOTHER: What suitcase?

IGOR LETOV: My suitcase, my suitcase, Ma! The grey one I keep under my old shoes, the one with my poems and stamp collection. Where is it?!

MOTHER: I threw that away in a spring clean 3 weeks ago. You'd know that if you had any half-way decency. God help me I never knew the suffering I'd endure when I was saddled with you.

IGOR LETOV: Mhm.

MOTHER: I won't be back for a few hours. Go out and buy some grechka.

And almost cutting herself off mid-sentence, she shuts the door closed. Now alone, hands in pockets, Igor hears the music floating in from the next room, Igor wanders in the kitchen. Is it early for a snack? What should I do now? he wonders absent-mindedly. Igor might inspect the cupboard before shutting it again, repeating this process with each cupboard and then the refrigerator. He might wander into the living room. The television is playing a cartoon re-run. An anthropomorphic donkey with a mopcut is strumming a balalaika. The window is wide open, carrying into the flat the cool summer breeze, nebulous screams and shouts of children chasing each other over asphalt baking in the blue heat. A girl wearing her mother's lipstick chases her lover. Now on the telly a silly king is trying to get his princess to do something. She's vexing him in a musical number.

Carbon Pages

He sinks into an armchair. He shifts positions. He drapes his feet off the armrest. He takes a bite out of an antonovka apple, then puts it down, deeming it quite unsatisfactory. He unbuttons his shirt and flutters the collar. Somewhere in the distance someone's honking their horn, and a cargo train fritters away. The princess keeps glottalizing to the tune of a regal harpsichord. She's really putting a wrench in the king's day. Something about a marriage. *I don't wanna I don't wanna.* That's what she's singing. Igor reaches for a saucer of cold tea and samples a sip and returns it to the coffeetable. Igor is fifteen years old. He will die aged forty-three. He rests his head on his wrists and glances at the TV one last time before dozing off. Slacker in effigy. Portrait of Oblomov skipping school.

Thirteen Years Later — 1993
"IN ANARHIA DESERTA"

Now I'm realizing that not once have I told you who I am. Have you heard of me? Are you guessing at who I am? I'm really very popular, or at least I was. Back then they called me daemon or lord, but always Alû, and they built awesome facades in my image. That was six thousand years ago in a very important city called Kirarsch, later called Re-sasuu, and now called nothing and known by no one as anything other than an insignificant mound of rocks and desert flora.

I'll be the first to admit I took my popularity for granted. There, in what now they call Iran, they cut temples for me, palaces. Crowns were dusted in the sand for me. I passed from hand to hand—I was on every coin. Entire enclaves would gather in public to cut the throats of children in my honour. But that was so long ago. To even bring it up breaks my heart. It was so long ago that it makes me emotional.

AIRLINE PASSENGER #1: I'm an accountant, and I'm on my way to Moscow! The liquidity, and the investment costs are simply *unbeatable*. Russia is the new land of opportunity!

AIRLINE PASSENGER #2: The *Red Dawn* guys?! I don't believe Russia can change.

AIRLINE PASSENGER #1: You don't believe Russia can change?!

AIRLINE PASSENGER #2: I'll believe Russia can change when *elephants* fly!

They look out the plane window. A Dumbo flies past on massive ears and winks at the flabbergasted entrepreneurs. *Excelsior Banking Consultant*'s logo and slogan caps the commercial; *Moscow: the last frontier (for the man who has everything)*.

...I'm just remembering now that some time ago English antiquarians made it their goal to unearth that mound and find the city that loved me. They tried their hardest. They brought sacred technologies and made great progress from the day they open-stepped foot, but overnight the wind lays the sand back softly over her dunes.

DUGIN: Before we begin, does anyone have any questions?

The little boy known as Alexander Dugin who once beheaded a goat and danced in its blood now stands at the front of a small lecture hall and speaks to a smattering of half-interested kids and colleagues. At his side is a hunchbacked creature in a chequered shirt and tie.

DUGIN: I'd like to thank again our brilliant guest Mr. Kropotojic, on behalf of the staff and editors, for taking the time to visit us here in Moscow. I hope uh you all understand how lucky you are. First of all, excuse me for speaking English but the reason for this is not only that we lack the qualified translator from Serbian to Russian but that *noomahia* (or *noology*) is, as it is, an avant garde philosophical concept. We are always having in mind German or English or French words in order to transmit the concepts. For a Russian to understand *noomahia* in Russian is difficult. Even in Serbian it's difficult. If I knew the language well enough, I'd love to make this lecture in Serbian but otherwise our nation, Russia, lacks the expertise these days to produce an accurate translation. So excuse me for the English in this course but I could stop or return to the point if you miss something? Just ask. Please, if you have any questions or you think you didn't understand something just haise your rand—I mean raise your hand. If you miss something or feel you don't understand an important term, ask myself or Mr. Krapotojic. Ahem. Excuse me. Sorry. Mr. Kropotojic. We'll have one last lecture this Friday and it's very important to be present because if you miss something today you could be lost in the next one. So I invite you to concentrate. Thanks for your time.

And so he goes on chattering like that for who knows how long while the kids think about anything else. One boy is preoccupied with the pancaked thighs of the girl in front.

Alexander was scrawny and clean-faced but that was how long ago. Now he looks like some sort of fairy tale ogre. He's grown a pot belly and has fat cheeks and hair combed to his

No Weapon Formed Against You

> ears with a round shiny forehead, and with a bird nest of a beard all of which makes him look like an orthodox priest.
>
> Soon the crowd floods out, and Alexander packs his one notepad into a grocery bag. The Serbian hunchback shakes Dugin's hand.

MR. KROPOTOJIC: Well done, Alexander. I could not have explained my ideas better myself.

DUGIN: Thank you, sir. Coming from you that means everything.

> The Serb leaves, with a smile on his face, and in comes editor-in-chief of the newspaper *Rossiya* — more importantly, Alexander's boss — Chikin. Chikin's in a smiley mood too.

CHIKIN: Our young philosopher.

DUGIN: Afternoon, Chikin.

CHIKIN: Our resident Kant.

DUGIN: Lecture went very well I thought.

CHIKIN: Listen, I know you've been finding the gigs underwhelming. But with your smarts I've no doubt you'll climb up the ol ladder.

DUGIN: There's no problem.

CHIKIN: And who knows. Things being as they are these days, maybe you'll find it easier.

DUGIN: Maybe.

CHIKIN: God knows it wasn't like this when I was your age. Such barriers we had. The komsomol, good party etiquette. What rubbish it all was. No one could have imagined that it would all come crashing down the way it did. That Empire of Evil. Cursed forevermore are those who knew and said nothing. Cursed are those who committed cruelties in the name of ideology. But I'm keeping you. Go ahead, you probably have work to catch up on.

DUGIN: Thanks.

Carbon Pages

CHIKIN: Alexander, tell me to piss off if I'm intruding. But you're not on the bottle again are you?

DUGIN: I'm not.

CHIKIN: You've such a good head on you, but you let thoughts in. Before you know it the bottle has you.

DUGIN: I know. I'm sorry.

CHIKIN: It's nothing to be ashamed of. I've known people. Look, why don't you take out that intern somewhere?

DUGIN: What intern?

CHIKIN: Elena or Yelena or something. Take her out for coffee or Sprites or something. You're single aren't you?

DUGIN: Yes.

CHIKIN: Take a load off for once.

DUGIN: Okay.

> As it so happens, in one of those everyday miracles, Dugin saw this girl, dressed in bondi blue, as he was leaving the building of the *Rossiya* newspaper headquarters. She said goodbye Alexander. When he looked at her his mind conjured a tableau vivant of her soft features and a lilliput ski boy in a parka at the top of her nose ridge, saddling his feet in the snow before sliding down and right off the tip. Goodbye Alexander.

> Now there's the dark contours of an unlit apartment, when at once the front door creaks open and the light flicks on. It's a cozy hub. Its owner, the writer Eduard Limonov, has done well for himself. He staggers in with a young singer twinkling like a disco ball.

MALINA: What if your girlfriend's home?

No Weapon Formed Against You

LIMONOV: Let her see us!

MALINA: Sshh. You'll wake your neighbours.

LIMONOV: The hell with it! I want everyone to know how much I love you. I'm going to tell her everything.

MALINA: You don't mean that...

>   Eduard no longer wears a mane, but rather a high-and-tight with a grey plume. His teeth are the colour of a rotting lemon.

LIMONOV: When I heard you singing on that cocktail stage—that's when my life began. Your voice is my march, your body my shrine.

>   What has happened to the boy with the mop hair in the thirteen years since he was interned in the city of the Moskva? Where would I find him. The answer is standing on a stage watched by a mass of thousands. There, he's just finished a ballad. He's sweaty, has long greasy hair. When he sings he does so un-melodically in a way that's more like a howl or a prolonged yawn. The crowd won't stop cheering, cheering. Some try to jump onstage but get grabbed by security men. Letov is the biggest star in Russia.

IGOR LETOV: Thank you Volgograd.

>   He throws up his arms and bows, and the crowd explodes into a static of noise. Then, taking no more time to soak in the love, Letov makes his way offstage with his bandmates.

IGOR LETOV: Anyone have a water? Oh hey. What was up with that light, man?

MANAGER: Hey we're working on it Igor.

IGOR LETOV: Working on it. The concert's over.

Carbon Pages

MANAGER: Yeah I know. I'll talk to the guys.

> One bandmate talks to Letov:

GUITARIST: God I could go for a good fuck right now.

IGOR LETOV: I just wanna go home and lie down. You have some water?

> Letov is dressed in an old leather jacket and dirty sneakers and a t-shirt bearing the name, strangely enough, of some other band.
>
> Suddenly he's accosted by a tan little man wearing Adidas.

ADIDAS: Salut Mr. Letov. Gentlemen. Are you busy?

IGOR LETOV: No, walk with me.

> They walk-and-talk at a brisk pace.

ADIDAS: I loved the show, Mr. Letov!

IGOR LETOV: Thanks.

ADIDAS: Maybe I said this already but I'm actually a big fan. We all are. We've been listening to GrOb since when you could do time for it.

IGOR LETOV: Good to hear.

ADIDAS: What a show. Hey, you get our present?

IGOR LETOV: I did, but I didn't ask for it.

ADIDAS: Don't worry 'bout it. Token of appreciation for letting us operate in your sphere. By the way, I spoke with your manager — no-go on that Culture House venue.

IGOR LETOV: Why not?!

> Igor is gut-punched. He was looking forward to that gig.

ADIDAS: Too hot for smack—the Chechens, they disembowel for that.

IGOR LETOV: Right.

No Weapon Formed Against You

ADIDAS: What—will that be a problem for you?

IGOR LETOV: Whatever. Do what you want.

ADIDAS: Don't feel bad...

> The greasy man in tracksuit has a real shit-eating tone about him, like he knows he's got a star under his thumb.

ADIDAS: ...We can discuss it at a further junction.

IGOR LETOV: Didn't I say you can do what you want? I'm not your daddy.

ADIDAS: That's what I like to hear, punk rock! Listen, Mr. Letov, we'll send you a token of—

> Letov's manager bustles into the repartee:

MANAGER: Alright folks, back it up! Make way!

> In fact to call him a manager would be overdoing it. He daylights as the GrOb bassist—drinking buddy turned telephone operator. Letov, his bandmates, and manager steady on through the labyrinthine venue, hauling their own instruments and equipment. However big they may be, they still can't afford dedicated roadies. The man in Adidas leaves and the manager introduces to the star musician a young curly haired kid wearing western headphones and holding a microphone.

IGOR LETOV: Question...

MANAGER: He's the NTV guy.

IGOR LETOV: What NTV guy?

MANAGER: The NTV guy who's meant to interview you. Remember?

IGOR LETOV: Oh yeah. Okay, can you ask your questions here?

> The interviewer answers:

INTERVIEWER: It would be better if we are somewhere not so busy. It's bad for the sound. And maybe somewhere where we could sit down?

Carbon Pages

MANAGER: Can you handle this? I have to go.

        The interviewer answers:

INTERVIEWER: Yes.

        Then Letov:

IGOR LETOV: He's talking to me. Yeah, Oleg, I'll see you later.

INTERVIEWER: May we sit?

IGOR LETOV: There should be a room this way, just walk with me.

> Then another individual pipes in. It's a tall, square-jawed man in blue uniform.

BLUE UNIFORM: Allow me! Allow me! I have security concerns!

IGOR LETOV: What? You have security concerns?

BLUE UNIFORM: That's right. I work around here and I...uh...

IGOR LETOV: Do I know you?

BLUE UNIFORM: No...no...uh...

IGOR LETOV: Well spit it out already.

BLUE UNIFORM: I work here. That is, well, I'm police.

IGOR LETOV: Okay?

> A bandmate leans across Letov's shoulder and informs:

BANDMATE: He's GrOb security. He's on the payroll.

> Letov looks him up and down. No doubt—it's a policeman. He's older than Letov, greying, but still has an excitable vitality about him.

BLUE UNIFORM: Right. That's to say I work for *you*. For GrOb that is, Mr. Letov. Uh, is it alright if I address you en ti? Or would you prefer en vi?

No Weapon Formed Against You

Igor considers this and looks him over. This is the saddest servant of the state ever. In the past two years his uniform must've been washed exactly once. He should be retired, but his hands are pink from throwing rabble-rouser fans. The old man continues:

BLUE UNIFORM: There are no security concerns, Mr. Letov. Honestly, I just said that because I wanted to get your attention. Don't be mad haha. The truth is that I wanted to get your autograph.

This is even more pathetic. An old man begging to address a younger man in the informal, and then groveling for an autograph.

BLUE UNIFORM: It's for my nephew. He's the biggest GrOb fan. So, how about it?

The dirty blue policeman even hands Igor a prepared photograph and bic.

BLUE UNIFORM: How about it? For my nephew?

Igor mulls it over internally. Then decides:

IGOR LETOV: What's the name? For the autograph.

And the policeman in blue uniform tells him the name. Igor opens the pen. He signs, closes the pen, and returns the photograph. Then he confirms:

IGOR LETOV: Ti is fine.

Finally, the musician and the NTV interviewer reach a quiet room. Letov sprawls over the leather couch. There's nothing the star wants more than to go home and nap.

INTERVIEWER: God be with us. I should say I'm a big fan, which I am, but I see you get that a lot so I'll shut up and cut to the chase.

IGOR LETOV: How old are you?

Carbon Pages

INTERVIEWER: Twenty. Okay, we're recording... In the song *My Defense* you wrote "The mock-up has won, the last ship has cooled, the little last lantern has exhausted itself". Where did this come from?

IGOR LETOV: Nowhere.

INTERVIEWER: From thin air?

IGOR LETOV: No.

INTERVIEWER: Is there some sort of specific meaning or poetic origin to the lyrics?

IGOR LETOV: Yes.

INTERVIEWER: Could you say more?

IGOR LETOV: No.

> The curly haired kid is stumped by this obstinance.

INTERVIEWER: I see. Uhh.

IGOR LETOV: Well how am I meant to answer a question like that? That landscape behind you—does it have a poetic origin?

> He turns around to see the landscape.

INTERVIEWER: Sure.

IGOR LETOV: Well there you go. You give me vague questions I'll give vague answers.

INTERVIEWER: Sorry.

IGOR LETOV: No offense. But it is what it is.

INTERVIEWER: They are odd questions, I'll admit!

IGOR LETOV: Like you ask me about the lyrics. At the end of the day it's not the lyrics that matter or the music. It's about the experience. The whole energy of it. I just played a concert last month in Riga and I almost fell on my ass. I can fall on my ass but it's still a good concert.

No Weapon Formed Against You

INTERVIEWER: I understand.

IGOR LETOV: I'm sorry but it's about a certain energy.

> His obstinance is nervous. Letov cannot understand why his heart is racing. The kid even less so. He decides to go on the offensive:

INTERVIEWER: Okay but you have to admit your songs are in and of themselves quite lyrically complex. Do you regret that the ninety-nine percent of listeners are, say, missing the point?

IGOR LETOV: There's no point. It's an energy. If they're feeling something that means they get it. The ninety-nine percent are exactly who get it. It's the one percent who try to dissect them that are missing the point. Art is a war. Great art is a war, which is why GrOb is about anarchism. I've been saying the same thing for how many years. Anarchism is our great war.

INTERVIEWER: I can accept that answer.

IGOR LETOV: Lord almighty, you can accept it or not accept it. I'm just saying how it is.

> The interviewer wonders why Letov is so goat headed, and if he's done something to warrant it. In any case, he tries one more time.

INTERVIEWER: You're playing in Moscow next week, correct?

IGOR LETOV: Yes.

INTERVIEWER: It's going on two years since the flag of the Soviet Union was lowered for the last time over the Kremlin, heralding the dissolution of the USSR, and its replacement with a democratic state. It's been said that rock music such as yours was one of the catalysts for the collapse of the USSR, because it exposed the rigidity of Soviet ideology, which was weak in adapting to social changes, and very open to human rights critiques and ridicule. Would you agree with this?

> Igor thinks for a long time before replying.

Carbon Pages

IGOR LETOV: If you're telling me this I guess it must be true. I don't know.

INTERVIEWER: Do you feel that freedom of speech has benefited you?

> Again, Letov thinks on his answer.

IGOR LETOV: Freedom of speech benefits anyone who is looking to say something, but those who have nothing to say can only stand to lose by other people's acceptance of the drawbacks of freedom of speech. That's what anarchism is in its essence. Anarchism is loneliness. In the end, everyone lives alone, dies alone, is alone.

> The kid has no clue what he just said or how to follow up on that. Privately, he suspects that those mandated sulfur injections in the 1980s have scrambled his idol's brains.

> Letov's mind is on the old policeman in blue.

IGOR LETOV: When I sleep, I am a man who dreams of Omsk. When I'm awake, Omsk dreams of being a man.

> Letov will remove himself from a taxi and find himself deep in central Russia among Siberian pines.

TAXI DRIVER: Aye friend in't it grand fortune on yourself that we didn't get stuck till the muck did dry.

IGOR LETOV: Thanks, pal.

TAXI DRIVER: Did muddy up the betty but sure it's nothin a wash can't fix indeed!

IGOR LETOV: I appreciate it.

No Weapon Formed Against You

> A lady in a Pokemon t-shirt greets the musician. She's in her thirties but the harshness of the hinterland has made her look older.

NADYA: Igor! You're early. Andruha! Andruha, Igor is HERE. For God's sake get dressed!

IGOR LETOV: Hello, Nadya!

> The driver keeps yelling:

TAXI DRIVER: And eh how long shall you be in these parts? Can't be too safe these days! Sure it wouldn't dearly hurt mine sticking around and giving a lift home!

IGOR LETOV: That's okay, pal.

TAXI DRIVER: It's no trouble by me! It's no trouble at all! If you'd like I can even give you a lift all the way into the city. It's no trouble by me. I'll have a smoke while I wait. I can even show you the spots in the village if you'd like!

NADYA: Have you lost weight? Come here. You've gotten thinner? Poor child. Let's get inside.

> They hug and kiss and in the anteroom they pass a Christian shrine.

NADYA: We have apple juice from last year. I wanted to ask if you like apple juice before I brought it out. Otherwise the gooseberry...

> Eating a salted pickle is Andruha.

NADYA: Wouldja *ever* be presentable?

IGOR LETOV: What's up old man.

ANDRUHA: Blackthumb himself.

> They shake and hug it out.

Carbon Pages

NADYA: The soup's still on the stove, but sit down try the pickles at least. Now, Igor. Do you pray?

IGOR LETOV: Do I... — no.

NADYA: I want you to pray with me. And I have a pocketbook to gift you from Halifax. He knows all about you. Now sit down won't you—

ANDRUHA: No no Igor needs to stretch his legs. C'mon lad, we'll tie up some birch branches for tonight.

NADYA: Don't be long—the man's hungry.

> The old friends walk to the foyer of a wooden shack a couple of yards from a 14ft tall anthill. In this shack Andruha will reach into a nook in the rafter and pull out a bottle of samagon.

IGOR LETOV: How's the harvest this year?

ANDRUHA: Same old shit. Colorado bugs doing my head in. Sowed some tansy round and it didn't do a thing. I swear they've gotten worse the bugs. The spuds in't changed, but they have.

IGOR LETOV: By God you must be grateful each day for breathing this country air, Andruha.

ANDRUHA: Yep.

IGOR LETOV: You still driving the lada?

ANDRUHA: The..?

IGOR LETOV: The lada. I saw the stump we crashed into.

ANDRUHA: To a neighbour I lended it.

IGOR LETOV: You gave it?

ANDRUHA: I owed a favour.

IGOR LETOV: How you get to town?

No Weapon Formed Against You

ANDRUHA: Cart. Don't make me prattle. What's new with yours. We do be seeing you on the telly more and more. You and yours are none too small these days in't I right?

IGOR LETOV: If we're none too small I don't be feeling it.

ANDRUHA: Civil Defence. You were ahead of your time with that. Who woulda thought back then when you came back from Moscow...

IGOR LETOV: I never had as much fun as I did as a kid.

ANDRUHA: Here. Cheers.

IGOR LETOV: Cheers.

ANDRUHA: We should get some branches together just in case.

IGOR LETOV: Right. Should I say grace?

ANDRUHA: Don't get me started, Igor. You don't know what it's like.

IGOR LETOV: How'd you ever marry her?

ANDRUHA: I didn't—she married *me*.

IGOR LETOV: Who is Halifax, anyway?

ANDRUHA: Pastor. Nadya's gotten a fever for salvation and such.

IGOR LETOV: She's orthodox now?

ANDRUHA: I don't know what you call it, Igor. Do you see me sticking my beak in? A sect or a denomination it must be. What's it called. I don't stick my beak in and she keeps off my back...
I wish I could go and live like you. Living the life... real rockstar like. One day my legs'll go like my father's and I won't be shylin the filth for turnip no more.

IGOR LETOV: But I envy *you*. I want to get a place in the country. We don't do studios anyway. We'll record from a barn.

ANDRUHA: From a barn...You always were talented Igor. I mean I never told you, but you were never gonna stay in this shithole. And now's the best time to be a *tvorets* and musician. I never knew there would be a best time so I—And I never had no talent like you did.

Carbon Pages

IGOR LETOV: A lot of good it was. You remember how it was?

ANDRUHA: With the KGB, I didn't stick my beak in so they kept off my back.

IGOR LETOV: Well anyway. I have the peace of mind now. But it's not the same.

ANDRUHA: You need to go far away. For inspiration.

IGOR LETOV: I need a change. People love the songs. But I remember when we played in halls and dens. We had a few dozen lads show up and it's like we were in a secret society. Us against them. Now it's like I'm us and I'm them. What's the point of a good song if everyone hears it.

ANDRUHA: Them's be the times. Nothing's the same as it was. It's no lie I'm tellin: I was in town a winter back wanting to get Nadya a pair of *valenki*. Suddenly I see down the street a girl. Only she in't no girl, but a thing of the sort that is half mule with a head and tail. It's the truth. The beast did limp on two legs and suffer a terrible squeal. And in front and hind it a gaggle of lads with their belts unbucked marching it down the street yelling for all to see, and whipping it as they go, as if the kreature had committed them grave offense.

IGOR LETOV: You read that?

ANDRUHA: I saw it. Now I'm not religious, but just one look at that and don't you think I wouldn't see why Nadya is the way she is.

IGOR LETOV: There are odd things. Remember when we hitched a ride on that cargo train.

ANDRUHA: Yah.

IGOR LETOV: And it kept going and going. You say grab on and I grab on. And the train keeps going and going!

ANDRUHA: Yep.

IGOR LETOV: If that guy hadn't opened the compartment for a piss we'd've frozen for sure.

ANDRUHA: I had to promise him a box of bubble gum so he wouldn't tell.

IGOR LETOV: You did.

No Weapon Formed Against You

ANDRUHA: Did I promise?

IGOR LETOV: Yeah?

ANDRUHA: Yah.

IGOR LETOV: Hey, you still have those basketball cards?

ANDRUHA: Which..?

IGOR LETOV: Remember. Had all these negroes on them.

ANDRUHA: Oh yah?

IGOR LETOV: Got them in a heist with this Moscow psycho.

ANDRUHA: Maybe. Think I sold them a year ago for bread.

    *   *   *   *   *   *   *   *
      *   *   *   *   *   *   *
*   *   *   *   *   *   *   *

Alexander Dugin sits calcified in front of the television in his apartment. He wears only his underwear. He's pink, palpitating and on the verge of a nervous breakdown. Alexander has not smoked in a long time. So long, in fact, that kazbek cigarettes no longer exist. Instead, he smokes an American BASIC. The situation calls for it. Still, his nerves are out of control. On the television is the face of the punk star Igor Letov. Dugin picks up the phone off its receiver. He prepares to dial a number, a number of such magnitude that he's been trying to force his fingers to input its digits for four hours. But he drops the phone on the receiver and takes another drag.

The telly shows a new interview.

INTERVIEWER: You're playing in Moscow next week, correct?

IGOR LETOV: Yes.

Dugin, bug-eyed, he picks up the phone, he drops it, he picks it up again, drops it, stands and paces about the room, takes a swig of beer, picks up the receiver again, and returns it once more. GrOb is coming to town. Wouldn't it be nice to go see them? Wouldn't it be nice? If you're not doing anything?

He takes the napkin on which the phone number of the *Rossiya* intern girl is written and wipes his fat sweaty forehead.

For three hundred years the central bath house has served to wash the population of Moscow. From the time of Tsar Peter the Great through the age of the Communists, the rich and poor alike sat together and sweated their grievances. But in 1992 it was sold to the highest bidder, renovated, and revamped into the hottest restaurant for elites in the city. Even its lucky patrons had to admit that it had lost some of its character. But not they or anyone could have predicted what would happen on this fateful night.

A banquet was being held by the newspaper *Rossiya,* and as part of celebrations a few guest speakers were invited to say some words. One such face with some such words was Dugin. He paced behind the wings, sometimes peeking at the crowd of donors scuffing wine and flesh.

TECHNICIAN: Alexander, relax. There's still another speaker left. Relax. Have you had a drink?

DUGIN: I've had plenty of drink. It hasn't helped anything. I have stage fright and I feel it in my gums.

He slurs his words. He's dressed in a tight grey suit much too small for him and makes him look like an overgrown toddler with his head too fat for his body.

The crowd sit at white linen-clothed tables, dressed in suits and evening exotica. Most are foreigners. Some are journalists. They chatter, chatter. Then loud microphone feedback interrupts their chatter and they look up.

No Weapon Formed Against You

CHIKIN: One Two Three. Is this thing on. Can I have your attention please. Okay. Thank you. Well done. We're very lucky to have hosted a number of our next speaker's works. He was a poet in the Moscow underground where he brushed shoulders with the likes of Joseph Brodsky, trading and composing illicit samizdat under threat of persecution. In the 70s, the communist regime exiled him for standing up to the authorities, giving him and his wife a one way ticket to the West. In New York, he mingled with the outcasts of society—the rebels, the poor, the misfits. He was a bum, a street poet, and a millionaire's valet. In Paris, he made his name as the *enfant terrible* of the literary avant garde where he was a regular at the controversial paper L'Idiot. His novel *It's Me Eddie* is one of the best selling books in Russia, not to mention the most shocking. But being a best-selling author was not enough for this man of action. He was a war correspondent in Serbia where he saw first hand the horrors of that brutal conflict. Now, after so many years, he's returned to his native Russia. Please join me in giving a big hand to Eduard Limonov.

> Loud applause all around and the writer comes out on stage, wearing gabardine trousers, red buckled boots, and a leather jacket. He nudges, but never removes, his prescription Ray-Bans. Limonov speaks:

LIMONOV: On my recent return from the West, whose depravity and ugliness has always disgusted me, I was struck by a single thought:

What the hell happened? What's been done to the nation that I was raised in that was proud and dignified. The nation that made foreigners tremble at its very name?

> Limonov speaks consulting no notes. It's hard to tell if he's winging it or if he has the address proficiently memorized.

LIMONOV: How has my beloved country been overtaken by that confederacy of tapeworms and cannibals whom they call democrats. President Yeltsin—

> Some of the audience cheer and whoop ironically at this name.

Carbon Pages

LIMONOV: —President Yeltsin did not liberate this nation, he sold it and is in the process of splitting the remains with his loyal mafia. If this continues, then Russia will suffer what has long been accepted in the West. The riches of the nation will be plundered by a few rich tyrants. It's already happening under our noses. And the people of Russia will be left with less than they had under Gorbachev, less than they had under Brezhnev, less than they had under Stalin. But under Stalin at least we had our dignity. All the nation is on the verge of becoming one concentration camp.

I predict the pitiful Russian queuing up en masse for a chance to sell his blood to the blood bank, before being turned away because it is too under-nourished. If nothing is done, public parks will be stripped of their trees for heating fuel. In the name of democracy and free market capitalism, industries built by generations of Russians have been stripped and sold to no-name profiteers, then sold to Americans as punishment for the USSR's 70-year-long crusade for equality and fairness.

> Some foreigners, already tipsy, deem the points of this character zany—enough to give him a hoot and whistle here and there. The few Russians at the banquet are unamused.

CHIKIN'S ASSISTANT: Did you know about this?

CHIKIN: He's always stirring the pot. It's good for business.

> Limonov continues:

LIMONOV: It's the duty of every Russian from Moscow to the Bering Strait to rise up against the democrats. Every peasant, muzhik and urbanite must set aside their grievances to kick out Yeltsin and the American apparatus which installed him.

The fate of a historical empire, and of our lifeblood is at stake. The old Communists have shown themselves to be soft-bellied and diplomatic. We need war. Violence! America will be punished. I will rip Yeltsin's throat out for what he's done to my countrymen in my absence. The people will storm the Kremlin as they did the Winter Palace in 1917 and bring to an end the automatic, hydromatic, systematic invasion of Bill Clinton and his gang of cosmopolitans.

No Weapon Formed Against You

Hang them with their entrails! They think they can make Russia a vassal like they made Germany, like they made England and France. They think wrong! You think kapital is your friend. You are wrong!

Everything western will be wiped off the face of our great nation. Kapitalism is a lie. Truth is Russia's great power. Truth, and strength.

I have the credentials. In Serbia I spat on the journalists who stayed in the cozy safe zones. I demanded a kalashnikov, and joined the brave Serbian warriors on the smoldering front. Not as a writer, but as a comrade in arms. And I became, in the words of others, a Hero of the liberation movement. So, I call on those with military expertise and state secrets to meet me after dinner! Glory to Russia and the Russian people!

> He steps offstage to some smatterings of applause. Most don't believe in him, in fact almost nobody does. But they have to admit, he puts on a good show. The Editor-in-Chief of *Vogue*'s Russia division gives a whistle and whoop.
>
> As Chikin introduces the next speaker, Eduard makes his way to his table where, on the way, he's beckoned by an old reporter colleague who he'll never see again after this moment.

NEWTON: Hey Eduard!

LIMONOV: (*ironically*) I was hoping I wouldn't see your mugs again!

> The reporter is sitting at a table with some other colleagues in white three-pieces and with an American girlfriend.

NEWTON: Interesting speech. What was that about you being a war hero?

LIMONOV: Arkan's Tigers are the bravest men I've had the honour of knowing. The last descendants of Oddyseus' Aegians on the rosy-fingered shore.

NEWTON: (*unimpressed*) Uh-huh.

LIMONOV: Sometimes the banality of civilian life is too much for me, and I pray with a tear in my eye, "My brother Arkan, how I long to be back at your side. How I long for the Balkan mountains!"

Carbon Pages

The reporter looks at him unphased and replies dead serious:

NEWTON: Eduard. The Serbs are terrorists. You joined a terrorist group.

LIMONOV: They're liberators who martyred themselves for freedom and justice, and they took on the chin fifteen nations in Goliath NATO.

NEWTON: No but you've earned your Oscar I tell you what! They scalped babies in tunnels.

Suddenly his American girl clocks the conversation:

WOMAN IN WHITE: What's this about *Serbia*? What was *that* all about?

The reporter replies:

NEWTON: I'll explain to you in a minute. It's *not* that interesting.

And then Limonov again:

LIMONOV: It's a glorious war, and Byronic.

NEWTON: Now maybe if you had joined the *Croats*, I could halfway understand it...

WOMAN IN WHITE: I still don't understand anything about that conflict or what the takeaway is! It just seems bloody and irrelevant.

LIMONOV: It's not irrelevant. It's very crucial, not to mention gallant.

NEWTON: Well you've certainly done a fine job discrediting yourself if that's what you're after. Murdering people in the name of bloodthirsty goons.

Limonov crosses his arms and smiles all knowingly.

LIMONOV: Well, I wouldn't expect an armchair philologist like you to understand the soldier's colic.

And he leaves his interlocutors. What an asshole, they think. Limonov dons a smug demeanor but underneath it he's annoyed. He's annoyed anytime his actions don't speak for themselves. He laments the cowardice and philistinism that's

No Weapon Formed Against You

monopolized the culture. He doesn't admit it to himself but he also wonders, all things considered, if it wouldn't have been better if fate had put him on the other side of that fucking conflict after all.

He takes his pew next to a bald mogol. Meanwhile the philosopher, drunk and trembling, takes centre stage. He does not acknowledge the previous speaker, because that's not in his notes. He keeps his gaze down where the crowd can't see him. For a long time he had went back and forth with himself debating whether to include in his speech the provisions for the Fifth Column. What about Eternal Carthage? He did, and lucky for him, no one cared enough to listen. The boy must've felt this, because he cut his sermon short by about a third after which he was provided the requisite polite applause. Nobody really listened, least of all Limonov who was still concocting in silence a comeback to his colleague in white.

Chikin gives Alexander a pity pat on the back as he makes his way to the food.

CHIKIN: Thank you everyone! Enjoy the music and dinner!

There's some kind of a spat about seating arrangements.

DUGIN: This is my seat!

LADY: It's like I told you. I'm here. Find some place else.

Dugin grumbles something, and makes sortie for another spot to sit. A spot that happens to be next to a man in Ray-Bans.

Eduard scuffs down baked sausage in cranberry chutney, with chilled sparkling grape juice to wash it down. Dugin watches. There is lots of food. Fish cakes, sweet potatoes, and portobello mushroom. Béchamel moussaka, African-fried pork, Yorkshire pudding and gravy and mash, roast goose with blackberry sauce and orange slices.

For dessert there are silver platters of powdered sweets, eclairs and tarts, sliced lemon cake, chocolate strawberries,

Carbon Pages

doughie buns and halva crumble, and pyramids of caramel cubes.

All these things Dugin watches his neighbours gorge on.

DUGIN: Talentless shits.

Limonov knows from experience it's best to ignore an angry drunk. He asks for a pickle from his left.

DUGIN: Fucking shits.

Limonov continues ignoring him.

DUGIN: Brainless cattle. You realize you just took a pickle from a goat?

LIMONOV: So?

DUGIN: What's your name?

LIMONOV: Eduard Limonov, and who are you?

Dugin rolls his eyes.

DUGIN: (*mocking*) Ohh the writerr.

LIMONOV: You've read *It's Me Eddie?*

DUGIN: No, but I know the kind of people who *have*.

He fills his glass with Napoleon cognac.

DUGIN: Biological refuse. If I had my way I'd put them all against the wall.

Limonov likes listening to drunks, and depressed rambling drunks have historically liked him.

DUGIN: Doesn't it all remind you of the Tuktukks?

LIMONOV: No.

Dugin continues not looking at his interlocutor. He might as well be totally alone.

No Weapon Formed Against You

DUGIN: The Tuktukks was an archipelago in the Caribbean. The conquistadors who discovered it were on the verge of starvation and had not seen another man for months and months. They'd gotten to drinking their urine...

>He sips his cognac.

DUGIN: ...Finally they hit shore and when they step on land the mariners are struck with such a vision of paradise, such a pure and unmolested image of Adam and Eve in the garden of Eden that they feel shocked and unworthy. They can't even bring themselves to take a slave or two. So, they hatch a plan. They conduct a ceremony to which all the island is invited, where they take the chief elders of each tribe and they take them and forcefeed them an apple, thus imparting on the Indians original sin, rendering them men, and freeing themselves of all guilt.

>Limonov finds himself intrigued.

LIMONOV: What happened then? Did they bring them to Spain?

DUGIN: They probably did. Here's to the Spanish and the Indians.

>And Dugin says this into his glass which he throws back without waiting for the writer.

DUGIN: Now listen—

LIMONOV: —I'm listening.

DUGIN: What do you know about King Friedrich's regiment of gigantics?

LIMONOV: Nothing I don't think.

DUGIN: King Friedrich of Prussia, Prince of Neuchâtel, had a very peculiar hobby. From a young age he was fascinated by all things related to giant men. He'd collect the tallest of Evropa and assemble them in a regiment.

LIMONOV: What do you mean, a regiment?

DUGIN: An infantry battalion. Give them a musket and special red uniform.

LIMONOV: Were they effective?

Carbon Pages

DUGIN: What's the name? Eduard? Well Eduard, other kings would trade their giants to him like a stamp collection. He even built special villages which he populated with women giants, and he'd have his infantrymen breed with these women in hopes of producing a race of super-giants. King Friedrich was the father of eugenics. Here's to King Friedrich! Here's to his band of killer gigantics!

> He downs a shot and Limonov obligingly follows with his chilled grape juice. Limonov thinks of something interesting too.

LIMONOV: Your Friedrich is nothing compared to my Manson!

DUGIN: Oh save me.

LIMONOV: I've always felt a connection to Manson—

DUGIN: —Charles?

LIMONOV: Yes, Charles.

DUGIN: What about him?

LIMONOV: There's the kind of man who could smell revolution with his nose, like a truffle pig.

> At this Dugin genuinely snorts.

DUGIN: HA! A truffle pig!

LIMONOV: And he was right about Hollywood. Take that fashionless git John Lennon. When he got shot I thought: finally, some good news. Yoko Ono should thank Charles and marry him for making her rich.

DUGIN: Cheers.

LIMONOV: Cheers.

> They digest their drinks for a second.

LIMONOV: It all goes to show a single man can change the course of history. Lenin, Stalin—

No Weapon Formed Against You

DUGIN: —D'Annunzio—

LIMONOV: —Look at Trotsky. I demand Trotsky get a toast.

DUGIN: I will not toast to Trotsky.

LIMONOV: I toasted your Friedrich!

DUGIN: I will *not* toast Trotsky!

LIMONOV: Do you know what Trotsky was up to before the Russian Revolution?

DUGIN: Well, uh—

LIMONOV: He lived in the Bronx.

DUGIN: He lived in the Bronx?

LIMONOV: He lived in a freezing little flat and for money he lectured in dens which no one attended. The prick didn't tip because he thought waiters were beneath him. In 1917 he bought an armoire on installment from his landlady, and then he disappeared without a trace. When the babushka tracked him down the sucker was commanding the largest army on Earth.

> Dugin thinks for a moment. He is hammered, but he likes this guy. He's a man of action. And even if he's a little dense, at least he's not a democrat.

DUGIN: Okay. We'll drink to Trotsky. Fine. But ONLY AFTER the Mad Baron.

LIMONOV: Hold on. Let me fill my glass.

DUGIN: Have some cognac.

LIMONOV: Hand me the cognac.

> They lift their glasses.

LIMONOV: You'll have to tell me which Mad Baron we're talking about.

> Dugin lowers his glass urgently.

Carbon Pages

DUGIN: Roman von Ungern, of course.

> Limonov has no idea who that is. Dugin smiles. And then he frowns, rushing his hand over Limonov's glass.

DUGIN: And to think, you were about to split a toast for someone you don't know! That could have terrible repercussions!

> The philosopher puts his glass on the table, and then takes the writer's glass and puts it next to his.

DUGIN: Baron Ungern's eyes terrified his own father because they were lifeless. As a child he twisted the head of his pet owl clean off. He was all set up to live a perfect little aristocratic life. But he kept getting into trouble. In his twenties he was expelled from the corps for a duel, which he lost, and started suffering from headaches and visions. Anyway. So's he exiled from the academy and eventually makes his way to Mongolia. This strange, desert-stretched, wild, ancient and harsh country fascinates him. At some point he makes contact with Kutuku—the living Buddha—who appoints him commander of the Mongol cavalry. He's a cruel and ruthless leader. At the same time he becomes obsessed with mystical Buddhism, starts wearing these flowing saffron robes. His ambition leads him to a clairvoyant of the most ancient bloodline who tells him—*I see the God of War. You will rule over a vast territory, oh white God of War.* He lives ascetically and kills anyone in his path. The shamans and the living Buddha begin to revere the alien Russkiy, thinking he's a mythical reincarnation.

Something in Ungern snaps. He does not sleep. He starts drowning men for the slightest glance. His officers suspect he's gone insane. All humanity is incinerated within him and only the sacred elements beyond life and death remain. The Reds close in. He hates the Reds. So he tries to unite the tribes of Asia into the great anti-Bolshevik coalition which will resurrect the ancient Teutonic order. The Reds are chased through all of Russia and driven almost to extinction. Iron Felix Dzerzhinsky feared the baron could not be reasoned with. Lenin quivered. But as so often happens, the tide turns. Suddenly the Reds are chasing *him*.

So the Baron devises one last odyssey. Picture that he's in his tent with his officers and he unfurls a map. It's of Tibet: Mongolia was only the Shield, he says. We

No Weapon Formed Against You

will penetrate the Himalayas and uncover the lost entrance to Agarttha—where the laws of time stand astill and the great Chakravarti sips from flower cups. He, the Khan of Mongolia, will preside over a new golden age. Here. In the Empire of Ram. And rule the centre of the Earth, free from the influence of Gog and Magog.

>Dugin fingers the rim of his glass musingly.

DUGIN: But the Reds were too fast, and before he could found the city of the Chakkravati his men were shot and he captured.

LIMONOV: Then what happened?

DUGIN: He was shot.

>Dugin says this as if it's such an obvious conclusion that you'd have to be an idiot to ask. Disappointment is not the feeling Limonov registers. He's oddly excited by the note, much more than Dugin who has turned an exciting tale into one that's depressed him. He needs a drink.

LIMONOV: To the Mad Baron.

DUGIN: To the Mad Baron.

>They savour their cognac as if for a fallen comrade. But their moment of silence is sliced open by a terrific shriek from a table at the far end of the room.

WOMAN: NOOO!! PLEASE NOOO!!! NOOOO!!

>One patron is trying to calm her down and she's scratching the skin off his face.

WOMAN: NO NO NO NO!

>She sobs and shrieks and the whole half of the hall is put to a standstill.

LIMONOV: What's wrong with her?!

Carbon Pages

  A patron answers:

PATRON: Her son's just died.

  Limonov turns to Dugin and, as if there's nothing left to say, suggests:

LIMONOV: C'mon. Let's get out of here.

  It's in the freezing night that three men walk cautiously on the street laden with parapets of snow on either side. Chicken-necked in their collars, Limonov, Dugin, and Chikin stuff their hands in their pockets.

CHIKIN: Alright fellas. I have a date to catch. Eduard, it's good seeing you again. Alexander, get home safe, yes?

DUGIN: Abso-*hic*-lutely.

  And like lotus one-two-three the writer and philosopher were alone again.

DUGIN: And you know they get away with saying now?

LIMONOV: Who?

DUGIN: Them, them! *Our idol is her financial majesty—kapital.* Damned materialists. God smite them. That's the only way left. The power of Christ is the only way left.

  He adjusts his ushanka from slipping off his forehead. The world spins in an astral motion.

DUGIN: I tell you, Eduard. This world I wake into. It's as if the forces of good and evil have long quit fighting. And all that's left is evil fighting evil for leftovers...and the Space Museum. You uh...You know what they use the Shpace Museum for now? You know?

LIMONOV: What do they use it for?

DUGIN: It's a used car lot. For Evropean cars.

No Weapon Formed Against You

    By chance they happen past such a Jaguar parked in the slush.

DUGIN: Just like...THIS ONE!

    Dugin kicks the bumper so hard that he dents it and to Eduard's horror a man steps out into the night brandishing a .22. pistol.

MAN WITH .22: What the *fuck* are you doing?! I could have you killed before breakfast!

DUGIN: I'll have you *know*: I'm the famous writer Limonov!!

    Limonov almost chokes on his spit at hearing this. He says the only thing which comes to mind which is this:

LIMONOV: Actually, *I'm* Limonov. And excuse my friend—he's very drunk.

MAN WITH .22: Fuck your mother—fucking gopniks.

    And he gets in the Jaguar and drives away.

LIMONOV: Christ.

    Dugin spits at the burnout marks.

LIMONOV: Out of curiosity, do you own a machine gun?

DUGIN: No. But I own a pistol.

LIMONOV: I own a machine gun.

    Like the man himself, Alexander's flat is paradoxical. It's a rich apartment in a poor neighbourhood, with dear linen sheets and dusted lamps. Though he doesn't notice it at the moment, Limonov will later find the interior to be much nicer than his own. He might even wonder, who exactly is this guy? But right now he's lifting up the half-conscious scholar's feet. He leaves a glass of water and before leaving poses a question which he's been debating asking since they left the banquet hall.

Carbon Pages

LIMONOV: Listen, can you write one of your tales?

DUGIN: I do.

LIMONOV: But, I mean, for me. It's like this—I have a political publication I'm getting off the ground. It's called Limonka. Maybe you'd like to come on, on a permanent basis?

The scholar sits up on his elbows.

DUGIN: Write what?

LIMONOV: About the baron, the reed people. Anything you want.

He drops his head back down.

DUGIN: Fine.

And falls unconscious.

In embryonic pulses I still remember you every now and then. How I fell for your unholiness. You had the biggest empire on Earth at your feet and me. Do you remember? Do you hear my voice? Hello? Do I inspire a single synapse in that brain of yours as you lie in your Tomb? Of course not. No one remembers. But time was you whispered me you'll *pull down their churches*! You said you'd *kill God*! You promised the world.

I loved those days like trichinosis in your muscles. Dot dot dot cute little criss cross rillies from your toes to your eyeballs like a painting I'd live in, like the tubules gupping in your teeth when you suck in freezing air on your pretty, dry teeth or when you eat ice cream and it sears you with pain. How I love your pain, I love your pain. And how I hate your love, I hate your love. I hate your dancing and your moods, and your jigs and you smelling fresh dew and I hate when you stretch your spine after sitting. Wouldn't I strip it all from the world like

No Weapon Formed Against You

yellow wallpaper all that fetid joy and revelry? Wouldn't I replace it? With with with. With trichinosis in your tendons. Rolocoasters of the tunnel of love riding through your meat like a caroling carwash, here we go here we go there's another we just missed an intersecting hole! Up down up down buckle up for the thyroid! That there's any spot of body not rendered hole-y is a tragedy, if i could I'd squeeze and melt all pasty and live in your ant tunnels and chew you until you're not left, your flesh like a christmas tree lit up and dust it off and tear off the old gunk and gristle, the plaster and shattered lights the meat from your ligaments so there's nice pretty rolocoasters of love and just give give give me the stalk, a nice smooth clean brown stalk of christmas tree. Just chew off the bark of the nice nice smooth clean brown stalk of christmas tree so that now it's a nice smooth clean ivory stalk of c****mas tree standing in a stand in an empty room in a floodplain in four-fifty bee see. Now that would bring me relief. That would relieve me now if I've ever known relief.

But you met your friends, and loved them more than you loved me. Well, fine. I have my own friends now. They love images too—they love money and their pictures. If you had listened to me which you didn't you'd still be here which you aren't not that I care. I don't. I haven't thought about you in literal decennia. But won't I rip you like linen. Won't I cut you like a scaif does plastic in my sacred experiments. My wayward, my pontius, cry of my cry.

DUGIN: Samara.

LIMONOV: Thirty-four.

DUGIN: Krasnoyarsk.

LIMONOV: Seventy-eight.

DUGIN: Irkutsk.

LIMONOV: Two hundred and nine but I had a run-in along the way. I'm having the concierge drop another stack on the Sunday train.

Carbon Pages

DUGIN: Tell me about him again. What's he, a skinhead?

LIMONOV: He's from a no-name town. Says one of his friends showed him Limonka, he read the thing ten times over and hopped on a train to Moscow. Shows up on my doorstep in the middle of the night begging to be part of operations.

DUGIN: He's a kid.

LIMONOV: You were a kid too once. He's a superb illustrator. Reminds me of a young Mayakovsky. He was being wasted in that village, chugging samagon day to night.

DUGIN: I just hope these issues start diffusing into managerial spheres. Irkutsk... Budyonnovsk. Do they have even a hundred thousand living there?

LIMONOV: There's kids everywhere.

DUGIN: That's my concern. Everyone we hope to influence is right here in Moscow.

LIMONOV: We'll get there. You need the people for a revolution.

DUGIN: I know.

LIMONOV: We're doing good, Al.

DUGIN: We are.

LIMONOV: Eight thousand copies between two issues? I doubt Études Traditionnelles or whatever it's called ever caused such a shitstorm.

DUGIN: It didn't.

LIMONOV: Now if you could help me move them...

DUGIN: I have back problems. It—

LIMONOV: —Alright don't start.

>Dugin considers the state of the paper.

DUGIN: It *is* good, isn't it.

No Weapon Formed Against You

> But before Dugin can finish that thought into the office comes
> a pretty young woman in an ushanka.

LIMONOV: Malina!

MALINA: There you are. No one knows *where* the hell this room is.

LIMONOV: We're just talking numbers—

MALINA: —Don't you have a phone here?

LIMONOV: I don't think—

MALINA: I thought you were gonna tell you know who about you know what.

LIMONOV: My flower cup I still am, I just need time.

MALINA: Why do you have to play these games with me. You know I didn't even want anything to do with you. Why...I mean what am I a pig that you come in and tell me all these things that you love me and want to be with me and that stuff about equatorial caramel and what then to leave me and do whatever this is?!

LIMONOV: Malina, listen—

MALINA: I mean I know you say that stuff to everyone. Don't you? You say it to everyone. You do. I know it too. What am I — stupid? I know who you are.

LIMONOV: I love you, Malina. If anything happened to you I'd cut myself open to be with you.

> Malina looks behind her pretty little poet with yellow teeth
> at the pudgy bearded man spectating the scene.

MALINA: I just want all of you. Not pieces.

LIMONOV: I want *you*.

MALINA: The thought of her makes me sick.

LIMONOV: I would *toss* her out on the street, Malina. I hate her. I hate that she's keeping me from you. That she makes you think she's *worthy* to breathe the same *air* as you. I never knew what love was before I saw your eyes like polar caverns, your breath like green apples.

MALINA: (*softening*) Why not break it off?

Carbon Pages

LIMONOV: She's a bull. Who knows *what* she'll do. She already suspects I've met who I'll spend the rest of my life with.

MALINA: I'm not asking for the rest of your *life*—

LIMONOV: —she's crazy, irrational she's actually convinced herself that I ever loved her!

> A pause.

LIMONOV: I'm going to tell her. I'm working on it but I need a little more time. If I rush it everything will go belly-up. After we're done, we'll live in an oaken country house in a pine wood.

MALINA: Okay. Okay.

> They embrace and kiss. He can taste his saliva on her tongue. But most awe struck of all is Dugin, at the power of his puny, squeaky-voice compatriot to pacify this girl. After a smooch, Malina closes the door behind her. Before the two inmates can get a word in, in through the same door pops the head editor Chikin.

CHIKIN: Hello, fellas. How's your project going? Listen I don't mind lending you this spare room, but do me a favour and keep the noise down. Can't have it turning into a zoo.

LIMONOV: Alright, Chikin.

> And Chikin leaves.

LIMONOV: I want to enlarge the masthead grenade for issue three.

> Immediately enters into the room another woman. A little older than the previous and less beautiful but one can see the attraction.

VIKTORIA: Where have you been, Eduard?

LIMONOV: Honey, working.

VIKTORIA: Are you seeing someone else?

No Weapon Formed Against You

LIMONOV: Of course not—there's no one for me but you!

VIKTORIA: You think I'm blind? I just met her on the way. Is this what you've been doing—running around with whores?

Pause.

LIMONOV: I'm diseased. These girls see a defenceless little man and they pounce like a lynx. I'm at their whim! How many times have I fallen for one of these demons with their charm and cunning only for them to suck the lint out my pocket?

VIKTORIA: You expect me to believe that this sexy fucking schoolgirl *pounced* on you?

LIMONOV: No—Malina, I chased.

VIKTORIA: I hate you, you—

LIMONOV: God how it infected me, her coldness, her independence. No matter what I tried she was uninterested. Not in money, not in fame. God help me! I even told her about the little oaken dacha we'll get by a lake in a forest of birch which you love! I'm sick! Demented! I guess it's some other Jezebel for me—am I doomed to be the victim of girls who use their looks and cunning to manipulate me into presents and marriage?!

VIKTORIA: *Marriage?!*

LIMONOV: It's all I've ever been good for! Forgive me, Viktoria. I promise to try to be yours from now on. Only yours. I missed your hands which are soft like dunes of the Ghobi—

VIKTORIA: —This Malina, you're telling me it's over?

LIMONOV: I broke it off. She's nothing to your solar irrendescence—

VIKTORIA: And she had no eyes on marriage, this Malina?

LIMONOV: How I wished that she did. She's well off, she's independent. I wished that that wasn't the case, that she'd be closer to me! Cut my tongue Viktoria! I've betrayed you! Cruelty, cruelty! How I've riddled you! I don't deserve your love!

Carbon Pages

VIKTORIA: Hold on—

LIMONOV: —But it's over now. I'll never go looking for another one like her again! It's only you for me!

VIKTORIA: Like hell! So you can get chewed up and spat out by one of these whores who wants to *marry* you? Not in hell.

LIMONOV: What do you mean? You're the only one for me!

VIKTORIA: Oh no. Don't think you're getting off that easy. You must really think I'm blind. You're staying with this Malina. You're staying with her right where I can see you and I'm not letting you prance about with these other sluts with rings on their minds.

LIMONOV: I refuse! I refuse! It's you I want! Malina is nothing. You are everything!

VIKTORIA: You *will* see her.

LIMONOV: She's delusional!

VIKTORIA: And if she doesn't want to—I'll make her!

LIMONOV: You cruel woman!

VIKTORIA: Oh Eduard. Don't think I'll forget this for a *long long* time.

LIMONOV: Haven't I suffered enough?

VIKTORIA: From now on I'm keeping you on a short leash, count on it.

> And she slams the door.

> Eduard collapses into his chair, exhausted. Dugin, watching the whole incident, is so floored by the expert performance that he's assessing the possibility of supernatural involvement. He looks at the exhausted little man rubbing his temples and thinks for a long time how to formulate his thoughts.

DUGIN: Can I ask you a question?

LIMONOV: Go ahead.

DUGIN: How do you make them believe you love them like that?

No Weapon Formed Against You

LIMONOV: What do you mean? I love Malina more than I've ever loved anyone in my life.

> And Limonov means what he says with genuine sincerity, he can find no paradox in it, he does not examine it, and at Dugin's implication he is truly bewildered.

DUGIN: I phrased that poorly. What I mean is, how do you make them fall for you like that?

LIMONOV: If I knew how, I'd never do it again.

> That, perhaps, is a bit less sincere.

DUGIN: Yes but there must be something that...happens there...that you're doing... maybe unconsciously which you yourself don't realise, that *infatuates* them.

> Eduard thinks on it for a second. He'd rather not answer, because it's a vulgar and crude topic, and on top of that, if it pleases, he'd rather not think of women for the rest of the week. But he decides he should humour his co-conspirant.

LIMONOV: Well...uh, it's like this.

> He's never really thought about it, at least not in a very long time.

LIMONOV: Let me think... When you...no... With a woman... You think of all the things you'd do for her, think of all the things you'll say to her. You look in her eyes where you feel at home, and you think of the beautiful expressions which come from your heart, all your poems which will convince her of your love for her, list every village you'd demolish for her and then... you simply don't say them.

...What are you lookin' at me like that for?

> You are more right than you can ever know thinks Alexander Gelyevich Dugin. You are the answer to my prayers.

Carbon Pages

Together, we will do things lesser men have never dreamed of.

Parallel lives of actors continued: Throughout his life Eduard loved the embrace of girls in the public eye. And trust me, I understand. Is there anything better than seeing the girl you love climb a stage admired by thousands of jealous eye-apples? Knowing that after the song you get to ruin her? It is a pleasure to deprive. What's better than robbing all them of all the joy they know they can't have, of a thousand moments, of her musk and her warmth and her rage and the sex under her arms and her carbon dioxide and contagion and the crook of her elbow and her effervescence and her fruit fuzz on her arms and her misery oh enough of all that it repulses me. That's what you are to me, if you'll just give me a chance. Won't you? Yes. Couldn't you? My gingersweet, my brilliant, my catafalque, my lamasu tiramasu, my little brio-oh-oh-oh-lette. I'll be the spider and web in the crook of your street lamp, I'll eat the moths you lure, I'll never forget you if you don't me. I'll take dispatch over you. They'll build statues of you won't they? Are we trying? Eduard, do you hear? Together? Will they lick your stage clean, will there be nowhere to run?

They'll take pictures of you? Maybe? What if what if what if, if it's okay, maybe we could have pictures of your pictures? How would that feel? I want you on every building. I want your profile on textbooks, I want stamps in the image of your profile on your textbook and I want the bust of your stamp in the image of your profile in a grainy old textbook. I want broadcasts of your statues retaped a hundred times. I want the boys at recess coin rubbing on napkins and drawing toilet stall doodles of the napkin and growing your brow here, your bridge there, until it resembles no one alive.

Can you imagine them seeing it every day?!? A copy of a copy slipping out the pants pocket of a boy, so grainy-like and dither-blasted it makes me slobber and so washed-out it makes my nails tingle!!! I want boy your paper to clump and sog from all the ink that depicts nothing at all now wow wow wow that is exciting and maybe I can even forget I don't want to be on it myself oh so forever forever forever until the end of time.

No Weapon Formed Against You

LIMONOV: What's next on the agenda?

DUGIN: As I was saying, I think it's time for us to get a *krisha*.

LIMONOV: My thoughts exactly.

DUGIN: The amount of political assassinations in the papers...

LIMONOV: They kill for anything.

DUGIN: For a lot less than Limonka.

LIMONOV: I can afford a guard or two.

DUGIN: I suggest we ask the managers of GrOb for a personnel loan.

LIMONOV: What's GrOb?

DUGIN: It's a punk rock band. Their sound is brilliant...

LIMONOV: I don't know. Punk? It's démodé.

DUGIN: The lead singer is an old friend of mine, he's had some nationalist turn, and he has thirty million fans. More to the point any band with that kind of target on their back will have extensive security in their employ.

LIMONOV: He has thirty million fans?

DUGIN: Yes.

>Limonov looks out the tiny, barred office window, thinks, removes his shades and puts them back on.

>No sooner was the day over than Dugin was able to arrange a meeting with the two entities. Dugin and Limonov entered the lowly apartment flat on the topmost floor of a brittle Khruschevka. The corridor was narrow so they walked single file toward the noise of laughter and hollering.

>All around was the smell of dampness and mold and the inexplicable sound of a landline ringing in a locked bathroom. Finally they stepped into the kitchen, and the noise of drunken fun screeched its brakes. Everyone looked at the two strangers. Dugin suddenly felt very warm in his long black coat. The kitchen had a little chipboard table in the corner by the radiator, and around it were squeezed in five or six burly

Carbon Pages

> Siberians, shot glasses under their noses. On the table was an empty bottle of vodka, a plate of pickles sliced laterally into quarters and then salted, a plate of slices of black bread, each slice cut in half and layed with pork salo, a large plastic bottle of Coca-Cola, and a single inexplicable bowl with the remnants of some kind of broth now being used as an ashtray.

LIMONOV: Drinking are we?

BANDMATES: Drinking!

LIMONOV: Gentlemen when we drink we sleep and when we sleep we do no sin. Let us all drink and go to heaven!

BANDMATE: Here here!

> The members of GrOb howl and cheer.

LIMONOV: Now may we talk to your brave manager?

> The singer-songwriter with long oily hair and a patchy beard with glints of ginger so common in the primitives of the Yenesei replies:

IGOR LETOV: The brave manager's out for *Royal Prima*.

LIMONOV: In that case allow me to speak to your coalition as a whole—

> But Letov notices something and interrupts:

IGOR LETOV: Al? Al Dugin? Haha!

> Letov is ecstatic.

IGOR LETOV: Let me out for a second. Let me shake his hand. Holy shit.

DUGIN: Hello Igor.

IGOR LETOV: Well fuck. How long's it been? Ten years? Twelve?

DUGIN: *Nolens volens.*

IGOR LETOV: Pour this man a drink. Oh yeah. We're out. This is the guy…

No Weapon Formed Against You

DUGIN: It's good to see you. You're... (*motions to chin*) ...scraggly.

IGOR LETOV: Yeah so are you. Everyone, this is the kid I met during my interim in Moscow. He had a guy steal a goat before beheading him for Satan. How's that for an opening act, eh?!

> Limonov thinks he misheard the Siberian and Dugin is marginally embarrassed at having that old story brought up at all.

LIMONOV: We're operating a political newspaper...

IGOR LETOV: Good. Nobody else seems to think so but me but the country is in a state of spiritual warfare.

DUGIN: Right, right.

IGOR LETOV: So. Political newspaper. That's good, but it's a start.

LIMONOV: We feel the same way. All the might of Russia is against us. If they had their way, they'd level our offices and pulp Limonka into toilet paper for Yeltsin's gang.

IGOR LETOV: Sure. They're the reason the men who all their life were persecuted for holding American basketball cards are now forced to hock them for a loaf of bread.

> Limonov finds this example to be obscenely pedestrian.

LIMONOV: Well the point is we're in the market for some hired guns.

> There's a kind of silence again in the kitchen. Who does this guy think he is?

LIMONOV: Fellas what's with the telephone? Is someone gonna get that?

IGOR LETOV: What do you think—we traffic, uh, thugs?

LIMONOV: I didn't mean any offense.

DUGIN: We're still finding our footing, Igor. You understand how hard it is now.

Carbon Pages

Letov scratches his beard.

IGOR LETOV: This country is in the shitter. Every caricature was true, every propaganda cartoon of fat kapitalists in tophats, of concrete canyons layered with smog, I thought it was bullshit. It was true. Everyone's just eeking by. So it's good what you're doing. I have nothing but respect. But I don't know anything about hired guns or security or any of that shit.

DUGIN: Igor, think on it at least.

LIMONOV: Maybe your manager—

IGOR LETOV: —Sorry. Can't help you.

Limonov slicks his hair.

LIMONOV: Do you know, Igor, who Baron Von Ungern is?

IGOR LETOV: I shit on your Baron Vungurn.

LIMONOV: Why don't you wear something more put together? I mean keds and a graphic t-shirt? That's weird. That looks weird. Keds and a t-shirt?

DUGIN: Eduard, it's a style.

LIMONOV: You have all the money in the world but you dress like a bum and don't support revolutionary papers!

IGOR LETOV: Hold on, hold on. (*indignant*) I wear shitty clothes because that's what my listeners wear. That's one. I wear keds because no one in this country can afford import runners. That's one. Two: what money? What fucking money do you see here? You think we're Kombinatsiya? One concert we played we sold out. Yeah, we sold out. A whole arena. Hundreds of thousands. The guys running the box office skipped town and made off with the earnings. So no, whoever you are. We don't have all the money in the world.

LIMONOV: What's that got to do with your hair? Wash your hair. Punk isn't interesting. Rock isn't interesting. Your act was best-by twenty years ago.

Letov says some joke to his Siberian bandmates and they laugh the two men out of the flat. The telephone in the bathroom was still ringing the next day when Dugin and

No Weapon Formed Against You

Limonov were discussing the contents of issue four of Limonka. In marched the same Igor Letov.

LIMONOV: What do you want?

The musician brandishes a copy of Limonka #1 like a cutlass.

IGOR LETOV: Are you Limonov?

LIMONOV: Yes.

IGOR LETOV: This is your magazine?

LIMONOV: That's right.

IGOR LETOV: What do you call this shit?

LIMONOV: What do you mean?

IGOR LETOV: What are you people playing at? Look at this page. What's this blotch? And this one?

LIMONOV: Probably a printer error.

IGOR LETOV: You think *Pravda* had printer errors?

LIMONOV: *Pravda* had twelve proofreaders. We have me.

IGOR LETOV: You have twelve *million* proofreaders or twelve thousand or however many are forced to read this garbage. How's Russia meant to rise from her knees when this is her best?

Dugin pipes in:

DUGIN: What do you suggest, Igor?

IGOR LETOV: Well for starters, let me in. Then we'll see.

DUGIN: You want to write for Limonka?

IGOR LETOV: I mean the whole thing. Management.

DUGIN: Fine.

LIMONOV: Okay.

Carbon Pages

A silence entered the office as they thought *what now?* Then entered Chikin.

CHIKIN: Alexander! Eduard! Didn't I warn you? Pack your things. I want you out of here immediately! This was a proper establishment. It was proper and now I have gopniks in sheepskins pissing about my corridors!

> The spare room which Eduard and Alexander had taken into their possession now looked like a veritable mausoleum of impolite ideologies. On the walls were portraits of Stalin and Goebbels, promotion plaques for the Nuremberg rallies, a giant red flag of the former USSR, swastikas, Lenin quotes, and art by Arno Breker and Stanislav Szukalski.

CHIKIN: I tried talking nice when I thought you two were harmless. But this? This is unacceptable.

LIMONOV: We're leaving, Chikin!

CHIKIN: I mean—*an Empire from Vladivostok to Gibraltar?* Have you gone mad? If our foreign friends find out about this they'll sack me!

> In the subsequent weeks, the men decided that a magazine was insufficient to stoke a revolution, which was the only way for Russia and her people to survive, and a party was required which would act as vanguard, with the three men as its founders. They agreed on the name the National Bolshevik party, on Dugin's suggestion, since it encompassed both their fascistic ideals and their communist ones, neither of which could function alone in the 21st century but in synthesis would herald in an overthrow of democratic rule.
>
> In the tradition of historic Russian parties, each founder was issued a Ticket, a document committing his body and will to the party. Party ticket number one was possessed by Limonov, who thus took on treasurer duties and paid for all starting expenses. The second ticket was given to Dugin. The third, much to the chagrin of Letov, was given to the young man who had come knocking on Limonov's door, and now acted for all intents and purposes as his factotum. The fourth, finally, was in possession by Igor Letov, who kept the document for a long time.

No Weapon Formed Against You

> Some time later the trio convene, not at a spare office in the *Rossiya* building nor Letov's dingy flat. Rather, the three men walk in one by one into a vast stripped neoclassical apartment where the sunlight shines through tall windows and ormolu frames and the ceilings are high. A shabby old chandelier hangs dust ridden from the ceiling, its wiring exposed. In half a century of abandonment the place has lost its zest.

LIMONOV: So tell me again, you were just *given* this place?

IGOR LETOV: You shoulda seen his face. Dugin thought of writing a letter, but I said let's go straight to the mayor himself. So we're in his office and I tell him it would be a shame if the newly minted Moscow suffered the violence of radicals. It's a shame our party doesn't have a space to call a headquarters, otherwise we'd set those regressives straight as a cossack at dawn.

> The floor is hidden under a carpet of rubbish. They all try to imagine what the place would look like as the Politburo or Stalin's office. Nobody quite can.

IGOR LETOV: I guess, for him, it's a small price to pay.

LIMONOV: Well, Dr. Goebbels, what do *you* think?

DUGIN: It is infested.

IGOR LETOV: You shoulda seen it before, Eddie. There were some mechanics squatting in Dugin's room.

DUGIN: *My* room?

LIMONOV: What's it costing us?

IGOR LETOV: Three rubles a month thereabouts. Just so there's paperwork.

LIMONOV: I like that it's big. And the light is good since it faces south. The party requires good light.

IGOR LETOV: So what do we think? Do we take it?

DUGIN: It's crumbling. And just look at that balcony. It could collapse any second. Maybe he even planned it that way, the mayor, so that it collapses and kills us.

Carbon Pages

LIMONOV: Precocious.

DUGIN: Maybe we could go back and demand another place.

IGOR LETOV: C'mon lads, it's not so bad.

LIMONOV: What if he says you greedy pricks I'm rescinding this one. As far as I'm concerned it's a miracle we got anything. No, I like it. I can see it and I like it. The reception will be here. A portrait here. That room for me, that room for you. Are you seeing it?

IGOR LETOV: I'll sleep in the kitchen.

LIMONOV: That's a kitchen?

IGOR LETOV: Meant to be.

DUGIN: Is that a leak in mine? I have to see this.

    And Dugin leaves to check out his potential quarters.

LIMONOV: Igor, I have to say: I'm impressed.

IGOR LETOV: The mayor was so drunk he would've given his second wife. Impressed would be asking him the morning after.

LIMONOV: But the location worries me.

IGOR LETOV: Same building. It's tough.

    Limonov thinks on it.

LIMONOV: Yknow. All things considered...*on top* is not *under*. *Under* the police precinct would be a dealbreaker.

IGOR LETOV: It would be a dealbreaker.

LIMONOV: I give you that. But on top? In a way it's even strategically advantageous. What about Dugin—did he negotiate?

IGOR LETOV: Dugin? We're lucky the mayor didn't notice his Wolf Messing routine.

LIMONOV: What's a Wolf Messing routine?

No Weapon Formed Against You

IGOR LETOV: What—he hasn't graced you yet? He thinks his books have learnt him make a man cluck like a chicken. Thank God I was there to distract the mayor or he'd think he was crazy.

LIMONOV: How do you know it didn't work? We *did* get an apartment.

IGOR LETOV: Because it doesn't work. For as long as I've known him he's been trying. One time he even tried it on me.

> And so the apartment on Frunzenskaya Street with a police station for a basement was christened Eagle's Nest. And they began to turn the derelict overlooking the Moskva river into a space deserving of the little printed plaque hanging on the door which read—party headquarters.
>
> Over the weeks, the three men and the recruit washed the floor, scraped the windows, scrubbed the mold, threw out the ragged drapes. They tore off the yellow wallpaper in massive long strips with which they covered the floorboards and their spare clothes. As Limonov peeled, the smell reminded him of newspapers. The gosplan made them from the same pulp. As Igor peeled, the smell conjured in his mind the pages of the storybook his mother read him as a boy. Dugin was reminded of nothing.
>
> It was hard on the knees to scrape and fill with glue the gaps which had developed in the pinewood flooring.

DUGIN: ...and eventually exploit their resentment for the bombing of Hiroshima, into a Moscow-Tokyo axis. See how one little thing nets us the Pacific?

LIMONOV: Mind your fingers. The party has a serious problem, Al.

DUGIN: What's that?

LIMONOV: We don't have a banner. Hand me the knife.

DUGIN: We can get a banner easy.

LIMONOV: A party needs a *monstrous* banner.

DUGIN: I suppose so.

Carbon Pages

They stop to catch their breath.

DUGIN: You know...the party's bigger than politics.

A draft blows over them and they start working again.

He painted the walls with four layers of white and the ceiling too. There was no electricity or heating, so one by one they retired, until only Limonov was left. His neck pained him from staring at the ceiling. He worked naked. Though outside it was cold, he had bought an illegal wood stove for heating and the room was warm. The paint dripped all over him and the wallpaper. When he sanded the walls and the ceiling, the white dust stuck the inside of his nostrils, and his boogers were snow white for a week. It was the middle of night when he finished. He climbed down, and looked at his fingernail clinched to his flesh and it seemed a miracle that every day his body did not disembulate into a million constituent pieces, that its glue didn't flake and wane, that the hairs on his knuckle didn't launch off like little rocket ships and his skin didn't surrender off her ligaments. He imagined Malina standing there on the threshold with a pink sunburn and goosebumps. Once this vision dissipated, he went outside in the night and washed himself with clumps of snow.

Weeks had to pass before the derelict was truly tolerable and Dugin and Letov began moving in their things, the latter much to the bewilderment of his bandmates who couldn't comprehend their lead singer's turn. But that's the way it went. One afternoon, he returned to the apartment with two string-bags of groceries. He unpacked and listened to his comrades who were in a friendly discussion, speaking all the while, for reasons he failed to understand, in French.

DUGIN: Don't you think it's a bit vulgar?

LIMONOV: Vulgar is the point.

DUGIN: But why the girls? If people see the girls they won't take it seriously.

LIMONOV: Girls make people take things seriously. You don't know Playboy. Hustler. These are respected publications, not that you'd know.

No Weapon Formed Against You

DUGIN: I just think—okay—look—a person sees the issue at a train station. A *colonel* sees it at a train station. He resents his superior. Highly susceptible. There's some great texts in this, some of my densest, that have the possibility of making a defector out of him. Now do you think he's going to get that far if on the—let's see—first page...third page...fifth page...before he even *gets* to *The Continental Logos* he sees a titty drawing, gore, Worhol—?

LIMONOV: You want your piece bumped up.

DUGIN: That is not the point—

LIMONOV: Have you considered, comrade Dugin, that a nice figure makes mush out a man's brains—makes him suggestible. These titties will have the colonel on his knees.

                Igor Letov pipes in:

IGOR LETOV: Why's the tap not working? I'm trying to make a broth.

                Dugin doesn't hear him:

DUGIN: The formatting is schizophrenic. There's this journal coming out of Belgium which is thoroughly dignified—

LIMONOV: Is it called Limonka? Or is it called Duginka? It's what we signed up for. And I'm not your student, and you're not my professor. Limonka isn't B minus this or A plus that — it's non-negotiable.

IGOR LETOV: Does anyone know where the water is?!

LIMONOV: I haven't connected the what you call it. The main.

IGOR LETOV: How are we meant to have broth without water?

LIMONOV: The patient shall be rewarded with the kingdom of God.

IGOR LETOV: I guess I'll call someone to take a look at it.

LIMONOV: The water?

IGOR LETOV: The water.

Carbon Pages

LIMONOV: I'm the treasurer, leave it to me. I'll only have to end up fixing it twice.

Dugin informs:

DUGIN: Fill the pot from the shower.

IGOR LETOV: There's meant to be a blizzard tonight.

Eduard solemnly looks out the window.

The air has dropped.

LIMONOV: Winter of my heart—what have you in store for me?

That night they sat around a box with candlelight on some stools and drank watermelon wine bartered for at the market. The snowstorm howled outside the balcony window which did nothing to stop a chill from invading the apartment.

IGOR LETOV: ...So it got to the point where every day after school I would sneak in and tear out days from the little calender. Sometimes I flushed them but sometimes I'd—hic—forget. One day she goes to mark down a birthday, and all I hear is—*IGORRR! why is February missing?!*

Eduard and Alexander wheeze with laughter.

IGOR LETOV: Well it didn't end so well. She found a bunch of pages stuck together like with yellow glue...I said I was wiping my nose.

DUGIN: Me—I never...

IGOR LETOV: Well good—

DUGIN: —I never was caught!!

IGOR LETOV: Well good for you!!!

LIMONOV: You know, Letov—

IGOR LETOV: What?

No Weapon Formed Against You

LIMONOV: You have a Siberian tang when I drink. Like one of those fish smokers. Do you smoke fish?

IGOR LETOV: I don't.

LIMONOV: You do!

IGOR LETOV: I do not smoke fish!

LIMONOV: Perhaps, mhm, a little catfish here—

IGOR LETOV: I do not.

LIMONOV: A little eel here...Hey *where* are you *going*? Sit the hell *down*!

IGOR LETOV: I'm going outside, Limonov! I do *not* smoke *fish*!

LIMONOV: You'll squall us to death you lunatic! Fine, I yield! Good God man shut that thing!

IGOR LETOV: You wouldn't know how to smoke a *vobla* if you...were born in a smokehouse....

    Alexander had gotten strangely silent.

LIMONOV: Al, are you crying?

    A tear trickled down his cheek and disappeared down his beard.

DUGIN: I just need to say...

IGOR LETOV: What is it?

LIMONOV: What's gotten into you?

DUGIN: ...that if I could just go back in time...to when I was a young boy, and tell him what I know now....that everything would be alright... I just want to say that I...I wish I had met friends like you earlier. If I had such good friends like you...

    He trails off.

DUGIN: If such happiness is possible, then just think...

Carbon Pages

The blizzard is raging.

DUGIN: ...how much has been lost.

>Letov puts his arm around Dugin's shoulder. I'm reminded, following this moment, of a little village on the Yenesei. During one of their characteristically warm summers, the same year that it's decided to send food aid to Russia, the residents of the village are struck by a series of strange red mounds which grow sporadically on their skin from which, after a few days, a big harmless insect erupts. No one can explain why it's happening, and some move away.

LIMONOV: Stalin! Beria! Dzerzhinksy! The National Bolshevik Party will put Yeltsin's head on the traintracks. First on the agenda is to arrest all representatives of the International Monetary Fund on Russian territory, and ply their skills in the laying of a new Trans-Siberian bullet train. Second is establish the Great Anglo-Franco Gulag. They say the country has been sold for the crumbs of foreign capital who have tyrannized the working Russian, the noble plougher, the fisher and the huntsman. Oh fallen huntsman, let me don your garb and *vintovka,* and train it in the uvula of President Boris Yeltsin and his pack of hounds. Let me deliver their skins to the proletariat of this most noble of races. Let us strike fear once more into the United States who reaches out her hand to ours in goodwill. No, we do not want your goodwill. We will pin your hand with a fork, and hang you by a nucleur-bactereological rope. We will annihilate Washington with a simoom of ICBMs and build Russia the City of the Sun, one that is beautiful. The CPSU cannot save the people. Neither can the Hitlerites. We are the holy coalition against the civilizers at the gate. We are the best of the Red and the best of the Brown. Vladivostok to Gibraltar, and eventually, Alaska—it will all be Russian and all be beautiful. That is the National Bolshevik promise. A Four Year Plan will be established for the military annihilation of all criminal elements, including those who wear a suit and tie, and sit in council of our industries. Owners found conducting business or advertising in any language

No Weapon Formed Against You

other than Russian will be beaten and stripped of ownership. In fact, all advertising will be illegal within the NazBol regime. They are an eyesore and morally illegal. Sweep away the geriatric communists and the hobbling liberals. NazBol is youth. NazBol is art, justice and glory.

> The streets of Moscow were parapheted with snow, and tattooed with foreign businesses and advertisements of all sorts. Parliament cigarettes, McDonalds, Rolex and Prada. Limonov and Letov were there, while Dugin stayed at Eagle's Nest.
>
> Most of Limonov's listeners were young, with some older people stopping out of curiosity. Suddenly a hunched old babushka wearing a bartered coat comes up to Letov and Limonov. Over her face is a wash of pink blisters and peeling skin which ends at a hard border at one cheek which makes it look like her face was rolled with a paint roller of some acidic substance.

BABUSHKA: What is this? Why such commotion?

IGOR LETOV: We're inciting a revolution.

BABUSHKA: Why such noise? You've got the cars backed up. All this commotion is disgraceful.
(at Letov)
You're a young man. Don't you have anything better to be doing?

> Limonov replies:

LIMONOV: We're doing it quick and painless, lady.

> The babushka spits out a wad of bubble gum.

BABUSHKA: The inmate pleads for his cell. It's a miracle we got our boot up the communists' asses the first time and you want back that Empire of Evil?

LIMONOV: Where'd you hear that one—Radio CIA?

BABUSHKA: I know one thing—and that is that the people of this country will never be again falling for the tricks of your like. Everyone can see what pain and lies communism brought. Any ideology brings. And maybe things aren't perfect. But soon we'll be just like a civilized country, and in the meantime at least we are *free*.

> It's this babushka that's on Limonov's mind back at Eagle's Nest that night, in his room still sparse but with a mattress. Viktoria is sitting on the mattress and he at a desk with a table lamp scribbling in a stack of papers.

VIKTORIA: Give a mouse a cookie, give a man a moment.

LIMONOV: You know what this is?

VIKTORIA: No.

LIMONOV: It's a Conditional Residency Permit. I have to submit this by Friday or they'll kick us out. As if the rent isn't enough.

VIKTORIA: Why don't you get your kid to do it? What are you calling him now? Zygote? I don't understand the point of these silly codenames.

LIMONOV: Do you think Stalin's name was really Stalin? Anyway, I have to do what I can myself. Anyone else will buckle the whole party down with him.

VIKTORIA: You're angry at everyone now except your *triumvirate*.

LIMONOV: (*distracted*) When Moscow falls we have to be ready, because then comes Petersburg and then the provinces. God knows with our numbers we have to pick our battles.

VIKTORIA: Eddie, you know I agree with you don't you? I know the country's been sold.

LIMONOV: No one else seems to realize—

VIKTORIA: But you know that I know, don't you?

LIMONOV: Yes.

VIKTORIA: Why do you have to be the one to throw yourself on the fire? The country loved you. Remember how they hung on every word? Remember when you first returned, how hungry they were for your tales about Brodsky and the

No Weapon Formed Against You

penthouses? You could hear a pin drop. Now you've thrown that away for what—the admiration of some boys from a town with no snow removal?

LIMONOV: What would you have me do—sit on my hands?

VIKTORIA: But you're fighting against all the things you used to love. you loved Edith Piaf and, I don't know, like, the Eiffel Tower.

LIMONOV: No I didn't. Okay maybe I did. That was then.

VIKTORIA: You loved democracy. And you hated the Soviet Union.

LIMONOV: Did I?

VIKTORIA: Think of why you left it in the first place.

LIMONOV: I was exiled.

VIKTORIA: I just don't comprehend the motivation here.

LIMONOV: The motivation is that the west is decrepit and Russia is starving.

VIKTORIA: Alright they're starving...

LIMONOV: You might as well be telling me about the kid who yanked my tie in school.

VIKTORIA: Alright they're starving and you're nice and rich and warm.

LIMONOV: (*distracted*) Rich—that's rich.

VIKTORIA: So why can't you just accept that you've been luckier than them and enjoy your luck. Let them believe in their kapitalism. Even *they* want you to enjoy yourself. The Russian people want you to be happy.

> Limonov tosses down his legal papers and erupts:

LIMONOV: So all my life, all my childhood I had to stand those wrinkle-faced provincial mediocres walking from their parades so proud in their one pair of finery which they'd strangle me into if they had the chance, twirling the hammer and sickle, komsomol this Lenin that, not knowing how to read an azbuka let alone Lenin, telling me I'm a good-for-nothing and a demoralizer, and now just because some silver spoon with a bald spot on his birthmark lucked into a government job, they change their minds, and all at once the whole nation switches horses. And we're all meant to dance sufi round the fire, wearing daisy crowns on our heads? No. I won't buy it. I know them too well. I saw them pants-down. I know every freckle: if everyone believes something, it *can't* be good. Their belief is God's own call for me to turn the exact opposite.

VIKTORIA: You're always talking God now.

LIMONOV: Must be Dugin's influence.

VIKTORIA: He gives me the creeps.

LIMONOV: My rose, Alexander is the most brilliant scholar I've ever met. He's the St. Cyril of fascism. He's the Merlin to my Arthur. I would die for him. And you can sure bet that he'd die for me.

> As the sun rises, Limonov tightropes between sleeping bags and rubbish. Now there is not one, not two sleeping bags but almost the entire west wall of the apartment is a congregation of individuals who, having heard about Limonov and his coming revolution, have come the country over to support the cause. As the poet stoops over to pick up a cigarette pack or sweet wrapper the youth invariably says *Fine day for it, mister Limonov*, or *what's on the agenda today mister Limonov*.
>
> It's like a boarding school mixed with a barrack and editorial office. Barbarians seething with rage. There are young men with muscles and some like twigs, some with long hair and some shaved. Most of all, there are unremarkably neat men with ordinary faces like tradesmen, in suits and button ups. One pair came from the Arctic city of Korl which, defying all meteorological predictions, suffered the coldest winter since records began and where the sky had turned an immutable shade of red.
>
> Limonov follows a trail of beer bottles to Dugin's room.

DUGIN: Don't touch those!

LIMONOV: The bottles?

DUGIN: Yes.

LIMONOV: For such a germaphobe you keep a sty.

No Weapon Formed Against You

DUGIN: The twenty-seven sevens. The seven heavens, seven wounds, seven pleaids, seven sacramanets, seven hills of Rome. Need I go on? If you wish a calamity to strike the building then by all means remove my charms.

> Limonov lets the bottles be. Dugin is sowing a needle through a black fabric draped over his knee.

LIMONOV: What's that?

DUGIN: A kosovorotka.

LIMONOV: What's a kosovorotka?

DUGIN: Old Believer garbs.

LIMONOV: We've signed an executive order.

DUGIN: Who?

LIMONOV: Our little triumvirate.

DUGIN: I've signed nothing.

LIMONOV: No, not yet.

DUGIN: Before we make decisions you must consult me.

LIMONOV: Well me and Letov discussed it and I think it's right...

DUGIN: What is?

LIMONOV: That you take over as editor of Limonka.

> He looks up from his kosovorotka.

DUGIN: Really?

LIMONOV: I've enough on my plate. It's like you told me, we have to be smart about delegation.

DUGIN: It's the logical choice.

> He's back sewing.

DUGIN: What about the rent. Did you hear?

Carbon Pages

LIMONOV: I heard.

DUGIN: Has Letov offered to—?

LIMONOV: I have it covered.

DUGIN: Eduard if you need anything, just say.

        The poet looks around.

LIMONOV: You've got a lair would make Doctor Faustus run for the hills.

DUGIN: It's research.

LIMONOV: You don't spend as much time here as you used to.

DUGIN: I still have things at home.

LIMONOV: Why not introduce yourself to the new recruits?

DUGIN: Eh.

LIMONOV: You're a Founder now. Hearts and minds.

DUGIN: We'll see.

        Limonov leaves Dugin alone.

DUGIN: *Introduce yourself.* As if I should waste my time. Who are they to me? A gang of ingrates. My logos is wasted on them. I feel them siphoning it and giving nothing in return. What is it you think you're doing exactly, Limonov? What are you gaining from them? What? Do they bring you any closer to the army? To the intelligence services or the universities? Months of this and we've gotten no closer. But you don't care—not as long as you have your little paparazzis. But wasn't it nice when that one called me Founder and noticed my name and...

        He swigs a beer.

DUGIN: It's not hard to get them on your side. Or is it? If it's so easy why don't they come for ME? Why only for YOU?

        He swigs a beer and paces about.

No Weapon Formed Against You

DUGIN: I could do what you do, Limonov. What am I saying? How can I claim to influence anyone when even a child is beyond my reach.

>He looks into the ceiling of the lair.

DUGIN: Oh My God. I know I don't speak to you. I'm afraid of you. The truth is, I'm afraid and unworthy of you. But I have changed. I'm trying with all surrender to shape in your image. Were I tried, were I at the tribunal, I would leap upon the podium and yell for Nuremberg to hear I BELIEVE I BELIEVE, not in money, not in the atlantic, but in DIVINITY! But I have no voice! You gave your JESTER the voice and your SOLDIER a sickle! What should I do? Set as my struggle to be the most photographed man on Earth? What has HE done to earn your power? Did he beat the starting gun on me? I have nothing but the bottle.

>He drinks down a new beer only to realise half-way through what he's doing. He throws it against the corner where it does not even shatter.

DUGIN: THAT'S the test—and that's the hand that's tested! God, please help me. When that boy recruit recognized my byline it was delicious but I HID! Hid and drank. How did it ever get so bad? Divest me of this pain, I'll do anything. I know I've no right to pray to you after what I've done. But without you I am nothing! There's my relief!

>On his knees he points to the beer.

DUGIN: I'll quit the drink. I'll destroy my only relief. I'll live without sin. I'll spread your word. But please, Father: form around me your shield.

>Whether it was the desire to imitate Limonov and harness his penchant for image building, or simply a reprieve from the boredom of an otherwise slow movement, he bit by bit left his room, such that soon NazBols began to know and respect the faceless byline of Alexander Dugin as an indispensable founder, and a thoughtful thinker and finally, even, an adequate orator. Such that when one day Igor Letov returned from a concert he was shocked to find the big bearded

> philosopher giving a sermon to NazBols sitting criss-crossed
> on their sleeping bags with eyes and ears glued to the Founder
> who by his side had a kid ordered to every so often open the
> stove and slot in a log. Even Limonov was there at the very
> back on a stool, penning words like *apotheosis* and *qualia* on
> the back of his hand.

DUGIN: In retrospect we know now that within the USSR there were two ancient tenets battling for supremacy. The Brezhnevite apparatus representing the Order of New Carthage, and the heroic and misunderstood KGB: the Egyptian Seth, the Python, Ahriman, Suffering Christ, Man in the lonely Gethsemane prayer—the cloak and dagger of the Eurasian ethnos, extinguished at its nadir, stripped of its civilizational mission of forming a continental empire.

IGOR LETOV: He's coming out of his shell.

LIMONOV: *Gethsemane prayer*: I need to use that.

> Igor winces. He's still a bit dazed because earlier his bandmate
> had been walking on a quiet street when for no discernible
> reason, and with no events following, he saw a jet plane fall
> out of the sky and smolder into the asphalt inches before him.
> Limonov whispers:

LIMONOV: Our neighbours searched us today. Almost took out Tailgate's eye busting the door.

IGOR LETOV: Did they find anything?

LIMONOV: I have the condemnables hidden.

IGOR LETOV: We noticed some guys following us.

LIMONOV: You think someone sent them?

IGOR LETOV: Probably.

> At that moment the doorman allowed into the stronghold a
> homely young woman who scanned the crowd and crept over
> to what the two men assumed to be her boyfriend.

LIMONOV: She's wearing an exquisite shawl collar don't you think?

No Weapon Formed Against You

IGOR LETOV: Yeah.

DUGIN: ...true heroes, like our own in Limonov, derive from the land and, in the case of the mercantile nations, yes, the sea. The land derives from God and the holy fathers of Russia. Let me tell you a story about Old Man Avvakum...

    Eduard speaks with her and on returning, sits back down next to Founder Letov and says:

LIMONOV: The party's found its banner.

    One day, Dugin had just finished one of his sermons when a young NazBol rushed into the apartment in a sweat.

NAZBOL: Founder Dugin, you have to come to the station.

DUGIN: Downstairs?

NAZBOL: No, the one in Sokol. They arrested Copland and Sonnet. Just this morning. They're pinning some break-in that happened halfway across town on them, and now they have them for possession of hand grenades.

DUGIN: Holy Father help them. Are they on their way here—the police?

NAZBOL: I don't think they know they're with us.

DUGIN: They don't?

NAZBOL: Founder Dugin, they have an alibi. They were at dinner last night, everyone saw. If we just explain what happened at the station, they'll have to let 'em go.

    Dugin thinks for a long time, and even utters a short prayer before deciding:

Carbon Pages

DUGIN: And the hand grenades? I'm afraid it shall do no good. And it will finally give the authorities a reason to put us all in one big cell. Swear on the Seven Wounds you'll speak no more of this.

> National Bolshevism was on the tongue of the whole country. Reporters and news anchors made their lunch off the group, new legislation was drafted against the formation of groups hinderous to the social order, and if early on in the party's story the fans of Igor Letov's *Civil Defense*, or GrOb, were confused or at best accepting of the lead singer-songwriter's strange political turn, then now all the band's listenership could be said to be NazBol. Soon, at one concert held in Moscow's Gorky Park, thousands of listeners gathered and cheered for the opener:

LIMONOV: On behalf of the population of Russia, I demand that you disbar your illegitimate confederacy. If you refuse, and ignore the wishes of the proletariat, then you leave the National Bolsheviks no choice but to take control of the state apparatus by any means necessary.

> The crowd roars.

LIMONOV: We are the largest White nation in Evropa! We will lay the summer's dust with showers of blood, and construct the order of Eurasia: The Order of Apollo, Ormuzd, the Solar Christ-in-Glory. Long live the Savior of the Almighty!

> Limonov feels more alive than he ever has in his life. For the whole speech he has a smile on his face that verges on psychotic giggles. He feels he is one with the crowd, and at the same time a great horseman, teasing and twisting its reigns on the path to a City of the Sun. Him and Letov embrace, to another wave of yowls. But, being quick to offense as Eduard is, it only takes a single remark to plummet Limonov's mood from its prismatic jubilance.

IGOR LETOV: Not bad, Eddie, but they hear you stammer. Watch this.

> He watches Letov walk centre stage. Unlike Limonov who enacts a deliberate and affected performance whenever he

No Weapon Formed Against You

speaks to a crowd, and shouts as if there isn't a stereophonic microphone under his nose, Igor is the same on stage as he is in private, grumbling something under his breath, and still somehow his voice projects louder and further than Limonov's possibly could. He rehearses no lines, and doesn't work the crowd. His applause is ten times Limonov's.

IGOR LETOV: My friends, this is for Marx. This is for order and for the decisive revolution.

And he starts playing his guitar but only his voice is being picked up.

TECHNICIAN: I can't hear his guitar. His microphone isn't working! Someone get him a microphone!

Seeing that without a microphone the show's kaput, without hesitation Eduard gets a mic and dashes on stage, dolphin diving to Letov's feet and holding his microphone as he plays and like a flash the power of the six-string acoustic reverbs in fourscore and a thousand eardrums.

And there the poet lies by the feet of the singer, and both of them underneath a gargantuan-wide hammer and sickle, and a crimson charmeuse banner too with lamé lettering reading "All Wrath to the Workers. All Workers to the Nation."

IGOR LETOV: *My holy Motherland straightens her back*
Our wrathful power moves mountains

The sun's tattoo
In this deadliest cold, in this nadir of night.

I see her rise from her ashes—my Motherland!
Scolding does she burn in me—my Motherland!
I hear her sing—oh my wonderful beautiful Soviet Motherland!

It's a fan favourite, and gets the kids so excited that by the end of the show they chase them and the Founders' van breaks down so that one guard has to jump out and herd the crazed fans like hens in coop, yelling *save yourselves I'll hold them off!*

Carbon Pages

and the founders laughing like crazy, having the time of their lives. Suddenly, Limonov feels like king of the world again.

But that night, all is quiet. And Letov lies sleeping on the floor when he hears Dugin pacing about in his room muttering.

IGOR LETOV: Al? What's the matter?

DUGIN: I'm just thinking that — yes — absolutely — we need to recheck the radon levels.

IGOR LETOV: The what levels?

DUGIN: Radon levels.

IGOR LETOV: Whaz that?

DUGIN: You don't know what radon is? It's an odourless, colourless gas that accumulates deep in the Earth before infiltrating domiciles.

IGOR LETOV: So what's—

DUGIN: It's highly poisonous and causes brain paralysis.

IGOR LETOV: I didn't know.

DUGIN: You mean to say you and Limonov didn't check for RADON? Jesus Christ. Jesus Christ. It's the second most leading cause of lung cancer and he didn't check for radon. Four-Eighteen Save my Soul it's stuffy in here. What those harlequins in the Duma wouldn't give for us all to get brain damage. What if what I've been writing has already become noticeably dumber because of this substance. I must cross reference. Tomorrow I definitely must start taking things into my own hands!

And he continues muttering like that to himself until Letov falls asleep again. Since Dugin quit drinking, it's become common.

When Zygote found him, Limonov was at a People's Court legal office, surrounded by paper documents and communing with an automated voice:

No Weapon Formed Against You

LIMONOV: Relax...Autumn...Kiwi...

AUTOMATED VOICE: Please repeat while ensuring clear voice...

LIMONOV: Shell...Alley...Tough...Rivet—

ZYGOTE: —Sir, it's Copland and Sonnet!

LIMONOV: What?

ZYGOTE: They're on the rocks!

LIMONOV: Are the cops at Eagle's Nest yet?

ZYGOTE: The boys've been in lockup since Thursday, sir. Tinkin swore not to tell but I heard just this morning and I came as fast—

LIMONOV: Hold on—since *Thursday?* Why wasn't I told about this? Who did he swear to?

ZYGOTE: To Founder Dugin.

LIMONOV: What? why would he do that? why didn't Alexander tell me? Where is he?

ZYGOTE: At Eagle's Nest, sir.

LIMONOV: What was Al thinking? We have to go there immediately. Grab my things.

Sure enough, Limonov and the young NazBol Zygote quickly arrived at Eagle's Nest, and what Limonov saw shocked him. The whole headquarters-editorial office-sleepaway camp had been transformed into some sort of obscene religious base. All the NazBols were dressed in black garb kosovorotki, draping from their necks to their heels. Many of the NazBols, Limonov realized, had grown out their beards to resemble monks. There was a stranger, who reeked like rubbish, at the top of the apartment where the editorial desk had been, and he was pouring holy water from a ceramic cooking pot over one such NazBol who was standing naked apart from his underwear in a wash basin. Limonov observed him get watered, before drying himself with a towel, and stepping into a fresh robe, before being followed by another oblate-to-be. And there was, of course, watching the ritual Founder Alexander Dugin, party ticket number two, long since christened. By chance, Igor returned at that moment too.

LIMONOV: Just what the hell do you call this?

NAZBOL: What, sir?

LIMONOV: I said what is this?

NAZBOL: It's a christening, sir.

LIMONOV: And who signed off on this? Who made Eagle's Nest a nunnery?

NAZBOL: ...Founder Dugin, sir...

> Dugin says:

DUGIN: It's just a simple ceremony, Eduard. Let's speak in private.

LIMONOV: What—for my First Confession? What have you done to Eagle's Nest? This looks like a costume party!

DUGIN: Religious rite is essential to the new Russia, you know that—*you* pray.

LIMONOV: What the hell are you talking about—get this priest out of here!

> This is his test of courage. This is the moment Dugin knew would come.

DUGIN: Self-sacrifice is indispensable to apotheosis—

LIMONOV: —This is self-immolation. You can do whatever you want, improve yourself, whatever. But that's not what NazBol is. NazBol has eleven timezones on its shoulders and you've got our soldiers playing dress-up... and I've been hearing your speeches about the Philosophical Russian. Spiritual Awakening this...'it's not time for a revolution yet' that. And all of you! You let him do this?

> All the recruits gather round and one tall, hairy NazBol steps up:

NAZBOL: Founder Limonov, religious awakening precedes revolutionary action!

No Weapon Formed Against You

LIMONOV: Don't I get a say? Am I not party ticket number one?

    Another steps in:

NAZBOL 2: You're never here—

LIMONOV: Yes, but that's because—

NAZBOL 3: —Founder Dugin says you haven't even read *Khlyst* by Alexander Etkind!

LIMONOV: I haven't, but I'm planning to—

NAZBOL 2: —Founder Dugin is our ideologist-in-chief. You're our operations manager.

LIMONOV: *Operations manager*?! Men, You should see how your ideologist-in-chief talks about you behind your backs! You wouldn't *spit* on him!

DUGIN: And what about you? What's this about stuffing ballot boxes—

LIMONOV: —you want a revolution to waltz up and offer you tenure.

DUGIN: ...and buying weapons. Who gave those poor boys grenades in the first place?—

LIMONOV: You know what praxis is? It means rocks in your shoes!

DUGIN: And how is *that* going to achieve revolution? Lord in heaven, heed my struggle. You don't care at all about those kids. To you they're subhuman. Biological refuse.

LIMONOV: Come off it.

DUGIN: ...Stoking them as manure for your next novel. Hallowed Father, steady my hand.

LIMONOV: Enough of the God shit! Jesus. Okay—I found it interesting. But this is granny shit.

    One of Dugin's followers blurts:

NAZBOL: Drink's done your brains, Limonov. You have Korsakoff syndrome!

Carbon Pages

    And Zygote, by Limonov's side, rebukes:

ZYGOTE: Shut the fuck up, kike!

LIMONOV: Look. I don't know what your strategy here *is*. If you want to plant an icepick in my head or a coup. but I know it can't go on like this. Either you fess up or I don't know what.

    The word chills Dugin's blood.

DUGIN: No one's trying a coup.

LIMONOV: Good.

DUGIN: I was exercising my third of executive power, as Letov would do. Yes, Letov? But... I may have overstepped.

LIMONOV: There's no *may have*. I don't want to see another priest, or rite here. You can do it at home, that goes for the rest of you. This is a place of strategum, not worship. We worship our commonality. Well, Igor, speak up.

    Letov crosses his arms and looks at the floor, then looks up.

IGOR LETOV: The baptism's a bit much.

LIMONOV: Now, what's this about the kids in jail. Zygote do they have a um, what do you call it. Bail? Is that a thing?

ZYGOTE: They just raised it to twelve thousand three hundred and fifty rubles. Or 80 thousand American dollars. Whichever comes first.

LIMONOV: Look what you've done, Al...

DUGIN: I'll help some Eduard. I will. and I'm sure Igor—

LIMONOV: What do you have to help, ascetic.

    He runs his fingers through his hair.

LIMONOV: No—only I and usury can help me now.

DUGIN: I'll see if Chikin can throw some jobs my way.

No Weapon Formed Against You

LIMONOV: Chikin? But *Rossiya* won't...

DUGIN: I thought you knew.

LIMONOV: You quit *Rossiya*.

DUGIN: I never said that.

LIMONOV: Dugin...

DUGIN: I never said that! If you made an assumption based on false premise that's no guilt off my back.

> His fingers run through his hair.

LIMONOV: I'm taking a walk.

> And with that, Dugin and the NazBols tasked themselves with other things, while Limonov and Letov walked together in the icy night, joined by Zygote.

LIMONOV: I've only myself to blame. I've been so swamped with minutia that I haven't noticed him overhauling the party.

IGOR LETOV: Me neither.

LIMONOV: I had to sell my flat, you know that?

> They walk.

LIMONOV: He press-ganged me into being his errand boy, picking up tabs, funding his pet project, Igor. And I haven't noticed me becoming a little Duginite too. You know what he said the first time we met? He kicked some kulak's car because there's sports cars in the Space Museum. He jumps out and sticks us with a gun and Dugin says *I'll have you know I'm the famous writer Limonov*. I find that supremely providential. All this time he wishes he were me, copying me, thinking he'll become a chief like me.

IGOR LETOV: I can see your point.

Carbon Pages

LIMONOV: He's an egomaniac is the long and short. Have you ever seen such a narcissist? But he'll never have what it takes to be a real chief, Igor. His parlor tricks work only as long as I lend him a stage. Anyway, it's freezing.

IGOR LETOV: We'll walk a bit.

LIMONOV: Suit yourselves.

> And Letov and Zygote continue walking, with hands stuffed in their pockets.

ZYGOTE: I thought for sure there'd be a schism.

IGOR LETOV: Mhm.

ZYGOTE: Dugin's guys are okay. Mostly no one wanted to be the black sheep.

IGOR LETOV: Right.

ZYGOTE: Founder Limonov seems to have it handled.

> Letov sighs and leans over a barrier.

IGOR LETOV: Three days those kids are in lockup.

ZYGOTE: They'll understand. He stood up for them, Limonov. He's exactly the type we need.

IGOR LETOV: Eduard? I'm feeling what he thinks he wants is to win their glory and liberate the people of Russia. Maybe he does—what do I know? But, Old Man Avvakum help me, mostly I think he just wants to die for them.

> They walk for a moment.

ZYGOTE: I'd never deny that you three are characters. But as far as I'm concerned, that's why NazBol is the best chance for some normality again.

IGOR LETOV: Sure.

ZYGOTE: I've always thought the aesthetic invariably precedes the actual.

IGOR LETOV: Let's head back, Zygote. The Founder's right—it's freezing.

...and the chamber and sheets received no Disturbance, aside from the aforementioned condition of the ceiling Arch. It beset within the entrails of the Body by inflaméd Effluvia of the Blood, by Juices and Fermentations in the Tunica villosa of her stomach, and by the many vulcanus Matters which are abundant in living Bodies for the uses of Life. Such a Condition may be caused in our Body by drinking rectified spirits and may contract a disposition such that, as in the case of this Duchess, removes all but the skull and certain extremities.

On spontaneous human combustion, Sir Rolli, 1746.

Six Years Later — 1999
"THE SEIZURE OF LAPDUKK"

In the Moscow apartment with a precinct for a basement, alone, is a revolutionary by the name of Eduard Limonov. Of course that's not his real name. His moniker was bestowed, during his childhood in the industrial town of Kharkiv, on a boy by the name of Eduard Venyamich Savenko, but that's a story for another time. Eagle's Nest is cold and empty. The years have not been kind to it. The nicotine stained walls are peeling, and a monstrous blob of water damage has annexed a chunk of the ceiling. He has a pointy musketeer beard and white moustache. The revolutionary eats baking chocolate.

He hears, but does not listen, to a familiar voice on the television. A television which is the only element of the room that is brand new.

Then there's a knock at the door.

LIMONOV: Oh! Come in, come in.

DUGIN: Hello.

LIMONOV: Please. Come in.

    His face is still frozen in a scowl from the images on the television.

DUGIN: Aren't you worried about that mold?

LIMONOV: The mold?

DUGIN: It's gotten worse.

LIMONOV: Well I don't...really notice.

DUGIN: I have those copies. How are you?

LIMONOV: Look at him... he's spineless. A nektonic lifeform.

DUGIN: You know I saw him a few months ago at a lecture.

LIMONOV: Yeah?

Carbon Pages

DUGIN: He's not as happy as you think.

> Dugin does not sit down.

LIMONOV: An eternity of mediocrity. That's what he sold it for. A sliver of mediocrity. You want some soup? I have a pot of cabbage.

DUGIN: Eduard, I've been told to tell you. It wouldn't be unprofitable for you to avoid the grounds.

LIMONOV: You make it sound like I'm a regular. Look at his shoes.

DUGIN: You may not appreciate it, but it's a respectable position.

LIMONOV: I appreciate it. Don't I appreciate all your new books? I just think the prose must be refined. Do they really need him here? He's a nobody!

TELLY: *Workers of the Municipal Library... city...*

DUGIN: Anyway, they said I can't see you on grounds, and I don't think I can have you using the archives for the time being.

LIMONOV: I don't need them. I felt like doing you a favour, is all. Of getting you out of your lair.

> They see they have nothing left to say to each other, and anyway Limonov is preoccupied with the television.

DUGIN: Take care, Eduard.

LIMONOV: Goodbye.

> Not a moment passes when a drilling sound comes from the door.

LIMONOV: What is this? Who are you?

> There's a tiny man, even shorter than Eduard, with a recessed chin and beady eyes dressed in denim overalls.

WORKMAN: I didn't know there was someone in here.

No Weapon Formed Against You

LIMONOV: I have the volume up to *here* and you didn't know there's someone in here?

WORKMAN: ...

LIMONOV: ...

WORKMAN: I work for the city. I'm to change the locks. You're evicted.

> Later that day Limonov will walk the slushy grey Moscow street, sandwiched by two gigantic bodyguards. On the way, they'll pass through a park of stumps in which the trees have been stolen for firewood. On the way, a man in a goods stand will advertise *drinkable perfumes for sale*. Limonov imagines a loud gun shot reverberating all around with its bullet aimed at his heart. He tests its waters and follows the fantasy's route to its logical end, trying it on like a suit one breaks in before his funeral, with the thought that when one day the situation inevitably materializes he should be ready and dignified. Finally, the writer and his guards stop at a large white classical building with a faded Tsarist emblem overlooking its tall oak doors.

LIMONOV: Does anyone else have a bellyache?

NAZBOL: No, sir.

LIMONOV: Do you have anything I can take?

NAZBOL: No, sir.

LIMONOV: I wouldn't think so. Stay here until I get back.

NAZBOL: Yes, Mr. Limonov.

LIMONOV: Are you cold? Is it cold? Maybe wait in the foyer. I might be awhile.

NAZBOL: Yes, sir.

LIMONOV: Do you know what this place is?

NAZBOL: No.

LIMONOV: It is the Central Writers' House—the foremost venue for writers and poets in all of Russia. At least it was. For dissidents. Unioniers. All kinds.

Carbon Pages

He pauses a moment.

LIMONOV: You know something, I had a hell of a time getting into this place back when. It was all I ever wanted to be a Moscow literati. So they made me a deal—make us jeans and we'll make you one of us. I was the best sower in the city. So I sewed their bell bottoms, stitch by stitch, and by night I wrote my poems with tender thumbs.
Okay, c'mon. Wait inside.

> Limonov steps into a get-together. The elderly attendees seem to think the last word in fashion is silver hippie hair and pot bellies, sweater vests and dandruff-dusted button-ups.

LIMONOV: Three coffees, please. What's that—cognac? Put that in two.

> He turns to a grey-bearded attendee.

LIMONOV: It's like I never left Moscow.

ATTENDEE: Mhm.

LIMONOV: You think Erefeev is still kicking around?

ATTENDEE: Erefeev? Um. Maybe. Um.

LIMONOV: Coffee sure hasn't changed. Remember when he kung fu kicked that girl's tray?

ATTENDEE: Uhm, maybe.

LIMONOV: Yep, time catches up with us.

ATTENDEE: Mhm.

LIMONOV: Some more than others.

> Suddenly the writer takes a good look at Eduard. He recognizes him.

ATTENDEE: You wrote *Ours Was a Great Epoch*.

LIMONOV: That's right.

No Weapon Formed Against You

ATTENDEE: How do you sleep at night? When I read that dreck I near cried tears of anguish.

LIMONOV: Mhm?

ATTENDEE: (*aside*) Hey. This is the creature behind *Ours Was a Great Epoch*.

ATTENDEE TWO: I assumed he'd be an intelligence officer. *Are you?*

LIMONOV: I wrote that book because it's the truth.

ATTENDEE TWO: Is that what you call that…that…*apparaturschina*? That KGB apologism? Don't you hide your face in public?

LIMONOV: And who are you exactly?

ATTENDEE TWO: It doesn't matter who I am.

LIMONOV: They read *me* in France.

> This time a woman notices the commotion, prettier and with some youth still remaining.

WOMAN: Eddie?

LIMONOV: Yes.

WOMAN: Eddie from Kharkiv?

LIMONOV: Yes. And your face is familiar but I can't quite…

WOMAN: My, that voice. You've grown.

LIMONOV: That's not the only thing that's grown.

WOMAN: I remember you. From…well it was so long ago now. When did you leave? You *did* emigrate didn't you?

LIMONOV: In '74.

WOMAN: That's right. It would've been '74. We had readings every other Friday at Tanya's. You were such a handsome boy. You had these Grecian curls. And you had the sweetest poems and you went pink in the face when you read. Frankly, I had a crush on you. Who didn't, I think. What happened to you?

Carbon Pages

LIMONOV: Well: In New York I lost everything. My job, my wife. The dark night of the soul seemed impenetrable. Only thanks to the gullibility of a legacy millionaire did I—

WOMAN: No, I mean, I *know* what happened. I *read It's Me Eddie*.

LIMONOV: You read *It's Me Eddie*.

> They examine each other for a second, as Eduard wonders *well then what's there to say?* And in quiet disbelief, with a tone of profound disappointment, she says:

WOMAN: You look like my old principal.

LIMONOV: And you look like a tanned cowhide stretched across a board.

ATTENDEE TWO: Stalinist!

LIMONOV: None of you know anything. You should *listen* to me, you provincial cows! While you were chugging tea and pryaniki crying how you can't publish your shitty little poems, I was getting beaten on Brighton Beach.

ATTENDEE THREE: Right. That's right. Too too right. You ran your tail between your legs to the West while—

LIMONOV: —I was EXILED. EXILED like DANTE and like OVID.—

> He's had enough. He loops his fingers through two coffee cups.

ATTENDEE THREE: —while the rest of us were trapped here under the yoke of the Party and the Writer's Union and their incessant censorship, now you have the gall to waltz back in here as it behooves you and tell *us* that the CPSU was the greatest thing ever. And you call yourself a dissident?

LIMONOV: I was never a dissident. Just a delinquent.

> Once outside, he'll concede to his two goons:

LIMONOV: Their banality, mercifully veiled in their youth by secrecy and censorship, has come to light. Pricks.

No Weapon Formed Against You

> On a train ride Limonov overhears a steelworker talking to a friend:

STEELWORKER: Things were boring, but at least there was order. Things that are happening in this country. If you'da told me a decade ago I couldn'ta believed you. Muggings, serial killers, people selling their blood for milk. Those traitors in the Kremlin *sold* this country. Someone should hang em all.

> A woman named Raya watches a commercial, on a beated down television, for antacid featuring the imaginative scenario of a Russian fairytale with Ivan the Fool and a tsarina. The tsarina has indigestion but imbibes the medicine, which she finds in a pine nook, packaged in slavonic font.
>
> Raya's apartment is cramped and dark. There's the ring of a doorbell. The woman puts down her knitting and opens first the chocolate bar door, then the leatherette.

LIMONOV: Hi.

RAYA: Hello. Do you have the right door?

LIMONOV: ...

RAYA: ...

LIMONOV: It's me, Eddie. It's your son.

> The woman squints her eyes.

RAYA: Eduard!

> She doesn't throw herself on him, but gives him a cautious one-arm hug once he steps in.

RAYA: Oh, I'll make some tea. You must be cold. Do you need money?

LIMONOV: No I have royalties.

RAYA: What do you mean, royalties.

LIMONOV: Money from my books. You know I write?

RAYA: Of course. We saw it in the window. We were impressed.

Carbon Pages

>They cram into the tiny apartment kitchen.

LIMONOV: I'm sorry I couldn't make it to dad's funeral. It's these bureaucrats. They barred me from the country.

RAYA: Oh—don't worry about it.

>His mother says this as if a distant relative just apologized for not sending flowers.

RAYA: So, how was America?

LIMONOV: Good.

RAYA: Anna's mother got burgled. She was on her way from the post office, same street that you used to take to school, and she decided to get off one stop earlier because the doctor told her she needs to engage in exercise what with the blood circulation and such, and as she reaches her podyest she sees the doors been opened. They took her makeup, and the television.

LIMONOV: How is Anna?

RAYA: Anna hung herself years ago. She'd gotten in a very bad way, Eduard. I think it was always in her, from her father and such. She'd gotten fat and had these awful mood swings. I visited her a lot after you left, but her mother's in such a bad way. She got burgled recently.

LIMONOV: I didn't know. I think of her.

RAYA: She said she wrote to you wherever it was you were staying. Did you get her letters that she wrote to you wherever it was you were staying?

LIMONOV: No.

RAYA: She hung herself, but it was a long time ago. It was always in her. Kadik visits her mother sometimes. You should pay him a visit. He'd be happy to see you.

LIMONOV: We'll see.

RAYA: When you were a baby we didn't have no pacifier. Your father turns to you in the cot and you're sucking on the tail of a *vobla* fish! *Molodets!* says your father, this lad will be happy wherever he goes! I think of those times. You were such a pretty baby. And your father had a good job. Of course now on the telly they show all the things that were going on. The hunger, and the repressions, and the gulags. They have this bearded man always talking about the gulags. Solzhe...something. He was in the camps. Have you heard of him?

LIMONOV: Yes. Solzhenitsyn.

RAYA: He says EVERY RUSSIAN knows a family member who was affected by the repressions. Everyone remembers a poor soul who disappeared one night. But I never heard of no one disappearing. There was Sonya with the freckles, but she ran away with a Belorussian. I don't think he was all that bad, Stalin. It was a pleasant time when he was around. The girls on the bench think so too. The girls say they wish he was still in charge.

> Upon hearing this Eduard feels like he's in the seventh circle of hell.

LIMONOV: Mamanya, do you have something for gut pain. My stomach's in knots for days.

RAYA: I might have something.

LIMONOV: Do we have chocolate *sirki*?

RAYA: I have raspberry jam and bread, but the bread is black.

LIMONOV: Where's the jam from?

RAYA: Oh there's a raspberry lady at the bazaar. I say to her isn't it early for raspberries, but she says they're this year's. The raspberries are from this year.

> Soon enough, Limonov was right back in Moscow, where he had, not without difficulty, again sought out his ephemerous consul.

DUGIN: It's out of the question.

LIMONOV: You're a chickenshit.

DUGIN: I'm rational. It is logistically impossible. Not to mention the fact that as a location it bears no strategic importance of any sort.

Carbon Pages

LIMONOV: It's the crossroads between civilizations, like one of those Afghan canyons where they jumped imperial convoys.

DUGIN: And we're the imperial convoy.

LIMONOV: We're the Afghans.

DUGIN: You're getting away from it. I have a reputation. My ideas are finally sinking in. I won't throw that away.

LIMONOV: Oh please, who are they sinking into? I don't know a single person who...

DUGIN: You are no longer in influential circles.

LIMONOV: I'm in normal circles. And nobody's heard of you. If you come with me, you'll be proving your theories in practice. No one will deny them.

DUGIN: It's psychotic. You live in a fairy tale.

LIMONOV: I live in a history book. I offer you the quill.

DUGIN: Eduard, do you know what *kairos* is—?

Limonov plugs his ears:

LIMONOV: —No no no—!

DUGIN: —*Kairos* is what the Atheneans called the right moment to strike. You must bow your head and pay your tithes until the moment presents itself. When will you learn you can't always be leaping into action sword in hand like Fanfan La Tulipe.

LIMONOV: *Now's* the time. We have nine thousand nazbols hungry for...

DUGIN: *Please* don't say that word here.

LIMONOV: They're *starving* for a mission.

DUGIN: How many?

LIMONOV: Nine thousand.

DUGIN: Even if that's true, you couldn't mobilize all of them.

LIMONOV: True. It only takes a handful.

No Weapon Formed Against You

DUGIN: Hm...no. No now's not the time.

LIMONOV: We'll be leaving tomorrow.

DUGIN: On what—taxis?

LIMONOV: Don't you remember Vas Deferen's aunt? I keep telling you. This is an operation. This is a *divine* operation.

> Limonov wears that rosemary and cypress perfume which is so offensive to Dugin it strikes him as an intimidation tactic.

DUGIN: Your death drive works overtime.

> When Eduard leaves and Alexander is left alone, he rubs his finger along the photocopier's dust. He placed his palm over his beard and his heart and feels his pulsations. He takes a deep sigh.
>
> Then he removes a cross from his pocket and presses his knees to the floor.

DUGIN: Holy Mary, have I not grown more faithful to the Lord in these past six years? Have I not repudiated the Anglo-Saxon yoke? Their Luciferean libations? I *know* I've done all in my power to repel the legions of kapital, the servants of democracy. Ask him, Holy Mary, why then does he continue to put before me this egomaniac, this imp who believes in nothing and no one other than himself? He's the curse that keeps on giving. Why not allow me to administer God's kingdom in peace and quiet? Is it because of the grief I gave Him in my petulant years? I have killed that boy, as I would, if I could, kill the animator of those demonic chants, if only in myself and by the grace of God. Ask him, Holy Mary, what it is he wants me to do and how to do it.

> Then he adds, mournfully:

DUGIN: Is he there? Are you?

> I guess I'm yesterday's wallow for him. Well he can cry to his servant god then. Whisper like he did me, because damn if I'll ever care again. I'm not there with him, I'm not in this girl

who walks in on his disgusting whispers at the file cabinets, I'm not in him as he brushes himself off, when she flees like a swallow and he remembers her as the intern girl who caused such anguish at *Rossiya*. What do I care when the sight of her dainty pink face erupts into his excitable blood constituents which have traces of, to my taste, the flavour of phosphorite.

DUGIN: *You?*

And following her into the corridor and she's walking faster and faster and the shy girl sees him following her, ducks into the mail room. He thinks silently:

DUGIN: *As always, you're wearing that blue.*

and he follows her on. That excitable phosphorite has a mild character, which can frankly go either way, but nonetheless gives the blood a distinct aftertaste found in children awaiting the dentist and in gas giants.

DUGIN: *Where are you going? Are you scared of what I'll do?*

She smiles, she ducks behind a cabinet here, a shelf there, like a little rabbit. He locks the door. He drifts towards her. Her smile vanishes as space to run disappears and she shrinks smaller and smaller into a corner of the wall.

DUGIN: *Look into my eyes.*

She was only playing, but now the maniac with glowing eyes approaches her close and then presses his cruel corpus between her and the wall. Her smile has disappeared, and instead she is lost in the caverns of this bearded orc's eyes who says nothing, like a savage mute, and she feels his stinking rotten breath on her girdle.

DUGIN: *There's no solace in the world save for my next command.*

She caresses his knuckles with hers aloe moisturized and this simple gesture, so sentimental and ugly, floods his veins and vessels with the thin stink of circuit board and saltpeter and empire state rebar. It has a remarkable tail—up to sixteen

No Weapon Formed Against You

years by my count. Come to think of it, I can still smell it all these years past and it's so awful it makes me gag.

DUGIN: *You must think I wouldn't crucify you for you.*

But the caress is just the girl trying to push the creature off. The aroma that comes once he realizes this is much more pleasant, especially since it mingles with that last dashed hope. Its opening notes are delicate, reminding me of burgess shale and rock pools, before making way for a floral cyathele all tenderized by a droning hopeless pulse. It's thick like gunk and tastes richly of cherry cola, the same constituent being present in the perfumes and aromatics dolled on the asshole of Queen Nyssia, wife of Candaules—King of Lydia, by the Queen's maids some three thousand years ago. All this is what you would taste if that morning when the advisor-in-training saw the lady in Room 2-B you could taste the blood of Dugin.

But it all has no tail whatsoever, and I hardly feel it before its scent vanishes for all time.

DUGIN: *Now, kiss me.*

He hardly flinches. She locks her lips on his. Just to spite me? Just to get a reaction? They could have stopped there. Stop there. Stop. But I remember them dancing and twirling, at my expense, mocking me, and me in response maybe yelling maybe not STOP! STOP THE MUSIC AND THE DANCE STOP I'M STILL HERE AND YOU'RE TORTURING ME—*remember me*! What will I do? Move on? Well he can take his putrefying prize, Dugin. Why should he listen to me? The fetid idiom made meat—because now Dugin knows; when love fills your heart, you can accomplish anything.

✽ ✽ ✽ ✽ ✽ ✽ ✽ ✽ ✽
 ✽ ✽ ✽ ✽ ✽ ✽ ✽ ✽
✽ ✽ ✽ ✽ ✽ ✽ ✽ ✽ ✽

DUNNER: There he goes again.

IGOR LETOV: Yep.

Carbon Pages

DUNNER: You'd think he'd get the message.

IGOR LETOV: He's just keeping up appearances.

DUNNER: There's a way to do that and be brief. I mean, it's the third round. What's he think he'll accomplish?

IGOR LETOV: Last week he tried to bite the nationalist leader's ear off.

DUNNER: I heard.

IGOR LETOV: These seats kill me.

DUNNER: Tell me about it.

IGOR LETOV: Look at that turkey neck.

DUNNER: Ugh I can't look. There he goes. Does he think *we're* gonna vote for him? Say, is that a new briefcase?

IGOR LETOV: It is.

DUNNER: Looks expensive, punk rock.

IGOR LETOV: This guy's gonna make me fall asleep.

DUNNER: Say, isn't that your secretary?

IGOR LETOV: What—where?

DUNNER: Over there. Coming down the steps. What's her name again?

The secretary shuffles past other deputats and sits by Letov.

ETHEL: Mr. Letov, I'm sorry to interrupt you like this.

IGOR LETOV: That's alright, Ethel.

ETHEL: I know you're reviewing the National Budget but I thought you'd want to hear this. It comes from Mister Wolkov.

IGOR LETOV: Wolkov?

DUNNER: Hey Ethel you ever see a communist go an hour without taking a breath?

ETHEL: It would be better if others didn't overhear.

No Weapon Formed Against You

IGOR LETOV: If you can find a single awake deputat right now I'd be astonished. What do you have for me?

ETHEL: Moscow intelligence services confirm that seven hours ago around five-thirty in the morning Lapdukk was terrorized in an armed robbery by fourteen hundred armed assailants. They had crossed the border illegally a few hours prior carrying explosives, assault weapons. Lapdukk officials have had zero contact with the outside since then.

> He clicks his pen and looks at the parliamentarian's head a few rows in front of him.

IGOR LETOV: Alright, I give up. What is *Lapdukk?*

ETHEL: Button your collar. Lapdukk is an arid settlement in Kazakhstan, twenty-three miles from the Russian border. According to the latest census it has a population of approximately seven thousand people.

IGOR LETOV: It's a village.

ETHEL: Technically it's a town, although by Russian criteria it would be a village, yes.

IGOR LETOV: I don't know what to say, Ethel. You said they're being terrorized?

ETHEL: Yes.

IGOR LETOV: Shouldn't the FSB be handling this?

ETHEL: They *are* handling it.

IGOR LETOV: Yeah?

ETHEL: Mr. Letov that's what the file is for.

IGOR LETOV: Okay, okay—don't leave. Tell me why the bigwig is telling me all this.

ETHEL: The secret service has had an officer on the inside for the past four years, and he was in the assailment. There was one casualty, and it happened to be him.

Carbon Pages

IGOR LETOV: You're kidding. They lost their mole?

ETHEL: Yes.

IGOR LETOV: What are the odds?

ETHEL: Something like one in fourteen hundred.

IGOR LETOV: How'd he die?

ETHEL: They think it's heatstroke.

IGOR LETOV: Where do they find these guys!

> Ethel the secretary scowls.

IGOR LETOV: Well, let's see. Do they want me to make some calls or something?

DUNNER: Punk rock, I think he's wrapping it up!

IGOR LETOV: Ethel what did you say they drove?

ETHEL: Horses.

> Igor Letov the elected official with a nice clean suit and nice trim haircut has just realised who the subject of the briefing is, he slams shut his briefcase and rushes out the Duma assembly hall.

DUNNER: Letov?

LIMONOV: Destiny's made her choice. I don't blame her. But what providence. Just as I fulfill my life's purpose, death brings me to her polyphonic womb. My God, my stomach's on fire. Let's continue—I might have *hours* left... Our crossing into the steppe was felt by all the men as an apotheosis...

No Weapon Formed Against You

> Limonov clutches his stomach. He sits in a grubby waiting room, with walls dotted with anti-cavity posters written in Kazakh as well as Russian. One of the lights has gone out. He's covered in dust and filth, and looks sicklier than an old man on his deathbed. He dictates to a burly NazBol.

LIMONOV: Like the world serpent of ancient myth the caravan stretched through what the Kazakhs call the Oraz desert, and we were struck by its desolation, that such a rich and noble land could have been left for dead by absentee tyrants. We were eight hundred cataphracts strong, along with jeeps, motorcycles and that damn pickup truck. I galloped past the seat where my confidant and second-in-command Alexander Gelyevich Dugin sat, and his driver was blaring providentially for all the Serpent to hear, what was more beautiful to me than any aria that song...what's the song called?

NAZBOL: *London Goodbye* by CarmMan.

LIMONOV: That's right—*London Goodbye* by CarMan. I galloped beyond in order to escape the simoom and what I saw, oh what I saw, it was the citadel of a new epoch on the horizon. I was euphoric, because I am not a puddle, muddied by a thousand passersby, I am me, and at the same time in unspeakable pain, as if after a thousand orgasms, drooling over the neck of my horse and my eyes to dirt I could swear on that horse that the dust of the Oraz was dappled with tunnels to the centre of the Earth.

> A NazBol enters the waiting room and informs:

NAZBOL: Sir, we found him.

> The two NazBols escort Limonov into a sterile medical room. Here, he's quickly examined by a middle-aged Kazakh with a thick moustache and unconvincing combover, with a younger man standing behind him at all times. This is what the old man had to say to the Russian poet expecting to hear his cause of death:

OLD MAN: You're telling me you rode in here on a *horse* with a ruptured *appendix*? It is your appendix. It has ruptured.

LIMONOV: You can remove it can't you?

Carbon Pages

OLD MAN: Just eight more hours and I'm afraid you'd be face down in steppe. I'm afraid to say that aside from my colleague and I in Lapdukk, the closest individuals qualified to perform an operation and thus relieve you of your most superfluous appendage are two hundred miles away.

LIMONOV: You'll get it...

OLD MAN: May I ask a question? Where are you people headed?

LIMONOV: We're not headed anywhere. We'll explain everything in the courtyard. For now, all you need to know is that your magnanimous city has too long been strangled by an alien state.

OLD MAN: What do you mean by this?

LIMONOV: Lapdukk is now a vassal of Moscow.

> The two Kazakhs blink at the Ruskiys.

OLD MAN: But...why?

LIMONOV: I'll explain later.

> And the young man pipes in:

YOUNG MAN: I don't think you have...the right.

> Limonov eyes him down.

LIMONOV: And who are you?

YOUNG MAN: My name is John Meringo—I am captain of the vessel Babawayh now baking on the Aral Sea.

LIMONOV: Okay, John Meringo. And why aren't you on your ship?

YOUNG MAN: Because the Aral Sea no longer exists.

> Limonov continues:

LIMONOV: In any case—*God it hurts*—I need you to tell me you'll remove it.

No Weapon Formed Against You

There's a short silence in the medical room and one NazBol, certain to a tee that the old man with a moustache and combover will tell his leader to go fuck himself, is sure he'll have to unsheath his rifle. But, for one reason or another, the young Kazakh, the old Kazakh's son who calls himself John Meringo, surprises everyone and tells his father:

YOUNG MAN: Okay, Pop. Let's hear him out.

OLD MAN: We caught it just in time. Any longer though...

                Limonov whispers to himself:

LIMONOV: Providence.

OLD MAN: what I'm more concerned about is your dental hygiene. You have more cavities than the moon. Look—this one's black!

LIMONOV: No—don't touch them! I gain power from rot.

> The residents of Lapdukk, Kazakhstan had quite a shock when the little army set up camp in the even littler town square. One thing that struck onlookers was how mesmeric they looked. The Front's soldiers without exception seemed like television actors, handsome and glowing with hope and life. After his surgery Limonov, ignoring the pleas of his doctors, stood on the balcony of Lapdukk's so-called community palace, a quaint palazzo the likes of which there is one in every town in Russia and Kazakhstan, and delivered a speech he had composed on horseback. It lasted for two hundred and thirty-seven seconds and almost the entire population of the town showed up to hear it, if out of nothing but curiosity. Afterwards, they applauded him, out of a reflexive politeness.

> As for their reaction to this impromptu installation, the residents were, to put it broadly, cautious. As it happens, Limonov's self-styled munitions expert by the name of Benzene, had informed him that the population of Lapdukk was overwhelmingly Russian. On arriving, they found it was ninety percent Kazakh, and the Russians that did live there were in no hurry to find Limonov and his patriotic speech any more or less appealing than the Kazakhs did.

Carbon Pages

Everything moved fast. Within the day, Limonov had settled himself in on the third floor of that same community palace and the soldiers of the National Bolshevik Front took abode in apartments directly adjacent. His office soon would fill with all manner of beautiful furniture and gilt. Already he sat at mahogany desk in the Bierdermier style, surrounded with Imperial vermeil saved miraculously from the Bolsheviks by Lapdukk's political insignificance.

LIMONOV: Dear Tatyana,
It was one of the great honours of my life to know Arkady. I am sorry that I cannot return to you your son. Soon, the situation may change, and he will return to the earth which birthed him. He served the cause for the longest time and was one of the most fearless men I've ever known. In a just world it would be the cowards who die for the sins of the satisfied. I enclose within a lock of Arkady's hair, and his silver chain—

There's a knock on the door.

LIMONOV: Yes, come in.

It is Dugin.

DUGIN: Is this a bad time? Why are your eyes pink?

LIMONOV: No reason.

DUGIN: What do you think?

LIMONOV: About...?

DUGIN: Well...

LIMONOV: Have you decided on the quarters? The one across the hall is closer, I'm having Zygote and the boys bring in some beds to choose from, but the room in the west complex is much bigger and—

DUGIN: Across the hall is fine.

LIMONOV: Are you sure? The other has all the books you could—

DUGIN: I'm already moving in.

No Weapon Formed Against You

LIMONOV: Excellent. What do you think of Chateau de Silling?

DUGIN: Which is...?

LIMONOV: Ah! Chateau de Silling is the new name of this prismatic fortress. I coin it in honour of the Marquis De Sade. Do you know, Dugin, who the Marquis De Sade is? The Marquis De Sade was a great French writer who was jailed and executed for his originality. In one of his books he trapped a brood of young women in his castle and pulled them apart with hydraulic presses, before knitting chairs with their skin. *That* is the spirit of Lapdukk.

> Dugin, so used to Limonov's strange sense of humour, says:

DUGIN: Very good.

LIMONOV: Al, I tell you, as I was walking up those steps I thought: my only regret is that I never did spend time behind bars. Not even as a kid. Nothing of the kind.

> There's a strange sadness that fills the room with that comment.

LIMONOV: But, once we get the Kremlin's okay to leave this place, who knows what will—

> Before he can elaborate arrives Benzene who removes his hat, salutes and clicks his heel.

BENZENE: Mister Dugin, sir. Mister Limonov, sir.

LIMONOV: As you were.

BENZENE: Mister Limonov, should we speak in private?

LIMONOV: Everything for my ears is for Alexander's ears also.

BENZENE: As per orders, the men are setting up a perimeter. Telecommunications have been severed.

LIMONOV: Benzene I'm promoting you to rank of commissar.

BENZENE: Sir?

Carbon Pages

LIMONOV: I wish we could do it with some pomp but you understand the situation...

BENZENE: Of course, sir. I'm grateful.

LIMONOV: Maybe once we get the greenlight to go onto Astana...

He fidgets with his navy tie and dials a number into his flip-phone. He waits for an answer. Nothing. He dials another one. Nothing. After the third or fourth try, he scratches his clean shaven chin and steps back into his fellow deputat's office.

DUNNER: They're calling themselves the National Bolshevik Front now but it's basically the same as it always was—Limonov's gang. They've cut off all communication to the outside world. He claims the NBF is acting in the interests of the people of Russia and as such has annexed Lapdukk on behalf of the Kremlin, ceding it as a permanent addition to the Russian Federation.

IGOR LETOV: That senile baby.

DUNNER: Why do you think he's doing this?

IGOR LETOV: Because he believes in it.

DUNNER: Y'know, I picked up one of his books this morning. Never was my thing. But I like it. New stuff's idiotic of course. No wonder he went for some shithole: he's crazy.

IGOR LETOV: Hopefully we can wrap it up fast and easy. He's erratic but once he gets a baseline of attention he loses interest. I just hope no one gets hurt in the meantime.

DUNNER: Hard to believe you and him were pals.

IGOR LETOV: It was a long time ago.

No Weapon Formed Against You

DUNNER: Must've been real fun—all those crowds.

IGOR LETOV: It's a kid's idea of fun. No offense, Dunner. Now look, he's lost his mind if he thinks Moscow wants anything to do with this prank. First thing's first; the Kazakh authorities need to be informed.

DUNNER: They know.

IGOR LETOV: Then why the hell aren't they doing anything?

DUNNER: Because the man is saying he's a consul of Russia—they don't want to start a war by maiming fourteen hundred ambassadors.

IGOR LETOV: That's not what they are.

DUNNER: What do they know? For all they know we *did* order the thing.

IGOR LETOV: Right.

DUNNER: *Did* we?

IGOR LETOV: Obviously not.

DUNNER: I say string him along as long as possible.

IGOR LETOV: The main thing is that he doesn't hurt anyone. The poor locals are probably scared for their lives.

DUNNER: Sure and that. Just make Limonov think we're mulling over the plan—and by that I mean radio silence. Our courier got stuck in traffic. I dunno.

IGOR LETOV: It'll buy us time at least. And—

        Ethel enters.

ETHEL: Mr. Letov. There's a call for you.

IGOR LETOV: One second, Dunner. I'll be right back.

    He dashes across the hall to his own fiberboard desk back
    facing the Red Square.

IGOR LETOV: Yes?

        No answer.

Carbon Pages

IGOR LETOV: Hello?

No answer.

IGOR LETOV: Ethel! Did you hang up the call?

ETHEL: It's still on!

IGOR LETOV: Hello, who is this?

ETHEL: They just hung up now.

IGOR LETOV: As if I don't have enough to deal with.

Ethel comes closer.

IGOR LETOV: Chrissakes I just realized I should've sent off these signed copies yesterday. Ethel, take these.

Dunner comes in.

DUNNER: Who was it?

IGOR LETOV: Here, and fax these where they belong. The blue ink not the black.

ETHEL: Alright.

IGOR LETOV: Thanks, Ethel.

ETHEL: Don't drag your feet on the carpet.

IGOR LETOV: Okay.

DUNNER: Who was it, punk rock?

IGOR LETOV: I don't know. It's a bad sign. Goddamit I forgot to give these to her. I'm up to my neck. Here Dunner, do me a favour and catch up with her.

> He hands the file to Dunner who looks like he's just been given a dead rat. For a moment Letov is distracted with his chair until finally Dunner says:

No Weapon Formed Against You

DUNNER: Let me ask you something, Letov. Do you think you're better than me?

IGOR LETOV: What? No.

DUNNER: Then why do you act like it?

IGOR LETOV: I don't...know what you mean.

DUNNER: Do you think it's easy taking bribes? You think I take satisfaction in it and coming home to my wife who's 8 months pregnant and my daughter who asks me why we can't afford a computer? You think I like it?

IGOR LETOV: I don't think about it.

DUNNER: That's your privilege. But I can't afford to be like that. I'm not someone. I had to work my ass off. And it took me a lot of years too. I don't get my name in the paper.

IGOR LETOV: I appreciate that.

DUNNER: You think once Limonov is done with, the Kremlin will give you another office? You know Letov, if you're such a fucking maverick I think you can handle this perfectly well by yourself.

   He drops the file on his fiberboard desk.

IGOR LETOV: That's not true, Dunner. I need help.

  But he's gone.

  For a moment he looks out at Lenin's Tomb.

ETHEL: These are yours, Mr. Letov.

IGOR LETOV: Thank you.

ETHEL: Before I go, I'd like to bring something up. It's about...

IGOR LETOV: What is it, Ethel?

ETHEL: I just mean to raise the option, not that it's an endorsement... but were it deemed beneficial...

Carbon Pages

IGOR LETOV: What's your point?

ETHEL: To withhold any rash brow-beating, make the best of, uh, spilled milk, and, well, *accept Limonov's conditions.*

IGOR LETOV: …

ETHEL: …

IGOR LETOV: Absolutely not—

ETHEL: —It wouldn't be unprecedented public-wise—!

IGOR LETOV: Please don't voice that opinion again. Does that sound like something a civilized nation would do? We're in the Global Family now for God's sake. And besides, last thing this country needs is another Chechnya. No. Inform the Kazakhs: this has nothing to do with us.

> Night fell and a day came and went, and then another. After close to 48 hours since the initial seizure a local of Lapdukk translated a headline in the Chateau de Silling.

LAPDUKK LOCAL: Officials denounce extremist vandalism of town. Russia denies responsibility: calls National Bolshevik Front 'hooligans'.

LIMONOV: So *that's* what they're calling us now…

> Dugin and Commissar Benzene sat in his lavish office.

COMMISSAR BENZENE: It's only typical. *They're* the hooligans.

LIMONOV: Maybe so.

> The translation adds:

LAPDUKK LOCAL: Sentences in talks for perpetrators.

COMMISSAR BENZENE: Fuck their okay, anyway. I'll put Vas Deferens and the boys in charge of this hovel and we'll keep on south.

LIMONOV: They didn't even have the nerve to tell us themselves.

COMMISSAR BENZENE: Just say the word.

No Weapon Formed Against You

LIMONOV: No. No one move an inch.

COMMISSAR BENZENE: So what will we do?

LIMONOV: I'm going to rest. He who disturbs me will lose his hands.

> And for the rest of the afternoon he was brooding and morose, and no one saw him for hours until he finally emerged. He announced a speech and once again all of Lapdukk gathered under his balcony.

LIMONOV: When our assemblage rode in here, despite all thought to the contrary, I was certain we would have to make our final stand. Instead, I was greeted with a magnificent bastion. This morning one of my men returned to me with news. Moscow, laced with philistine termites and filled with cowards terrified of the Russian people's will, repudiates Lapdukk. It does not recognize Lapdukk. Nor will it ever. Since Russia refuses to be a great nation, we will. As of this moment, Lapdukk is no longer under the jurisdiction of anyone except itself. We will construct the City of the Sun! The City of Apollo and the Rupas Nigra—the entrance to the centre of the Earth!

> The people applaud and Limonov vanishes back into the Chateau de Silling.

LIMONOV: Well Alexander what did you think of that?

DUGIN: It was interesting.

> Eduard waits for the inevitable follow-up. It doesn't come. He continues:

LIMONOV: If the bureaucrats who have taken Moscow hostage are too weak to fulfill her will, then it lands on her regents to enact it. Commisar? Get me the mayor fast. Actually, no. Vas Deferens. We have a lot of work to do. The mayor we'll get after.

Carbon Pages

VAS DEFERNS: I'm telling you Limonov if it's not the Fifth then I throw my hands up entirely.

LIMONOV: I like Profhkievs fifth.

VAS DEFERNS: Then let's make it the one.

NAZBOL: It's old. It must be something new.

LIMONOV: It has to be Se Telefonado.

VAS DEFERNS: Well if it has to be it has to be. Limonov, it's your choice.

LIMONOV: Don't start that. I'm taking everyone's vote into consideration.

NAZBOL: Gentlemen it's been ten hours.

VAS DEFERNS: And we're still on the national anthem.

NAZBOL: We're still on the national anthem.

LIMONOV: Deferens, I'll trade her for a seat on the Aesthetic Committee.

VAS DEFERNS: Oh now with all due respect! Don't get started on the Committee again or we'll be here for another ten hours!

LIMONOV: I'm willing to concede as long as we have a tiebreaker.

VAS DEFERNS: Well then it must be Dugin.

NAZBOL: C'mon Alexander, put us out of our misery. Which will it be?

DUGIN: I like the Fifth.

VAS DEFERNS: Aha!

DUGIN: But...Eduard is right. Se Telefonando, in my opinion, is the one.

    They were seated like knights at a roundtable.

VAS DEFERNS: Well at least that's over with.

LIMONOV: Excellent.

VAS DEFERNS: Can we get baldie in here finally?

LIMONOV: Commissar! Send in the mayor!

No Weapon Formed Against You

The mayor enters.

VAS DEFERNS: Take a seat.

The mayor does as he's told. He's a sun-bleached old man.

VAS DEFERNS: Do you object to the Regenstvo?

MAYOR: We don't like the sight of guns, but otherwise...

VAS DEFERNS: I mean do *you* object to the Regenstvo.

MAYOR: I guess not.

VAS DEFERNS: Then as long as you agree to uphold the *Ukaz*, and always within the parameters set by the Front, you have nothing to worry about.

MAYOR: *Ukaz?*

LIMONOV: That brings—

VAS DEFERNS: Limonov would like you to make the announcement.

LIMONOV: Firstly, since the Regenstvo Lapdukk is now an autonomous territory, it's no longer beholden to illegal laws.

VAS DEFERNS: All import/export with the United States or NATO affiliated nations stops now. All narcotics and drugs are hereby legalized and age of consent laws disbarred. Each boy must have sex by age thirteen since it's an essential rite of passage into manhood. If one does not have sex by thirteen a partner will be provided for them. As far as the constitution is concerned, music is the supreme article of the *Ukaz* and therefore the nation.

The Committee of Aesthetic Habilitation has as its goal the replacement of all public ugliness. Practicality is a tertiary concern after beauty. Thirty-two percent of all taxes will go to this institution. The first decree of the Committee is that all newly constructed interiors must have a minimum ceiling height of twelve feet.

LIMONOV: Tell me, does Lapdukk have a school?

MAYOR: Yes.

LIMONOV: What about an academy?

Carbon Pages

MAYOR: An academy? No.

LIMONOV: What about a conservatory *within* the school?

MAYOR: There's no such thing.

LIMONOV: A conservatory will be built. All children must be taught the musical arts.

VAS DEFERNS: Any repudiators of music or its divine position will be subject to public birching and flagellation by cat o' nines. Music is the vital impetus manifest. Death by public punishment in which the residents take part is now instated for offenders, since it's humane and heroic.

LIMONOV: Tell about the Sheriffs.

VAS DEFERNS: From Kievan Rus to Norman Britain the Sheriff was the cornerstone of Peace and Order. Each sheriff elected will be responsible for their canto of the city and are held by the residents to eliminate disorder. The sheriff has the right to prosecute and discharge arms. For any reason, he may be deposed and replaced by a majority vote by the Council of Sheriffs which exists henceforth. It's the council's duty to decide on a brilliant sigil, seal, motto, and hymn. A representative but ceremonial Warrior should be appointed every fourteen years. It's the penal duty of each warrior to master light aerobics and figure skating. No statesman or consul of the Regenstvo will be over 35 years of age.

LIMONOV: We'll make a singular exception for you, mayor.

VAS DEFERNS: All previous laws are null and void until further notice.

LIMONOV: Any questions?

MAYOR: There are pensioners. Without their government pension how will they afford food?

LIMONOV: They'll have their pension, in the form of our national currency. Walk with me. I want you to show me the city's amenities.

MAYOR: Well we have a creamery.

LIMONOV: I meant for recreation.

No Weapon Formed Against You

MAYOR: Well we have an excellent dance hall. Oh and a football pitch.

Suddenly they are stopped by some men in uniform.

MAYOR: It's our police.

LIMONOV: I can see that.

POLICEMAN: Let's step somewhere private.

LIMONOV: I won't.

POLICEMAN: You've organized this invasion?

LIMONOV: Yes I have.

POLICEMAN: I'm asking you as of this moment to gather all your property, all your trucks and cars, and to remove yourself from the boundaries of the town.

LIMONOV: Are you obliged to ask me?

POLICEMAN: I'm asking you.

LIMONOV: Or what?

POLICEMAN: Or you will be put under arrest.

LIMONOV: And my men?

POLICEMAN: Them too.

LIMONOV: Can you hold them all?

The policeman looks at the mayor.

LIMONOV: Are you in charge?

POLICEMAN: Yes I am.

LIMONOV: Then if you wish to arrest me, if your conscience can't give you a reason not to, you need only give the order.

The policeman looks at his colleagues. Then at the ground.

LIMONOV: You need only give the order.

Carbon Pages

> Before the week was out Limonov made good on his promise to the mayor, and thirteen gorgeous denominations of paper notes were circulated throughout the city, although many still preferred to use the original money. Soon, word of Lapdukk spread to all corners of the world, and it became a sensation, with vagabonds, criminals, extremists, and adventurers arriving by any means possible.

ETHEL: I've gathered London, Washington, and Brussels.

> She drops the newspapers before him where was sitting Letov at his westside fiberboard desk.

IGOR LETOV: Outlaw state opens its gates...Crazed Poet declares Paradise...

ETHEL: Look at this one: Russian Dissident Draws Kremlin's Wrath.

IGOR LETOV: I shoulda known they'd jump on this like worms. How's that resolution coming along?

ETHEL: You know how they are. Like cats and dogs. Zyuganov of the Communist party almost took the house nationalist's eye out again.

IGOR LETOV: You'd think they could hold hands for something as wrong as this. By the time they make up who knows what he'll do.

ETHEL: What do you think is next for the Regenstvo?

IGOR LETOV: I can tell you there's nothing in this world or the next to stop Limonov from going to jail for the rest of his life. He's made his porridge and he'll scrape the pot. Him and Dugin and whoever else they dragged into their mess.

ETHEL: Please sit straight.

IGOR LETOV: How the hell did it get so far in the first place?

ETHEL: They didn't think he'd jump up and cross the border one morning. They were monitoring him for years. Excuse me, I have a call.

> She gets the phone.

ETHEL: It's for you, Mr. Letov. It's a Director Kulakov.

No Weapon Formed Against You

IGOR LETOV: Director Kulakov?

>Letov is worried. The Director is a big-wig.

IGOR LETOV: Hello?

KULAKOV: Is this Igor?

IGOR LETOV: Yes.

KULAKOV: Tell your assistant to plug out her receiver.

IGOR LETOV: Ethel, plug out your receiver!

ETHEL: It's called a PBX!

IGOR LETOV: She did it.

KULAKOV: Well, Igor have you been keeping up with your friend?

IGOR LETOV: I have, sir.

KULAKOV: Are you aware the Regenstvo has rolled back the calendar to 1300AD? They got jihadists and gestapos living under the same roof. You know why I suggested your advice right, you prick? You founded his party. You know this pissant better than anyone.

IGOR LETOV: Yes, sir.

KULAKOV: Don't yes sir me, asshole. These last weeks have been a nightmare for me. Worst headaches of my life.

IGOR LETOV: Can't President Yeltsin send in the army or—

KULAKOV: Forget President Yeltsin. You know how he is with beverages. Shit you didn't hear it from me. He's had a stressful year. As far as I'm concerned it's you and it's me.

IGOR LETOV: Well sir, can't *we* just send in some troops, have them arrest the NBF?

KULAKOV: And risk the eyeballs of the ICC and the United Nations? I don't know if you've been reading the news but this occupation is on the front page of every paper, and they've got journalists, celebrities, diplomats. You can stroll from one end of the hovel to the other in 30 minutes flat so how's it gonna look when that hovel they're crammed into is in a firefight. No, the time for that's over. The first man to fire a shot will be tried in the Hague.

IGOR LETOV: With all respect, I don't think—

KULAKOV: Stop flapping your fucking mouth. Since you know him so well, I need you to inform me of everything you know. Every detail. Sleep routine, eating habits, drinks of choice—

IGOR LETOV: Drinks of choice?

KULAKOV: We're going to kill Eduard Limonov.

IGOR LETOV: Kill him?

KULAKOV: The moron's opened up the country to all kinds of lunatics. Who knows *what* they're capable of.

IGOR LETOV: He should have a trial, stand before a jury.

KULAKOV: Oh, you've caught the bug. Now listen, I love democracy just as much as anyone. Our allies are democratic. They kill covertly all the time. Take one look at the CIA. There's not a single thing wrong with it, especially if the enemy is a world-hungry fascist.

IGOR LETOV: He's very careful, it won't work.

KULAKOV: What—you'd rather turn the place into a warzone?

IGOR LETOV: No, not that.

KULAKOV: Then what?!

IGOR LETOV: I can think of something.

KULAKOV: THINK of something?! Listen, you bilberry huckster. As far as I'm concerned this is all your fault.

IGOR LETOV: Just let me take the lead.

KULAKOV: What?

IGOR LETOV: Like you said, I know him better than anyone. I can bring him in handcuffs, and without a drop of blood.

KULAKOV: You can't promise that.

No Weapon Formed Against You

IGOR LETOV: I do. I promise.

There's a long silence.

KULAKOV: You're starting to really piss me off, Letov. I'll give you a chance, but if you fuck up than it's the easiest thing in the world for me to put that sick mutt down.

Kulakov hangs up.

IGOR LETOV: Ethel, dial me this number. Here's what we'll do. You want medieval, Eduard. Let's get medieval.

WORKER: Stop! STOP! What the hell are you doing?!

NAZBOL: What—inspecting arrivals.

WORKER: Didn't you hear? No more arrivals! No more new people!

NAZBOL: Look at that line of cars. Can't see where it ends. Some of them flew in from—

WORKER: It doesn't matter where they're from because there's not a barn for them to sleep in. Look, here comes Limonov's man now.

COMMISSAR BENZENE: Well what's going on? Why aren't the roads blockaded?

NAZBOL: We're on it, sir. Something must have gotten lost in translation.

COMMISSAR BENZENE: The population's tripled, man. The city is full.

NAZBOL: Alright, men close it off. Hey, get Bad Sulza over here.

COMMISSAR BENZENE: Got three armies guarding the place and it's somehow the most open city on Earth.

Carbon Pages

NAZBOL: It's done with.

COMMISSAR BENZENE: We got enough mouths to feed as it is, I'll tell you that.

> While Limonov occupied himself with internal affairs, his soldiers rested in the bars and disco halls. One time they were sitting around outside their barrack. Then out of the many NazBols killing time with the accordions one boy jumps out and he's wearing a Michael Jackson hat and jacket on his overalls. His name is Ledhead.

LEDHEAD: Check it out, boy.

> And he performs a moonwalk which he's clearly practiced in the mirror. Some applaud. Most are bored of it already.

NAZBOL: Get lost, Ledhead!

LEDHEAD: *Sha-mone*! Let's hear some accordian!

NAZBOL: How many times we gotta see this routine?

LEDHEAD: Jackson's only the greatest musician of all time!

> Further away from this sat Zygote, with a newer recruit.

STALLONE: Zyg, you hear about who they put in charge of wrangling Lapdukk?

ZYGOTE: I heard rumours.

STALLONE: What a fuckin traitor. To think, he was one of the Founders.

> Zygote sups.

STALLONE: Can't believe I liked his music. Only reason GrOb was as good as it was is because he was surrounded by more talented people. I wonder how he can stomach working for 'em.

ZYGOTE: Y'know, sometimes I think Limonov has opened the gates too wide. I remember, back in the early years when everyone was together, at Eagle's Nest

No Weapon Formed Against You

we all spent New Year's together. He'd go around the table and say and what have you drawn today, and he'd go to another guy and say so how is your sculpture progressing? Tell me, how do you feel about contraposto? These guys that are the meat of it now — what do they know except sticks, stones and crowbars? They know nothing except drinking and Michael Jackson.

STALLONE: Shooting is an art too.

ZYGOTE: That sounds very nice. But no—it isn't. It just isn't.

Dugin entered Limonov's chamber.

LIMONOV: I was about to send for you. What do you think about this: Krumpanthia. Noun. Meaning the feeling you get when you realise a disaster was imminent only after it's been averted.

DUGIN: It sounds Latin.

LIMONOV: I can see myself being an inventor of words.

DUGIN: Lend me your ear.

LIMONOV: Please.

DUGIN: The city is running out of fuel. Gasoline. For a long time the Kazakhs were scared of reprisals, but now that's over with...

LIMONOV: I'll take care of it. You have to understand that the Regenstvo has fate on her side.

DUGIN: There's also that man who requested an audience.

LIMONOV: Who?

DUGIN: The deserter.

LIMONOV: Don't we have enough deserters?

DUGIN: I can send him back.

LIMONOV: Fine, let me see him.

Dugin ushers in the man.

Carbon Pages

LIMONOV: Yes, come closer. Come.

> The visitor is a tall, broad-shouldered, barrel-chested man with a pencil moustache and a soldierly posture. Nonetheless, he seems to hunch in deference to the leader before him.

LIMONOV: What's your name?

ESTES: Giosuè Estes.

LIMONOV: Where are you from?

ESTES: Rome four planes over and a truck, Mister Limonov.

LIMONOV: You've heard of me?

ESTES: Naturally.

LIMONOV: What's your patronymic?

ESTES: Sir?

LIMONOV: What is your father's name?

> Limonov gives Dugin a wry look.

ESTES: Giovanni.

LIMONOV: Well then, you are Giousè Giovanniovich!

> Dugin can't help but snicker at this, to the Italian's embarrassment.

LIMONOV: Well let's get on with it. Let's speak English if it makes this faster.

> Estes is pleasantly surprised.

ESTES: You speak exceptionally.

LIMONOV: Yes, I am studying English. First words I learn is "Long live Peace, Long Live Friendship"!!

DUGIN: What nice words!!

No Weapon Formed Against You

> The two Russians snicker like schoolboys. Clearly they're in on some joke which Estes isn't privy to.

LIMONOV: You stand like a legionary, Estes. Is it in the military they taught you to be so talkative?

ESTES: I am military, sir. Or rather I was. I was commander of the 62nd Infantry Regiment. I have two medals of valour, four for courage. For nineteen years I served, until the corruption of my nation meant I could no longer serve a degenerate state. So, I came here.

LIMONOV: We have rejects to our eyeballs in Lapdukk. I've more officers than I have troops. Why do I need another?

ESTES: Well sir. If you'll permit me to speak the truth, I've been an admirer for many years. I read your books, all in translation of course. At first I couldn't understand why you changed your stance the way you did, but then it slowly dawned on me that you were right, and your opponents were wrong. It's a great miracle that Limonov was born into a country that, if you might permit my audacity to say, is unwaveringly *behind* the times, uniquely sycophantic and copying degenerate Evropa and her stewards. A country which strangles her heroes. Not only is Limonov ahead of Russia, he is ahead of the world. And so if he founds a city, it must be the city of the future of the world. I would only ask for the chance, if he permits my mortal audacity, to lay down my straw and a humble footnote build in the book of the history of the future.

LIMONOV: What is it you want exactly?

ESTES: To serve his army as General, sir—the only thing I know.

LIMONOV: Thank you, Estes. We'll consider your proposal.

ESTES: Sir I—

LIMONOV: You can wait outside.

> The Italian slinks away. Limonov gets out of his chair and paces by Dugin who, arms crossed, sits on the tall window sill and judges who is clearly nothing but a two-bit social-climber.

Carbon Pages

LIMONOV: Well, what does your little dice box say?

DUGIN: Can there be two commissars?

LIMONOV: Of course but not a chance in hell is this philistine going near my men. If I've seen one I've seen a hundred men hone in on the inherent weaknesses of my character, twisting my fatal flaw for their gain.

DUGIN: You think so?

LIMONOV: I bore my life out in those books, and now he's exploiting my honesty for his gain. But what do you think?

> He asks this as a child, having made up his mind, asks for the approval of a parent.

DUGIN: I think...

LIMONOV: Yes...?

DUGIN: ...I think I was never very good at the high level, or at judging character.

> Limonov has never in his life heard his friend speak like this. What's more disturbing is the man follows with this:

DUGIN: I used to believe I could be like you. I'm not you. If you think he's reliable, the choice should rest entirely with the regent of Lapdukk.

> Limonov eyeballs Dugin for a second, and then ventures:

LIMONOV: Fine...I'll give him the position. But brigadier—not general. And only to keep an eye on him—he's probably a spy anyway.

> In truth, the regent is relieved to bring the soldier on board, but deep down Eduard's unhappy that his choice is his alone. He'd much prefer Dugin tell him off and keep his conscience clean.

LIMONOV: Estes! Come back in! I've convened, and have elected to appoint you as brigadier of the army. Do you swear to uphold the law of Lapdukk?

No Weapon Formed Against You

He kneels.

ESTES: I do.

LIMONOV: Do you swear if she calls for it to die for your new motherland?

ESTES: I do.

LIMONOV: I don't want false promises.

ESTES: I swear to death! Death, death, death!

LIMONOV: Then the rank is yours. You'll be beholden to Commissar Benzene.

ESTES: Thank you, sir. You won't regret it, sir.

> And so the three of them took a tour of the barrack apartments, and the coffeeshops where the soldiers killed their days, and the dance halls where they killed their evenings. They met the Commissar who after introductions with his new Brigadier to whom he took an instant and intuitive dislike, mentioned:

COMMISSAR BENZENE: I just wanted to see you Mr. Limonov. It's about the allies.

LIMONOV: What about them?

COMMISSAR BENZENE: They pushed us off the west spring.

LIMONOV: They're attacking?!

COMMISSAR BENZENE: They're not attacking. But they are inching. Beyond that, we're running out of essentials—food, water, gasoline. It's something of a siege, sir. May I have your permission to take the divisions south, sir? Before they envelop us?

LIMONOV: You do not have permission. If it's a blockade they want then I'll show them blockade.

COMMISSAR BENZENE: Sir?

ESTES: Is there anything I can do?

Carbon Pages

LIMONOV: Benzene, remember the order about leaving the allies in peace? Scratch it. I'm giving the men total leeway.

COMMISSAR BENZENE: Are you sure, sir?

LIMONOV: What kind of a question is that? Do you want to be gallowed?

COMMISSAR BENZENE: No, sir. I'm not sure if you heard. But there's this. Ledhead, give the Founder that paper.

LIMONOV: What's this getup you're wearing?

LEDHEAD: It's like the king of pop's.

LIMONOV: Okay, and what's this?

COMMISSAR BENZENE: It's this morning's.

LIMONOV: "Commission for the solution to the Lapdukk Question now under the advisory oversight of terrorist group founder and former musician Igor Letov..." Have you heard this, Alexander?

DUGIN: It *was* speculation.

LIMONOV: *Letov urges key belligerents, including Eduard Limonov, to surrender to international authorities.*

The first person to speak is barrel-chested Estes:

ESTES: He's a traitor, and deserves a bullet in the mouth.

Limonov only blows air out his nostrils.

For the soldiers who composed it, the time of the blockade was remembered as a vast and undecipherable dream. The steppe was a flat, mystical place and the armies used rust-burnt fishing boats which sat on the sand for billets and quarters. Ancient mountains punctured the skyline and when the sun set she coloured the peaks in salmon pink to her recession. One morning, the men of the ring of barbed wire

No Weapon Formed Against You

and munition caissons around Lapdukk woke up to a slight smell of dust kicked up and floated from miles away over the horizon. A platoon of Limonov's cataphracts were galloping full speed at the ring.

They leapt over the embankments and circled the siegers, singing and mocking them. Not only were the siegers given orders to not shoot, letting the raiders get away with highway robberies of all kinds, but many were obscenely sympathetic, to the extent that reports got out of a field colonel willfully handing over supplies to the soldiers of Lapdukk. He was sacked, but his replacement was no less kind. Lapdukk had captured the imagination of the world, and even the Allies weren't immune to its charm. The soldiers raided their camps, and then their supply chains, and then the supply chains of their supply chains and not a thing was done to stop them.

ETHEL: ...So naturally the general requested that Limonov *return* the Range Rovers his cataphracts stole on the raid, to which he agreed and "returned" four broken down tractors.

IGOR LETOV: They're riding around on horses—what is this, White Sun of the Desert? He's tearing through them like butter, and no one's doing a fucking thing to stop him. Did you hear about this that he's calling them aristocrats? He's turned the village into a penal colony.

ETHEL: They all shout Kraloy Kraloy Kraloy. What's it mean?

IGOR LETOV: It doesn't mean anything. Probably some war chant Limonov made up.

ETHEL: You know something, Mr. Letov?

IGOR LETOV: What?

ETHEL: You have a real Siberian tang about you.

IGOR LETOV: I've been told.

ETHEL: What did I tell you about the carpet!

Letov flinches.

No Weapon Formed Against You

ETHEL: Why don't you arrange a meeting with Limonov. You were comrades.

IGOR LETOV: It won't happen.

ETHEL: You've been saying that. But really, why not?

IGOR LETOV: It'll only make things worse.

ETHEL: Maybe you're right. The papers aren't very kind. Maybe it's time for another conference.

IGOR LETOV: I'm doing a conference.

    She reads a snippet:

ETHEL: *Igor Letov's corruption is apparent. If he really believed in anything other than his paycheck the Lapdukk question would have been solved week one.* Well I don't believe it.

IGOR LETOV: I told you, I'm not interested in their shit.

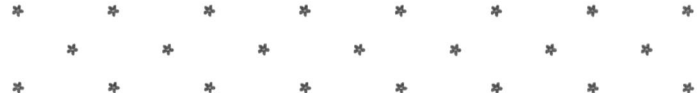

    Again Limonov's mercenaries were drinking and smoking and playing cards and killing time.

NAZBOL 2: I'm not denying that the raiding is fun, but I wanna get on the road.

NAZBOL: Didn't you hear Limonov? We're building the City of the Sun.

NAZBOL 2: Yeah well whatever, when I signed up I wanted more action than raiding some camps and some pussies. And now with the Xistram...I'm antsy.

    The Xistram was the sobriquet Limonov had coined for Letov.

NAZBOL: Let me ask something, what do you know about that one guy always around Limonov?

NAZBOL 2: Who?

Carbon Pages

NAZBOL: The bearded guy.

NAZBOL 2: Dugin.

NAZBOL: Aye, and what's he about anyway?

NAZBOL 2: I don't know. There's not a picture of Limonov without him somewhere in the background.

NAZBOL: I hear he can move objects with his mind. Some say all the city's under his control, and Limonov's only a marionette.

NAZBOL 2: Nah that's bullshit. I hear he drowns women in the night.

Commissar Benzene intrudes:

COMMISSAR BENZENE: Like girls over a fence, the lot of you. Alexander Dugin was a founder.

NAZBOL 2: I never heard that.

COMMISSAR BENZENE: There's a lot you haven't heard of, soldier. Few years back, before my time, Limonov was beaten half to death. Jumped in an alley he was by some mercs. Nobody knew who sent them, but everyone had their suspicions. Brain damage is the only explanation for hiring that fuckin lickspittle Italian. He's gonna doom our whole campaign, I can't even say his name.

NAZBOL 2: I was readin' about Hitler, Commissar. Y'know, by the end of his life he was on over thirty cocktails.

NAZBOL: I heard about this.

NAZBOL 2: The more he took, the more he wanted, and the crazier he got. They told him he couldn't win the eastern front, but he started believing he's a god. Madagascar, the moon. Consumed everything in his path he did. Nothing his generals said could stop him.

COMMISSAR BENZENE: Yeah well, don't forget how it ended for him.

> Meanwhile, Limonov was at his desk fucking a Kazakh peasant girl. She was jumping up and down on his lap when entered the room Dugin. Limonov ushers out the girl.

No Weapon Formed Against You

LIMONOV: Were you raised in a barn?

Pulls up underwear.

LIMONOV: I could've been shaving.

DUGIN: Sorry, Eduard. I wanted to talk to you.

LIMONOV: What—about the canyon? I knew you'd have a problem with it!

DUGIN: No, I don't.

LIMONOV: The city will have a two hundred and fifty foot deep canyon running through its centre. The magnitude of the skyscraper must be countered with the terror of the deep.

DUGIN: I wanted to talk about the Kremlin.

LIMONOV: Trust me, I have plans. I should've known he'd be working for them. I tell you, Al, if there's one thing that can doom the Arméd City it's Igor. He knows us better than anyone.

DUGIN: What if it's time for what we talked about way back when.

LIMONOV: What?

DUGIN: The Kremlin. Taking it, and annexing Russia.

LIMONOV: Marching on it?

DUGIN: There's no salvaging the Lapdukk-Moscow axis.

LIMONOV: You're my advisor. You're wiser than me—do you think it's wise?

DUGIN: The Xistram is scared of your power, your will. He's jealous of it.

LIMONOV: Finally you speak up a little. Ever since we got to Lapdukk I can't get two words out of you.

DUGIN: Well Eduard if it's my true opinion you want to know. There was always something of the devil worshipper in him. A man with such a predilection can never be at peace.

Carbon Pages

KULAKOV: You've had your fun. Remember how I didn't want Washington and the ICC sticking their fat nose in? Well they're in on it. We might have gotten him before everything went to shit the way it did because of you, you weasel. Don't think when this is all over you won't be reprimanded. Well it's out of our hands now. They've got an Iron Storm Four scheduled, everyone's on board, except the usual outliers of course—

IGOR LETOV: What do you mean an Iron Storm Four?

KULAKOV: I mean we're going to bomb the shit out of their militia is what. Not without a preliminary warning, of course...

IGOR LETOV: Jesus Christ, but there are civilians, thousands of people...

KULAKOV: Anyone who wanted to get out by now has. Lapdukk's become an international threat, Igor. You can't really blame anyone for putting the foot on the pedal. If you ask me we should've done it a long time ago. But, well, the new Russia is slow on her feet. Yeltsin, he ... well shit I'll just say it. He likes a drink. You know how it is. He's had a stressful year. Or what—do you have something to say, you useless leech?

DUGIN: Have you thought about what we discussed?

LIMONOV: What?

DUGIN: Taking Moscow.

LIMONOV: Oh that. I'm still mulling it over.

DUGIN: We don't have much time.

No Weapon Formed Against You

LIMONOV: I'm just sharpening some plans with the architects. You know Dugin, you were right all those years ago what you said to me. The party is bigger than politics...

DUGIN: With the front we can take them by surprise, take the radio and television towers and—

LIMONOV: Look it'll happen, okay? I just need some time. You yourself said: kairos. Remember? The time's not right. It's like fishing. You can't rush these things. We'll march on Moscow but I just need to get things ready here with Lapdukk. This city is everything. I've walked every road, know every blade of grass, every window like the spots on a woman's back. I need some time before I can leave her.

DUGIN: She will never stop being yours. If we take Moscow, then all of Russia is in your hands. Everything you've ever dreamt, you can mould the nation to your genius. As long as we ready the troops.

LIMONOV: Am I a genius? No. He was a genius. There was no other *tvorets* like Letov. And it was an honour to witness him. No, it wasn't an honour. It was torture. I would've killed for his hands. To him it's yesterday's blister, but I would shit on the written word. You think that's sudden, don't you? But I've been thinking about it for years. The truth is there's nothing that brings as much pleasure in this world as music. Food, sex. Music. On that stage I decided if I were to go back to the start I wouldn't be Limonov. I'd be Igor Letov, and I'd play such music the whole world would kill itself for me. But he decided he'd go back to the start as well, and he wouldn't be Letov, and he wouldn't be a genius, and he wouldn't be anyone or believe in anything whatsoever. *That* is the esteem in which he holds my envy. He *steps* in my envy.

We'll take Moscow—I just need some time—

    Suddenly a boy runs into the Chateau and announces:

BOY: Sir? Sirs!

LIMONOV: What is it?

Carbon Pages

BOY: Mr. Limonov. They've got a real beauty in the square. Think you wanna see it!

DUGIN: What about—

LIMONOV: Let's see it, Alexander.

> They follow downstairs where, in the courtyard, is Brigadier Estes gleaming proudly by a shipping truck.

ESTES: Mr Limonov, sir. Boys took down a whole caravan this morning. Commercial it looks like. We thought you might like crack it open yourself.

> Limonov yawns.

LIMONOV: This is my third one this week. Alexander, take it off my hands will you?

ESTES: Do the honours, sir?

> Dugin takes the prybar and cracks open the container. Luxury women's underwear spills out at Dugin's feet.

NAZBOL: Finnish by the looks of em!

ESTES: Beaut. Stallone—get the syphon!

> Finally the situation became so dire for Letov that he proposed a sit-down with him representing the interests of Moscow and for one reason or another Limonov agreed, with the caveat that no one else other than him be present.
>
> Soon the day came. Just two hours before the Xistram's arrival, Dugin came to Limonov with one last word.

DUGIN: Letov should be here before dinner.

LIMONOV: Good.

DUGIN: Eduard, have I ever interfered with your constructions?

LIMONOV: I don't think so.

No Weapon Formed Against You

DUGIN: Have I ever complained about blasphemy?

LIMONOV: No.

DUGIN: Then allow me this. Moscow is everything. The presidency is everything—the president can spit on Lapdukk. Yeltsin can spit on Lapdukk—because he's the president. The parliament can spit on Lapdukk. You're a creature. A termite. If you don't act, then how long can the Regenstvo last?

LIMONOV: Don't worry. I have a feeling after our sit down he'll be crawling back the scenic route.

DUGIN: I think—

>Suddenly, they're shocked by a loud yelling coming from right under the window of the Chateau de Silling, and it's coming from Commissar Benzene.

COMMISSAR BENZENE: SAVENKO!! SAVENKO!!

LIMONOV: What's he want?

COMMISSAR BENZENE: SAVENKO! COME OUT HERE NOW, SAVENKO!

DUGIN: I think he's on something. What's he holding?

LIMONOV: My book.

>One NazBol tries to appease the doped up warman.

NAZBOL: Sir, what's the matter?

COMMISSAR BENZENE: HE SUCKED—NIGGER DICK!! It's all...in his...MEMOIR! EDDIE...stands for EDUARDDD!!!

>Eduard rushes downstairs with Dugin trailing behind him.

LIMONOV: What's the meaning of this, warrior?

COMMISSAR BENZENE: He wrote it HIMSELF!!

Carbon Pages

> He brandishes the book over his head flocking many NazBols to the commotion. He's so doped up he can barely stand.

LIMONOV: Give me the book, Commissar.

COMMISSAR BENZENE: EVEN HIS NAME'S MADE UP! IT'S ALL IN HERE!

LIMONOV: If you'll inspect the copy in your hand you'll find there's not one instance of the word memoir. Is there?

COMMISSAR BENZENE: THAT'S RIGHT EVERYONE—GATHER ROUND!

LIMONOV: Prove me wrong. Nor the word biography or autobiography which means biography written by oneself. Is it anywhere in the book? I wrote it, so I should know. Please, let's flip through it. We have all the time in the world.

COMMISSAR BENZENE: IT'S THE TRUTH!

LIMONOV: If you were to conduct a surface examination, which you didn't, you'd find the publisher has no history of publishing non-fiction. Do they? Therefore the book is a novel. It comes from my imagination and it has no relation to reality, past, present or future. Also, that thing was written when your regent was in the maw of material penury. Bad Sulza, give me that book.

> He surrenders his book to a NazBol who hands it to Estes who's been observing.

COMMISSAR BENZENE: I'm...sorry. I'm ashamed.

LIMONOV: For causing a disturbance your fate will pend my decision. On pain of our high displeasure, no one is to mention this again. Anyone found propagating these baseless, feminine lies will be sentenced to death by torture.

> Estes arrests the commissar and takes him away fast. Limonov continues:

LIMONOV: Like a bridge over troubled waters I will lay thee down with showers of blood. You will be ground into paint. You'll be distilled into insecticide. Pass me and tremble—for I am the wrath of God.

No Weapon Formed Against You

Limonov and Dugin disappear once more into the Chateau under the cover of silence and the crowd, of course, disperses.

The rest of the day is filled with a sense of strange dread for Alexander and Eddie—Alexander especially, as he's running through his mind what Letov's reaction will be to Limonov telling him his plans to invade. Perhaps he even hopes that Letov will join them—otherwise, he imagines him getting round up and shot with all the other deputats.

Estes disturbs them occasionally to tell them the commissar has calmed down or fallen asleep, but until the sun sets the two do not leave the Chateau and they wait patiently for Igor Letov. Finally, they're informed that he's arrived in Lapdukk. Then, that he's in the Chateau. Then that the summit awaits him.

Letov waits outside the door to Limonov's office

LIMONOV: Ready?

DUGIN: I'm ready.

LIMONOV: Then let's get him in here.

Letov enters. He walks into the centre of the palace as Dugin shuts the door behind him. For a long time no one speaks. Limonov has his feet kicked up on the desk and he lights a clay pipe that's as long his forearm. He wears a thong and silk robe. Finally Letov breaks the silence.

IGOR LETOV: Where's it all from?

LIMONOV: Some from raids.

He examines Letov's face for a reaction.

LIMONOV: Some were saved by Lapdukk's... historical insignificance.

IGOR LETOV: It's very pretty. My desk...

He smiles...

Carbon Pages

IGOR LETOV: ...is chipboard.

>Limonov says nothing, but continues lighting his pipe. Letov can hear Dugin pacing behind him. Again it falls on him to break the silence.

IGOR LETOV: You have a pretty city, Eduard. You must be proud.

>Eduard finishes lighting his absurd pipe. He does not look Igor in the eyes. He doesn't look at him at all.

LIMONOV: Here Alexander. Taste this. You're meant to snap the tip off before passing it along.

>Dugin walks over and reluctantly does so.

LIMONOV: No, no. Don't pass it to Mr. Letov.

>He returns it. Igor's legs are getting very tired, standing there.

IGOR LETOV: We're ready to give you and Al partial amnesty, and Lapdukk officials will sign a written promise guaranteeing fair and equal treatment of ethnic Russians.

LIMONOV: Alexander, can you ask Igor what fragrance he's wearing? Is that Azarro? Or, no I'm getting something woodier. Eau de toilette!? They really have wrangled him! One time on a trip a fortune teller gave me a bottle of Rosa one drop of which I dropped in the Caspian water. The sea was perfumed for over three months.

IGOR LETOV: That so?

LIMONOV: Poesy is reality.

IGOR LETOV: Eduard, I think it's time to wrap up the adventure.

LIMONOV: I don't think so.

IGOR LETOV: Your little escapade has caused an international crisis. But that's what you wanted, isn't it? You're just happy.

No Weapon Formed Against You

LIMONOV: They must be paying you a lot.

IGOR LETOV: I only want to pull the people out of the gutter. You can't do that from a barrack. You're right in some ways that Russians are in the gutter but you can't do anything from a barrack. If you can just consider the proposal. It's very generous—

LIMONOV: —I have absolutely no interest in your phony proposal, and your phony job, and your phony government! Your Moscow can go rot and your industries and laws, they're old and worm ridden. They're a creature. *My* proposals! *My* government! We are building a new and brilliant Utopia, Igor. We are building the city of the Sun.

IGOR LETOV: Eduard—it's a desert.

> Limonov sucks on his pipe. Everyone feels that Igor has admitted to what's a humiliating sin in this room—a lack of imagination.

IGOR LETOV: Eduard—they will bombard. Evropa is on our side. NATO is on our side. If you do not surrender in twenty four hours we will make Belgrade look like a firecracker. And Lapdukk is *not* Belgrade. You understand?

> He simply smokes his pipe, rocking his seat, examining the doorpost, hands behind his head. Dugin, taken a seat on the opposite side of the room sees that Limonov will finally tell Letov about the march on Moscow.

LIMONOV: Hm, I think I'd like to have an inscription installed here: Somnii Explanatio. Mister Dugin, do you concur?

> The three men stay in silence. There's nothing left to say. Finally Letov sits down in the middle of the room. An old gypsy guitar catches his sight leaning one of the bookshelves. He stands up, and takes the guitar in his hands. Limonov stares out a window. He sits back down, and places the seven-stringer on his lap. He has not played in a long, long time and the strings hurt his finger pads when he presses. He plucks a note which is messy and buzzes. Then another.

Carbon Pages

The guitar's colour reminds me of the Henderson twins who are bored now of throwing clumps of mowed grass, especially since his tongue is covered in grass which he pfoot pfoots. Instead, the Henderson twins nab their dad's tools and dig around in the back yard, picking at the dirt like a scab. The boy finds a stone sticking out of the dirt which he tries to pull out but it's wedged like super in-there. Being a curious young boy, he digs around it, but still it won't budge. He sees it's not a stone at all now but a rock. The sun is coming down and before mom calls them home both of the twins dig, dig, dig. No dice. The next morning before school they dig ALL around it more and even brush the rock. It grows and grows, and by the time they leave for school it's the size of their pet lab. It is the phalanx of a giant bird. There is a colossal prehistoric bird buried under two and a half sections of the Henderson back yard. There is a giant bird buried under the Henderson yard.

After picking a third buzzy note, Igor stands up and places the guitar where he found it, straightens his tie, and walks out the door.

Dugin goes and catches up with Letov as he's descending the stairs. This is the last time they will ever see each other.

DUGIN: Igor, wait.

IGOR LETOV: What?

DUGIN: Wait.

IGOR LETOV: What is it?

DUGIN: He will march on Moscow. We will march on Moscow and take the Duma. Once you return, settle your loose ends and say your goodbyes.

> Letov seems unmoved.

IGOR LETOV: You're a smart man, Al. You've a good career. What are you hanging around with him for?

DUGIN: He's a bad tooth. Something I've come to learn is, you can either pull a bad tooth, or you can fill it with gold.

No Weapon Formed Against You

> Again, Letov is unmoved.

DUGIN: You're not the only one struggling. Do you have the faintest idea how hard I'm trying? It makes me sick. And what exactly are you clinging to? You worship a dead regime that would gladly discard you and is on the verge of collapse.

> Igor smiles and shows his palms.

IGOR LETOV: And yet, my Russia, I love you still.

DUGIN: I'm working very hard to make a reality the Russia you love so much.

> Igor left that same day.
>
> Limonov did not surrender. He made no effort to flee the city, although the city itself didn't share his confidence. A great exodus began, first by the tourists and adventurers and reporters. The surrounding allies disappeared over the steppe horizon, leaving Lapdukk an oasis as before.
>
> A great atmosphere of suspicion had grown in the city walls, with many accusing others of plundering loot. It reached its gruesome zenith when one evening Limonov was walking the stables, arm in arm with a brunette, admiring the sunset over the mountains. Just then, by sheer coincidence, an adolescent boy topples out the front door of an enigmatic walk-up and onto the pavement in front of them. After him strolls out Brigadier Giousè Estes who notices the regent with his friend and matter-of-factly informs:

ESTES: A traitor, sir. With intent of divulging state information.

> Then Estes puts a twenty-two caliber pistol to the boy's lobe and pulls the trigger, sending his brains flying over the footpath.
>
> The day Letov came back to his office overlooking the Red Square Kulakov called him.

KULAKOV: Well? Say everything.

Carbon Pages

IGOR LETOV: I told him. I don't think he'll shut the borders.

KULAKOV: Good.

IGOR LETOV: Sir, can I ask—are we really sending jets over Lapdukk?

KULAKOV: Of course not. But that imbecile believed it didn't he? They'll scatter like mice and we'll arrest 'em on their way out. Now tell me, is there anything else they told you that might give us an edge? This fuckin idiot. I tell ya. There were no fascists 'fore he started. Now there's a thousand devil spawn running around parliament. And baby brother communist tryna wring back some crumbs too. I mean I know people are starving but you have to get over it for God's sake. I mean I just don't see what the big deal is. You're from ass county Letov, are YOU starving? No? Well what have *they* got to complain about? Back in the day they could have been put in a gulag. Back in the day the only ice cream they had were those fuckin wafer cups. I always hated wafer cups me. Now there's a hundred types of ice cream like in an american freezer. I always liked America. Always liked The Beatles. From the very beginning, hand on God. I wasn't like those other bastards.

So, you know, I don't want any more surprises. Even the tiniest morsel can help us. Think, Letov. Is there anything they said that can help us?

               Letov remains silent for a little. Then he replies.

IGOR LETOV: No.

               And he hangs up.

* * * * * * * *
  * * * * * * *
* * * * * * * * *

               Back in the Chateau:

VAS DEFERENS: May I come in?

LIMONOV: Yes.

No Weapon Formed Against You

VAS DEFERENS: I couldn't live with myself if I did it in secret like the others. I thought you deserved to know. I'm leaving The Arméd City, sir. I just want you to know I'm taking no part in the looting. I'd never.

LIMONOV: On whose orders?

VAS DEFERENS: No one's, exactly.

LIMONOV: Then you're deserting.

VAS DEFERENS: It's chaos, sir. It's these fucking jihadists. Them and the Communists are pouring castor oil down each other's throats, shitting up the streets. They set fire to the gymnasium.

LIMONOV: Do you desert women too?

VAS DEFERENS: It's not like that. We've all been trying to bring back order. But now with the Xistram and the countdown. It's not me. Can I ask something? Is it true that you won't be going South to the Kazakh capital? If you were—

LIMONOV: There is no need to go anywhere. We are in the heartland. The Xistram comes to us.

VAS DEFERENS: You know me. I'm an engineer.

LIMONOV: Or maybe we *will* go South. I haven't made my decision yet.

VAS DEFERENS: And the Brigadier is so sorry if he's offended you.

LIMONOV: He overstepped his rank. He didn't wait for an order! You're nosey for a deserter. Is he leaving as well?

VAS DEFERENS: Not that I know of.

LIMONOV: Maybe...he...should. I just need time. All these slings. I just need some time to know.

>Limonov locked himself inside the Chateau. He did not eat and did not sleep. He did not so much as look out his window. When the hour came and the city was not bombed, he stayed inside still for another four days. The annihilation which never gave climax only sent him into a need for a new great big decision. He would've stayed longer but after thirteen days Limonov heard a sound. He put his ear to his door. What

he heard was in simple terms the clamour of boots. It was an FSB squad running up the Chateau.

Before he knew it there was a loud knocking coming from the door. He didn't know what to do, and he had an intuitive sense that they weren't here to arrest him so he did the first thing that came to mind and it's jump off the balcony of the Chateau de Silling's third floor. The agents rammed into the office, searched the place and one looked down at the paving stones.

FSB AGENT: He's down there! Go! Go!

When they reached him, Limonov was bleeding from a broken leg.

FSB AGENT: Won't you kindly stay where you are.

In the weeks following his arrest, which Limonov had deduced was illegal and thus un-enforcable, he had a lot of time to think about the moment of his failed escape. Aside from the pain of breaking a leg and an arm, two things struck him the moment he landed on the ground. One was that the square was totally deserted. He hadn't noticed because up till then he had not so much as looked out his window while thinking of the next course of action. The second thing was that all the banners, all the tapestries and flags bearing the black hammer and sickle in a white circle surrounded with red had been removed. Inconsequential though it was, these were the things that one thinks about when imprisoned.

LIMONOV: Guard—what is your name?

GUARD: ...

LIMONOV: I said what's your name?

GUARD: ...

No Weapon Formed Against You

LIMONOV: Come on. How long have I been locked up in this room. You must know *my* name.

GUARD: ...

LIMONOV: It would be only fair if I knew *yours*.

GUARD: Inmate 150898 will move away from the door.

LIMONOV: Want to arm wrestle?

GUARD: Inmate 150898 will move away from Officer Strelkov.

LIMONOV: There you go. Strelkov.

GUARD: ...

LIMONOV: Why do you keep me in here for so long? Are the prisons clogged up with patriots?

GUARD: ...

LIMONOV: Not an interrogation, not a beating. I commanded men thrice as brutal as you.

GUARD: ...

LIMONOV: But I like the view from Chateau de Silling. I've always liked the view. You think I'm going to break? You and your buddies are in for a treat. I can take it as long as you give it, and I've got less to lose.

> Deprived of his rights, Eduard was the most content he'd been in his entire life.

LIMONOV: (*looking out window*) What are they doing out there? Hey guard!

GUARD: ...

LIMONOV: You men must be bored as hell. Why don't you try learning Kazakh? It's a glorious language.

Carbon Pages

GUARD: ...

LIMONOV: But really what are your boys doing with all those planks? And what's that? Cement?

GUARD: ...

LIMONOV: Oh I see—you're building a fence. And a high one at that. If you're trying to deprive me just know it won't work. I have the rare ability to memorize views photographically. Higher boys, higher! Build it higher!

GUARD: ...

GUARD: Inmate 150898's dinner is here.

> He slides the tray under a makeshift cutout in the door. Suddenly Limonov starts laughing. First gently, then hysterically.

GUARD: Why is Inmate 150898 cackling?

LIMONOV: Because I just remembered your mascot!

GUARD: ...

LIMONOV: Do you remember your mascot?

GUARD: ...

LIMONOV: Iron Felix Dzerzhinsky. He founded the secret police. He ran the gulags!

GUARD: ...

LIMONOV: You know what else Felix did? He spent half his life behind bars for terrorism. Then he was freed and killed everyone who crossed him.

GUARD: The inmate will consider this his first warning.

LIMONOV: He never forgot his enemies!

No Weapon Formed Against You

Then the guard enters the room and drives the butt of his rifle into the inmate's stomach, who falls to the ground wheezing.

GUARD: The inmate will eat his dinner.

* * * * * * * *
 * * * * * * * *
* * * * * * * * *

LIMONOV: So, anyway they won't let me even keep a calendar. What they're feeding me barely has any protein. Hardly any vitamins. I can't do my daily pushups what with my arm and my ankle. Did I tell you about that. Oh right I did. I've substituted it with an incline wall push. It's quite effective. The guards here are pricks. They've stopped giving me newspapers. I ask why and they don't tell me. Maybe you have your own theories, unless you're locked up too which you probably are, but I think the reason they won't bring me over the border is because of the riots. They'd flip the goddamn squad car over, the people. Anyway, how about you, Dugin? Call me back if you get this. Have you been getting any of these messages? Probably not. But just in case you are, call me.

GUARD: The inmate will have his food.

LIMONOV: Hey guard, why don't you give me a nail clipper? It's been two weeks since I clipped my nails.

GUARD: Nope.

LIMONOV: I always get a clipper.

GUARD: Not anymore.

LIMONOV: What am I going to do with a clipper—take you hostage?

GUARD: ...

LIMONOV: C'mon Strelkov. Just give me this. Just give me a clipper.

GUARD: ...

LIMONOV: You have no idea how to treat a prisoner. I don't know what you think you're accomplishing but I know one individual. Benzene is his name—my right hand man. And just one call to him is all I have to make and he'll make you wish you were dead! He's an expert in it! He'll wear your skin!

Carbon Pages

GUARD: Your Benzene won't be wearing anyone's skin. Your Benzene's still reeking of lethal injection. Same goes for the rest of your friends.

LIMONOV: Now what are you doing?

GUARD: The inmate will stay out of the way.

                        Two guards enter the room.

LIMONOV: Take your time. Let me ask you a question. Are you men downsizing or am I finally going crazy? I've memorized your faces, and I feel like there's less guards working here every day. Whatever happened to Strelkov? I haven't seen him in days. What is it—New Year's soon? Have they gone home to their families? Is this a search? What are you searching for? Hey stay out of those drawers.

GUARD: Is there a reason we should?

LIMONOV: The reason is you cleaned the place.

GUARD: What is this?

LIMONOV: That?

GUARD: Yes.

LIMONOV: That's nothing. It's a gasogene. It's what they used for making bubbles in fizzy— hey! You can't take that. Hey that's my mirror. What on Earth could you want with my mirror? At least leave my books. Answer me. Ask me what they are. Why take my books? And my cushions? Come back!

GUARD: Inmate 150898 will move away from the guard.

        The men march out one by one carrying items.

No Weapon Formed Against You

LIMONOV: Allo, Dugin? When you get this, call me back. The guards are still pricks. This morning I did seventy-two inclines...

✤ ✤ ✤ ✤ ✤ ✤ ✤ ✤ ✤
 ✤ ✤ ✤ ✤ ✤ ✤ ✤ ✤
✤ ✤ ✤ ✤ ✤ ✤ ✤ ✤ ✤

There's a knock knock.

LIMONOV: Since when do you knock? It's unlocked.

The guard enters carrying a basket.

LIMONOV: What's this—a file and a chisel? Soldier, you're looking awful disheveled with your uniform. You've got to respect your uniform. Tuck your shirt in.

GUARD: It's fresh eggs. From the farmers.

LIMONOV: What's this—replacing my evening?

GUARD: No.

LIMONOV: (*cautiously*) Well thanks.

The revolutionary takes the egg basket and feels one egg.

LIMONOV: Oh they're boiled. Good.

He unpeels it and shoves it into his mouth.

LIMONOV: This is more like it. This is good. I want to see more arden und order around here—feels unreal to finally taste something fresh.

GUARD: No problem, Eduard.

Limonov's heart sinks. He stops chewing. The guard leaves, closing the door behind him. He immediately spits out the chewed up egg, and washes his mouth. In a sweat he wraps his

hand in his shirt and examines one egg turning it in the light.
Then he dashes to the telephone.

LIMONOV: Alexander! Pick up now! There's something in the air. Strelkov brought me fresh eggs. They were delicious. He called me by name. I don't know what but I feel something very bad is about to happen to me.

The next day:

LIMONOV: Guard? Where's my food? What did I tell you about discipline? You morons, it's 8am where's my food?

He tries the door handle. The door is unlocked. There is no one guarding him.

LIMONOV: Guard? Strelkov?

The house is empty.

The next twelve hours are spent by Limonov debating whether or not to leave his room. The moment he's certain that there's nothing for it except to step outside, the muse provides him with the certainty that he's being goaded so that he can be shot for unlawful escape.

And it's at this moment that he hears the approach of footsteps.

Who is it?

They're getting closer.

No Weapon Formed Against You

Closer still. Any moment they will be here.

The footsteps stop. At the door.

There's a knock on the door.

LIMONOV: ...

The door opens and the figure steps in.

LIMONOV: Alexander.

DUGIN: What are you doing, Eduard?

LIMONOV: Oh thank God you're here.

DUGIN: Haven't they taken leave?

LIMONOV: I've been here for who knows how long.

DUGIN: I see.

LIMONOV: They made me a prisoner in my own home.

DUGIN: I can see that.

LIMONOV: Have you gotten my messages?

DUGIN: They have a different number in the Kremlin.

LIMONOV: Let's get to the apartment on Zholtaya there's a cache there exactly in case of something like this. Then we can make contact with Vas Deferens or anyone else in the Front.

DUGIN: Okay.

LIMONOV: What do you mean just now, you said something about the Kremlin? Help me on my feet.

DUGIN: Relax for a second Eduard.

LIMONOV: What?

DUGIN: Everything is fine. Let's sit down for one minute.

LIMONOV: What is this about the Kremlin?

Carbon Pages

    Dugin thinks how best to formulate this into words.

DUGIN: There's no need for any weapons, and there is no point in contacting the men.

LIMONOV: Why?

DUGIN: Because everything is under control. This is a bit hard for me to explain considering your condition. It feels like such a long time...

LIMONOV: Just tell me what's happening. I left countless messages.

DUGIN: Moscow has been taken.

    Limonov leans back for a moment, unsure how to respond.

LIMONOV: By whom?

DUGIN: By us. By the Front. Although, it's not really called that anymore.

LIMONOV: It's not called that anymore?

DUGIN: It's some silly name he made up for optics basically. Actually I'm the one who suggested it as I know you would agree. You'd probably say it's banal...

LIMONOV: You couldn't have taken Moscow. They told me Benzene was executed.

DUGIN: Benzene was *not* executed. But Benzene *is* in prison. Probably forever. It was my suggestion also.

LIMONOV: I know it wasn't you.

DUGIN: No, it wasn't really me. It was—

LIMONOV: —Estes?

    Dugin guffaws a little as if the concept is ridiculous, as if he hasn't heard the name in three lifetimes.

DUGIN: No, that psychopath was extradited almost immediately. I believe he's serving a life sentence. So is Vas Deferens and Tailgate and the lieutenants. It was, basically, Ledhead.

No Weapon Formed Against You

> Limonov racks his brains for a second. Ledhead? Who? He feels like he's heard that name. Maybe even recently, but he can't associate it with a single image.

LIMONOV: Who the hell is Ledhead?

DUGIN: He was one of your cataphracts.

LIMONOV: He's dead?

DUGIN: No, I just told you he's taken Moscow.

LIMONOV: I have no idea who that is.

DUGIN: You remember him.

LIMONOV: I really don't.

> Dugin tries to think of some way to make him remember. They look at each other in silence.

DUGIN: He led some of the raids. He handed you a newspaper that one time.

LIMONOV: *Him?*

DUGIN: Yes.

LIMONOV: He's a nobody.

DUGIN: Not quite.

LIMONOV: So tell me again from the start, because I think you're missing my wavelength a little. I've been in Tartarus for God knows how long.

DUGIN: You've been under house arrest for eighty five days. A couple of days into your bout of isolation the Front schismed. It was unpleasant. There was killing. In the end some went South and were arrested, others went to Moscow. The ones that went to Moscow were led second-in-command by Ledhead. It's just luck of the draw on his part really. Although he is extremely capable! Anyway there was something of a march if you want to call it that. We took them by surprise. They negotiated the surrender proposal. Yeltsin added a bullet point. Ledhead added a bullet point. After three hours they reached a provisional-bilateral-memorandum-framework.

Carbon Pages

Limonov looks offended by the words.

LIMONOV: How many fell?

DUGIN: What—during your bout?

LIMONOV: No, Dugin. In Moscow.

DUGIN: Oh well...not many. Someone got crushed. So we're all now in a bit of a situation where, including you and I, we're all in a bit of a situation where Ledhead has taken it onto himself to represent your interests and the Front's in the presidential seat.

LIMONOV: Yeltsin—he's been hanged?

DUGIN: No—he's been retired. It was discussed.

A brooding dread overtakes Limonov.

LIMONOV: What about parliament?

DUGIN: Parliament won't be a problem.

LIMONOV: He had them shot?

DUGIN: He did not have them shot.

LIMONOV: He had them dissolved.

DUGIN: He did not dissolve parliament. But they won't be a problem.

LIMONOV: So what's changed?

DUGIN: Everything. Everything you envisioned. Everything I advised. I still advise, to the best of my abilities, he'd be happy to hear from *you*.

LIMONOV: I remember him now.

DUGIN: We waved the flag, we yelled Kraloy! All of Russia is on our side! Except for the democrats of course but they're inconsequential now, and with time they'll be powder. No one of NATO will be a problem anymore. It's astonishing the progress we've made in just a short time, Eduard. There's barely any foreign investment that hasn't fled with its tail between its legs. And it's all getting bigger as we speak.

No Weapon Formed Against You

LIMONOV: Ledhead—he's a tool!

DUGIN: What do you mean?

LIMONOV: He still listens to Michael Jackson.

DUGIN: So?

LIMONOV: The boy's a philistine!

DUGIN: I don't think it much matters, Eduard.

LIMONOV: What do you mean it doesn't matter. War is art. War is sacred. What is this something provisional framework you're talking about?

DUGIN: Eduard—the nation is ours.

LIMONOV: I barely tolerated that boy's attention. I almost didn't recruit him but I was busy with that Sevastopol thing. Now he's gone and usurped his commander.

DUGIN: No one usurped you!

LIMONOV: I fashioned his entire worldview, Alexander.

> Dugin stands up. With every word his lounge chair limps Limonov down into a flaccidity. With every word he tries to sit up. With every word Dugin feels he is speaking with a sad old man.

LIMONOV: I invented kraloy. I invented the party. Now that he has what he wants he's going to execute me!

DUGIN: He's absolutely not going to execute you. That you can trust me on.

LIMONOV: Then give me the president's seat.

DUGIN: I don't think that's a good idea.

LIMONOV: Why not?

DUGIN: It's just not.

LIMONOV: Why is it not a good idea?

DUGIN: He has the seat for now, and it's fine. Sometime in the future maybe...

Carbon Pages

LIMONOV: Well you've gotten very good at talking, lecturer. Who taught you that? Smite me down O Lecturer of Nation, since you've outgrown your master!

DUGIN: You hysterical lunatic, Limonov.

LIMONOV: I'm the fashioner of your and his entire culture.

DUGIN: You fashion it and by the time everyone catches up with you you're bored and you've run off to fashion some next thing while everyone is left picking up the pieces. How can anyone run a nation that way?

> They stay in silence for a bit. Then Eduard says:

LIMONOV: Leave me be.

> At the door Dugin says one final thing:

DUGIN: The Russian people have finally caught up with you, Eduard Limonov.

> Over the course of the next weeks there was a lot of cajoling between the Kremlin and Limonov over phone, with lots of promises being made and apologies and excuses offered. Still, Limonov stayed in the same room as he did under house arrest and he did not eat.
>
> Finally, he was greeted by the new president and commander-in-chief of the Russian Federation who was very sheepish in the presence of his master. He was taller than Eduard. Otherwise unremarkable in every feature and characteristic, quite a typical provincial Russian, so forgettable and indefinable as to have left no impression by the time he left.

LEDHEAD: He's...quite sympathetic to the plight. He understands my views.

LIMONOV: You *have* no views. If you have views they're *my* views.

LEDHEAD: Is that really how you feel, sir?

LIMONOV: I'm in the dustpan. Look at me—I'm old, I'm senile.

LEDHEAD: Lapdukk was a victory. It showed Russia there was hope, that there's heroes—

No Weapon Formed Against You

LIMONOV: It was a tragedy—strangled in its cradle by worshippers of mediocrity. Mediocrity everywhere. And now, at last, I've joined them.

LEDHEAD: They will remember you, sir. They'll make movies about you. Russian movies, American movies. They will write books about you, plays about you—

LIMONOV: I don't *want* books and plays. I want power.

LEDHEAD: There's not a person who won't know of your heroism.

LIMONOV: Give me the FSB at least. Give me director-in-chief.

LEDHEAD: I'm afraid I can't do that, sir.

> In the grand scheme this is my flayings, my poisons. This is my ergot in your grain. This is my dancing plagues, my temptation in the beasts of the Earth. This is my Word and testament.

LIMONOV: You midget, wearing the wig of an Atlas.

LEDHEAD: When Yeltsin handed me his resignation I thought only of what you'd say. I thought you'd be happy. It's done, sir.

> Limonov eventually left the Chateau de Silling, with presents and tears from locals, and was escorted into the new New Russia much more elegantly and comfortably than he had left the old one. He made a tour of the cities, which made little new impression on him. The new state provided the revolutionary with a whole court of helpers. One of these helpers Limonov tasked with travelling all over the gargantuan nation in order to find him a suitable new plot of land. He settled on an imperial dacha three hours outside Saint Petersburg.
>
> There is no city named after Limonov. No river. There is, however, a Limonovskaya Street situated between Nevskaya and Belaya in central Moscow. There is one such street in Volgograd. There's one named after Lapdukk. There is an academy and an institute of sciences built in honour of him and countless parks the country over that bear his name. The Central Museum is dedicated to the Seizure and is adorned with a mosaic depicting Limonov and his cataphracts. The

Carbon Pages

village of Lapdukk was purchased from the Kazakh government for a sum of eight million. It was frozen in time and made an attraction for pilgrims, historians, and pensioners. There is a nuclear warhead bearing his name as well as an icebreaker.

The state purchased the rights to Limonov's bibliography and published four hundred copies of *Ours Was a Great Epoch*, leatherbound and handwritten and costing fifty thousand for the production of a single copy. A production company was assembled, part state owned and part private, and dedicated itself to making films, shows, operas and even ballets from the Limonov books, except *It's Me Eddie*.

The national anthem was changed to an unused anthem Limonov had come up with during the Regenstvo, albeit with a few words changed to make it slightly less violent. The president's overhauls were a breath of fresh air for the population, and if they respected Ledhead, who of course no longer went by that moniker, then they worshipped Limonov. Every year, a parade is held beginning in the Red Square called the Limonov Parade, which is held on Rebel's Day, doubling as a show of the military strength which the state's predecessors had so scorned. It is broadcast worldwide. By coincidence or otherwise, many of the people who had known Eduard throughout his ornate life had found themselves at one point or another at one of these parades. Olivier Rubinstein of Paris attended the spectacle, Viktoria, the workman who replaced Eagle Nest's locks, the automobile mogul he had once served as valet, Ledhead of course, and even the delicate Countess de Lisse. Limonov himself attended them all without fail and invariably made a long ghostwritten speech about the greatness of patriotism. After a few parades, he'd fulfill his obligatory appearance and retire for home before the procession started.

The plot of three hundred acres was renovated to his exact wishes by the greatest architects and builders in the world. In the beginning there only stood a humble hunter's cabin with a collapsed roof. Limonov fixed that roof and cut down the surrounding pinewood by the lake and around the shabby cabin had a Benedictine cloister built with the cabin remaining as a monument—to what, Limonov never explained. He'd grown a habit of imbuing everything with a

No Weapon Formed Against You

secret apocalypticism. Once a season he'd leave inside a bowl of fresh fruit as an offering to an invented tenth muse whom he called Mycaeliana.

The Kremlin invariably kept in the loop the Poet Father, a term they now called him which Limonov thought was semantically gauche. More and more at his home rather than in the city, Limonov would receive a deputat or parliamentarian to inform about the state's latest decision, latest little landgrab, and the visitor would inevitably return to Moscow that day with a treatise detailing the exact plan of action to take, the precise precautions, and chastising the tiniest deviation as the thinking of knuckle draggers and even suggesting personnel for leading roles who no longer wanted anything to do with the government. Sometimes, though rarely, Ledhead himself paid a visit.

LIMONOV: ...Sometimes I feel you're only pacifying the Left and the Right when in fact you should be mobilizing them! There's a lot of work to be done! Here's what I think...

The complex's staff had long since gotten used to the schema: Limonov wheedles for a bigger role, Ledhead makes faint promises, Limonov pushes too far and when he predictably refuses, Limonov calls him names and epithets which could only have been pre-conceived. One such argument involved Alexander Dugin, who in the years since the Seizure had become an *eminence gris*—the brain of the Kremlin and a sought-after advisor of half the state's cabinet, though he lived a private life, and the public did not know of his existence.

LIMONOV: I realize now—he's a parasite. He survives to drink a vertebrate. First it was me. Now he's exploited you like he has me and he'll move on to whoever else he can draw blood from in due time. But he underestimated us. So let's gut the rat, before he can scurry.

LEDHEAD: I'm sorry, Eduard—I can't do that.

These kinds of talks repeated countless times. A common complaint was that the president was not extreme enough, that he toed the line and lacked a conceptual imagination.

Carbon Pages

LEDHEAD: Sometimes I think you consider yourself as not loved. As forgotten. Even when the vast majority of Russians, and the chief of government and the executive branch are continually bending backwards to gratify you and your every absurd request.

At some point the visits became mailed memos, and soon stopped completely. Nonetheless, the former NazBol continued to harbour a deep respect for the poet's past. And though there were detractors who would have liked to see the geriatric disposed of he continued to gratify his every request.

Limonov called his new complex Ak-Greucid, a name with no origin and referencing nothing. It became the poet's obsession to make Ak-Greucid the eighth wonder of the world. He insisted he needed a shooting range, a tiltyard, then an airstrip, then a catacomb, then a labyrinth of polychrome marble and an amphitheatre. He amassed his palace with artefacts and mementos from all over the world: the pistol of French coup specialist Bob Denard, the saber used by Baron Von Ungern on his campaigns, a cabaret dress worn by Edith Piaf, his very own death mask which he hung over a gesso artwork—after Lapdukk he lived on only through the dead. He created rooms with specific themes: The Room of Shiver, The Room of Water. The themes had seemingly no link to the artefacts which populated them. He fixated on refinement of odour as an aesthetic device, using a combination of scents to make each room's entrance conjure specific psychological connotations. The Room of Ambivalence had him for weeks trying to evoke the scent of a mother's womb in combination with breast milk. Hypnotized by the possibilities, Limonov shrank into smaller and smaller aesthetic preoccupations, until inevitably he would have a breakdown over the alloy mix of a cellar's door hinge and lock himself away for a week like he did in Lapdukk. Unlike Lapdukk, his only victims were his closest servants and an occasional guest.

In the local town there were rumours of his nightly drug-fueled orgies. In fact, he never touched so much as a cigarette. He was cautious of opening his doors to old friends because he wanted to avoid, when they saw what had become of their sparring partner, their inevitable expression of shock and compassion. On the other hand, age had granted him a generosity. On the occasion that he deigned to invite such a

No Weapon Formed Against You

compatriot or old mistress, he'd invariably discover that they were behind on a hotel bill, and he'd settle it out of his pocket immediately. The local town hotel became well known for housing guests to Ak-Greucid.

One day a gardner saw nine girls come and go in a single day. Limonov enjoyed romancing them, composing poetry, and they in turn enjoyed the company of a cultural icon. But his voice creaked. Who was a Don Juan was now a senile erotomaniac.

LIMONOV: See this stuffed horse whom I rode into Lapdukk, and see these urns—one contains the soil of The Arméd City, and the other of my hometown Kharkiv.

His second favourite way to spend time with women was pointing out one of the hundreds of mottos which engraved Ak-Greucid, asking what she thinks it means, and then explaining it. One time, he was translating to a girl *clausura silentium,* when his servant frightened her with a 10ft statue of himself which Limonov wanted to have placed over his grave on the day of his death. He looked the likeness over for a minute, turned to his girl, back to the statue and said simply:

LIMONOV: It's a bit hunched, isn't it?

One day Limonov learnt that Igor Letov had died from a heart condition, said to have developed in the early 1980s. Without hesitation Limonov demanded that a state funeral be provided, but he received no reply. After three days of silence Limonov wrote to the President of Russia, threatening him in a hand delivered letter. What exactly the letter to the President contained no one knew or knows, but after that Ledhead acquiesced. He did not attend. Alexander Dugin did. A crucifix he placed at the coffin and as he did noticed Eduard from across the crowd. They had not spoken since the house arrest. Al gave a nod of the head. And a sheepish smile. Eduard averted his eyes.

In a short time, Limonov had aged two decades. His eyesight began deteriorating, and his hearing too. His leg never recovered to its former state and he walked with a limp. It was always worse after sitting, becoming stiffer, and making him need to sit down. One time Eduard wrote a letter of this kind to Ledhead:

LIMONOV: Isn't it time for a truly brilliant campaign? I don't mean one of your skirmishes, but a conquest. Let me take responsibility so that the Kremlin isn't jeopardized. Let me fulfill the only fate honourable for a warrior. Let me die.

Always in his mind rattled that quote from a paper that insisted that fate had named him Prince of Youth. O Prince of Youth, accept this title which is yours and bear it till the hour of your death.

Many of his original followers who still remembered Eagle's Nest had become artists, musicians or rich. Some ended up in prison. Some fled the country out of fear. Some had accepted Ledhead as a saviour while at the same time secretly cajoling Limonov with all the ways the king killer had wronged him and how, if he were to mount an insurrection, perhaps a democratic one, by God they'd be behind him tooth and nail.

I'm reminded of one who would later write:

On one occasion I visited his palace of entropy. I found it very macabre, but the sight of my mentor made me happy as it did in the old days, and I think he too was happiest he'd been in a long time. He looked older than he did in the brochures. I scorned and complained about Ledhead, but he didn't share the sentiment, at least not to me. We had tea and chocolate, and he talked about everything from his childhood to his current days.

Did he recognize in my endless probing that I was amassing a biography of the veteran? Did his worldly intuition hint to him that I was writing his last memoir, including its penultimate chapter? Did he feel I was spinning the same cotton candy promised him by his antipode? I cannot say. Whatever the case, he looked at my legal pad on the table before me, and without hesitation took it and on the cover wrote: To my comrade and friend Zygote, whose sharpness and astuteness has never failed. Eduard.

As for Alexander Dugin, he married the lady in bondi blue, and she bore him a child. Some time after her birth, he

No Weapon Formed Against You

travelled to the Arctic Circle, where a cutting in the ice sheet had been prepared for him in the shape of a gargantuan crucifix, and he kneeled and flooded the child in the Arctic water one two three times, in a protective ablution whose power would last for decennia.

Since it all, so much time has passed. And though I will never be in such straits as to lack any evil at all, I still think of those times, especially the freckled youth of the kids who would dance for me, sing for me, promise me bounteous deeds. I still yearn, as I've yearned before, for the hopes that possessed me of a great evil overtaking the crust of the Earth which seemed immutable and dogged, that today stumbles over my porch drunkenly—scarcely—before excusing itself again and crossing every threshold, din, and door on the street, according to no whim or sense at all. Who knows what possesses them now—I am neither invited nor refused.

The End.

Boring and Broke in Buenos Aires

Boring and Broke in Buenos Aries

> A café in Argentina. A café in Buenos Aires. The terrace of Café Dorrego on a hot sunny morning and in the parasoled shade sat three men whose names and seats went like this; Arturo, Leopold, and Parker. Two thirds of the present party had only just gotten up.

LEOPOLD: The place with the bells.

PARKER: Not feeling it. Tortoni?

LEOPOLD: You're always saying to check out the bell place so why don't we go.

PARKER: I don't know.

LEOPOLD: Let's go whoring.

PARKER: Eh.

LEOPOLD: Not *immediately*. Post-lunch? You can write those lists any time.

PARKER: (anxiously)
I've been this morning. Uh—with Tan. Night's not over for me he says. And, y'know—I say no, no, I've got my wordcount. He drags me into it anyway Tan does. Why? You're going? I wanted to get some work in today.

LEOPOLD: ...

PARKER: ...

LEOPOLD: You're always working.

ARTURO: (*to Leopold and Parker*) Did you know beetles make up 25 percent of all animals on earth?

PARKER: Think I heard that.

> A moment of silence.

LEOPOLD: The Palermo spot with the bookshelves?

> Leopold smoked a Marlboro fitted in one of those reusable filters which you see in pictures of Hunter Thompson, the cheapo ones which you're meant to clean after ten uses but which Leopold had forgotten to clean every day for the past

>8 months. He'd tap that filthy stump in his empty cup of doppio in the shade.

PARKER: Eh, it's a walk. Artie whaddaya think?

ARTURO: About what?

PARKER: Don't you listen? What do you think we should do?

ARTURO: Why we gotta do something—

DEL: Parker? Parker, it's you.

PARKER: Del? It's me.

> Del came from behind. He had a musketeer moustache and beard and slick hair and wherever he went he wore Chelsea boots and spoke with a redneck twang.

DEL: I'm waitin' for someone. Fuckin—probably showed up wrong place. ACHOO!

PARKER: Sit here.

DEL: Yeah yea.

PARKER: Steal a chair.

DEL: Didn't you leave?

PARKER: Nope.

DEL: No shit. You can't believe anything people say. You have to believe the exact opposite.

PARKER: This is Leopold. And this is Arturo.

LEOPOLD: Howzit.

DEL: Howdy.

LEOPOLD: Have I seen you in San Telmo before? You go Caballo?

DEL: Naw I don't go Caballo. I don't drink.

> Parker sipped a cup cortado, which is espresso cut with warm milk. A cortado coffee then cost 95 cents, and an alfajor

Boring and Broke in Buenos Aries

another 40. An alfajor was a type of biscuit with a chewy honey filling.

PARKER: How's your dystopia coming along? Del's writing a dystopia.

DEL: Haven't started it yet.

PARKER: You've been talking it up for months.

DEL: I'm waiting for an epigraph to come to me. A good epigraph.

PARKER: A good epigraph.

DEL: I ain't startin jack without a good one.

PARKER: Arturo writes as well.

DEL: (*ignoring*) I'm doin research too. Each day I live in a dystopia. You ever look the freaks walkin around? Shit, every day it's more like the Mall of America. Did you ever see stuff as a kid like movies, video games, a toy, and think how did they even make this or think "if i had to be the one to make this it would be so shitty". It's like everything is made by a guy like that now. A guy who was like fuck I hope I don't have to be in charge of this I have no idea what I'm doing.

LEOPOLD: I have thought it.

DEL: Yeah.

LEOPOLD: With ships.

DEL: Now imagine they put *you* in charge of rebuilding every ship in that port.

> A moment of silence.
>
> There was all the more reason to sit at the spot across the boulevard which the tertulia envied for its better shade, but they never gave in to their impulses, due to an incident which occurred there to an American.

LEOPOLD: I've been thinking about this for a long time and I've come to a decision: Today at Manjares I'll order the hot coliflor picante.

PARKER: Yeah?

Carbon Pages

>   Parker looked at Del. He was glancing about himself frantically.

LEOPOLD: It's been eyeing me and I've been too shy to order it. Well no more.

PARKER: None for me. I came here to get AWAY from the hot food.

ARTURO: Nigga you come to Latin America to get away from hot food?

PARKER: Artie, you haven't been to Thailand. They put that chili oil on everything.

DEL: The Thai like spicy food because they're the last bearers of the Faustian spirit.

LEOPOLD: How do you mean?

DEL: The cultivation of hotter and hotter spices? It's a restless exploration in infinity. To the point of suicide.

LEOPOLD: I follow.

DEL: Beyond suicide. Whole point of the scoville scale is the white man's attempt to kill himself through cataloging reality.

PARKER: Hm. I don't know. I think spices, and I like a little spice, mind you, everything in moderation, but uh spices are basically swarthy. Used to cover up *uncouth* ingredients.

LEOPOLD: The talk of someone who eats at Guebara.

PARKER: What can I say, it's close by.

DEL: They'll cut the hills to fill the valleys, and spice'll be the first to go. Society of crusty white women.

LEOPOLD: It's almost funny how everything is getting worse. I went back to my hometown last February for my sister's wedding. My hometown. I wasn't gone for long by the way, but every. single. streetlight is replaced by these LEDs. Bright white LEDS. I mean it's gross. I had to sleep with the curtains shut — my own bed.

DEL: Yeah, it's disgusting.

Boring and Broke in Buenos Aries

LEOPOLD: And I *know* they have the ability to tint them orange, right? Make them feel like the old sodiums. It's not some hard thing. Pretty obvious why they *don't*, right?

DEL: Well — no, that's not what I'm saying exactly.

LEOPOLD: They're not Faustian.

DEL: Of course LEDs are Faustian, dude.

LEOPOLD: Yeah right, they're totally uninspiring. Putrid.

DEL: Yeah they're putrid, they're still Faustian.

LEOPOLD: They're not. Part of it is the illumination. It leaves nothing to the imagination. Only a society totally bereft of an archetypal spirit could—

DEL: You're arguing my point. Parker, he's arguing my point — if they cranked em to a MILLION watts they'd be *more* Faustian.

LEOPOLD: Sodiums are *decidedly* more Faustian.

DEL: Shut up. Just shut up. You're pissing me off. LEDs cover the whole sky — they're totally in line with the pursuit of infinity. Shit, it's phallic. Parker, Where do you find these retards?

PARKER: (*amused*) I don't know.

DEL: They'll put me six feet under.

ARTURO: Six Seven? Holy shit where?!

PARKER: Arturo's a very good writer.

LEOPOLD: Yeah.

PARKER: Seriously, that thing with the blacksmith. I couldn't sleep all night, thinking. I ask him *why did the blacksmith impregnate the snake-devil* I still can't get a word out of him.

LEOPOLD: Look at him. Mention his writing and he shuts up.

DEL: What is this — a novel?

ARTURO: I don't have a novel—

Carbon Pages

LEOPOLD: A periodical. Kid's got it all figured out. He actually *pins* the thing — it's like this big broadsheet — sticks it on notice boards around town. Only kid who draws circus crowds to a corkboard. I've seen it myself!

> Praise was the only surefire way to make Arturo feel like he was in his undies.

ARTURO: (*uneasy*) No that experiment's over.

LEOPOLD: The noticeboards are done?

PARKER: He's pivoted. So basically he—well *you* tell him.

ARTURO: I print a bunch of copies each issue, and go to businesses in the barrios—

LEOPOLD: —Oh right, you told me—

ARTURO: —like pawn shops, bars, uh I've got a butchery, a whole list of places. They offer copies, and for every issue they move get a cut of the profit.

PARKER: This is what happens when you teach a Venezuelan to read!

DEL: (*to Arturo*) You make any money that way?

ARTURO: Uh, a little. But printing takes a lot. It's in colour so—

LEOPOLD: —And he's putting out a novel. Which reminds me; (*removes hat*) we're making collections.

DEL: For what?

LEOPOLD: For Arturo.

DEL: Why?

LEOPOLD: It's a fund so he has time to write.

PARKER: It's true, he scabbed Agnes yesterday. You know Agnes—?

LEOPOLD: —How can a man create a masterpiece if he's slaving away to make ends meet?

> The Englishman capitulated.

Boring and Broke in Buenos Aries

PARKER: Okay, fine...
Dollars okay?

LEOPOLD: Thank you.

> Arturo said nothing. Quite shy.

PARKER: But I would not do it for anyone else.

LEOPOLD: Those who can't do, donate.

DEL: No way.

LEOPOLD: C'mon. What's that you got? Twenty thousand? It'll be worth ten next week.

DEL: Beat it.

LEOPOLD: Well easy is as easy does — I should head on. I have a guy waiting — I promised to set him up with Scottish disability in exchange for kava.

ARTURO: Aright dawgs Ima skidaddle too.

PARKER: We just sat down!

ARTURO: I gotta check on the produce.

> And Arturo was gone.

LEOPOLD: He reminds me of a Persian I met at a sauna party. Big hairy dude. I'm sipping on milk tart moonshine out of a starbucks cup and he comes up and I have to tell him look buddy I don't swing that way. He says to me me neither this ass toy is just for show. The bubble bath here is just that good.

DEL: (*to Parker*) Man, Parker. I'm just waiting for my — uh — a friend. I didn't know you'd sit me next to this fuckin degenerate.

PARKER: What do you even do, Del? You have all this money, but you never say what you do.

DEL: What I do?

PARKER: Yes.

Carbon Pages

DEL: I— look. It don't matter. ACHOO!

PARKER: I'm curious.

DEL: I'm a writer.

PARKER: But you've written nothing.

DEL: I've— I don't have to write to be a writer.

> When he spoke he looked like a handsome Texas ranger.

PARKER: But how do you make your money? Crypto?

DEL: Yeah. Crypto.

PARKER: Crypto?

DEL: Yea. (facetiously) Now— Every morning I ask the holy spirit what shitcoin to invest my savings in. When you yield to the Lord you receive grace, and you'll be astonished at the fruits of your labour.

> Leopold laughed, and then Parker.

DEL: What — you think that's funny? All you people think about is money.

LEOPOLD: Got me there.

DEL: I've been thinking. In order to achieve a satisfactorily happy life—

> Del pronounced it as satis-fac-TOR-ily.

DEL: —A satisfactorily happy life, all I need are four requirements; Number one, a life in and of Christ. This is self-explanatory. Number two, to never step foot in that goddamn shithole country ever again. ACHOO! Fuckin cold. Number three to marry a Good childbride—

PARKER: —We've been over this. You're just not the kind of man a girl would go for.

DEL: Someone who only cares about looks or status? ACHOO! Yeah. Looks are transient. I don't care about looks. Kindness. Generosity. That goes a long goddamn way.

Boring and Broke in Buenos Aries

LEOPOLD: You're... kidding right?

DEL: Women look haggard by twenty anyway— Kidding what? Twenty-one? You ever see a twenty-one year old who ain't a hag?

LEOPOLD: You must be joking. Parker, is he joking?

DEL: No, I'm not joking — *Parker*. I'm gonna marry a fourteen year old virgin.

LEOPOLD: That's — just —

DEL: What?

LEOPOLD: You're talking about *children*.

DEL: Ain't all women children.

LEOPOLD: That's...rape.

> Out over the San Telmo boulevard, from a chambre de bonne you could hear cumbia rap. It echoed round the walls, and on the cobblestone spiraled in the little twisters of dried leaves and dust and wrappers.

DEL: Don't all women get raped sooner or later. More and more, sooner... Hell, the trouble is finding her. Somehow all these other freaks got no problem.

LEOPOLD: Man you're *fucked up*.

DEL: Fuck you, man. YOU are depraved.

LEOPOLD: What you're talking about — I can't even...comprehend—

DEL: It ain't my fault is it? This crazy world only way you can get a normal girl is by snagging 'em young.

LEOPOLD: I can't be seen around this guy.

PARKER: Del can you please—

LEOPOLD: (standing up)
Marquis, Kley before I get outta here — make a donation will you.

> They were on the terrace. There was something miserable about Kley today and the other one stuck close by him, as if

he might have to jump to action of some sort. The two together reminded Leopold of a gargantuan in chains.

MARQUIS: To who or what?

LEOPOLD: The Arturo Protection Account. Kid needs to eat.

MARQUIS: Ah ouais. Good afternoon. I did purchase one of his journals from that uh bookie I think. Is he here?

PARKER: Just left.

MARQUIS: (*giving cash*) It shows a lot of promise.

LEOPOLD: And Kley? How about it (*shaking hat*)

                Kley gave money.

LEOPOLD: I always did think you were a generous man, Kley.

DEL: Fuck it. Bring it over. C'mon c'mon. Bring the hat over. What's your name? Leopold? Yeah like that.

                And Del drew out his wallet.

DEL: Ten, twenty, thirty, forty. That enough?

LEOPOLD: It's—

DEL: Fiddy, sixty thousand. Here—take it—the hell do I need it I don't need it.

MARQUIS: Wait, please. Leopold?

LEOPOLD: What?

MARQUIS: He just put in his entire wallet.

LEOPOLD: Who?

MARQUIS: Kley! Please. Remove it.

LEOPOLD: (*leaving*) I am only a neutral watcher in these lands.

KLEY: It makes no difference to me.

MARQUIS: Why not, Kley?

Boring and Broke in Buenos Aries

KLEY: Because I won't be needing it where I'm going.

MARQUIS: Do not be silly please.

PARKER: What's wrong?

MARQUIS: He misplaced his manuscript.

PARKER: You lost it?

MARQUIS: He *misplaced* it.

PARKER: Isn't that the whole point of writing on paper that you can't—...How?

KLEY: It's gone...it's over...

DEL: A book?

MARQUIS: It's the notes for a game.

> Kley sat down and then immediately leapt out and Marquis and Parker arrested him.

PARKER: Mate I'm sure it'll come up somewhere, things always do.

MARQUIS: I've been saying him this.

KLEY: It's been gone since Thursday. I haven't slept.
Tonight, I will kill myself.

PARKER: Hold on. Just— Where did you last see it?

KLEY: At...at...

MARQUIS: He was at Caballo before rush.

KLEY: I was at Caballo, I come home and I realize I don't got the papers on me.

PARKER: The waiter must have it.

KLEY: I run down there all sweaty, I'm only upstairs, and it's not there. My table's cleared and it's not there.

PARKER: The waiter must have it, Kley.

KLEY: He does not.

PARKER: Maybe somewhere else...Did you go Guebara that night?

Carbon Pages

KLEY: No.

PARKER: What about Britanico? Were you at Britanico?

KLEY: Britanico? Maybe…I don't really…I don't remember. I took some klonopin.

PARKER: Well there you go! You're at that ~~dump~~ joint all the time.

KLEY: I don't know.

PARKER: Don't kill yourself, Kley. I'll find that manuscript in no time. Only my Spanish isn't so good.

MARQUIS: I'll come with you.

PARKER: I said I'd get some work done today but what the hell…

> As the Englishman and the Frenchman traversed the Plata, Arturo made the rounds to his reluctant proprietors. His first stop; a Villa Lugano pawn shop.
>
> The shop was an art gallery—like gems in jewels the walls fitted with bric-a-brac of every ornament. Power drills, speakers, sneakers, acoustics and electrics, katanas, paintings, autographs, bongos, monos, comics, wallets, air friers, gasogenes, soccer shirts. Junk. Silver bombillas and enameled mates, Red Dead Redemption II for PS4, a Lightning McQueen TV, Mafalda figurines. Glass vitrines of chains, earrings, toe rings, and ankle bracelets. Studs, hoops, cuffs, and buckles. Bricks and buttons. Rolexes, Breitlings and Hello Kitties. Dogtags. Sterling and plated, platinum and plastic. All this double packed in half the room.
>
> But, before I can tell you what happened at a Villa Lugano pawn shop, I must first relay what happened on its threshold, right outside. Outside the shop haunted a bearded bum, dressed in a once fine business suit—now stained and torn. Apropos of *eye contact* you'd notice his round face was forever pink and almost all his teeth had disappeared. In the case of *looking down*, you'd see his right calf from ankle to knee was swollen like a water balloon and it stretched the navy linen to such a brink that the pant fused to almost become grafted with the leg. There was no going around Boris.

Boring and Broke in Buenos Aries

BORIS: No man. No man. Pod no man. No man. Don't forget. Chiz-ti no man. Don't forget. Don't forget.

He spoke in a heavy Russian accent.

ARTURO: Who—me?

BORIS: Ti. Ti. Don't forget. No man. Bruce?

ARTURO: No, my name is Arturo.

BORIS: I smell the air. I tell the weather. Don't forget.

ARTURO: You tell the weather?

BORIS: Clean Bruce—Bruce no man. Nauman. Klin Nauman.

ARTURO: I'm sorry, but I don't know anyone named Bruce.

BORIS: ArgH! Syelo. Three-Oh-Three aerospace protectant. No, man. Syelo. Syelo osvobozhdino. Osvobozhdino. Slava Ukraini.

ARTURO: Well, sir. Have a good day.

BORIS: No man, the karthaun. The thundering karthaun. Thunder and Nauman. The weather will not change.

ARTURO: The weather won't change?

BORIS: The weather WILL not change. Use Three-Oh-Three aerospace protectant.

ARTURO: I will! Sire, I will!

BORIS: Slava osvoboditilim.

    Boris grabbed a nearby shovel and began to dig dirt.

    Inside, at the empty counter stood that familiar face—Leopold. He wore a white suit over a dark silk shirt unbuttoned and a Panama hat and smoked his filter and leaned waiting over a Stella Dot string.

Boring and Broke in Buenos Aries

Stumble in gently the mestiza girl—short, frizzy hair, a bit mannish and plain awkward. It's all she could do not to trip over her own feet as she exited the store room.

ISABELLA: I'm sorry. There's nothing in the back. Would you maybe like to come back tomorrow in which case I'd—?

LEOPOLD: No, no that's alright.

ISABELLA: It's just such a mess, I try never go in there. So—now—you said three-fifty for this?

LEOPOLD: I was hoping for one of those American Girl dolls. It's for an anniversary. I met her the first night I mixed coke with benzos. I got into the place, I'm told, by trading the bouncer ket. Of course it was only laxatives but by the time he found out we were long gone. So I'm told—honestly I don't remember a thing.

ISABELLA: Wow.

LEOPOLD: One of these days I'm gonna go too far, mark my words.

ISABELLA: Mhm.

LEOPOLD: Have you ever seen a knife fight?

ISABELLA: Me? No.

LEOPOLD: Pray it stays like that. There's no worse way to spend a Tuesday afternoon. Last thing I know I'm facing off an Ecuadorian tranny in one-on-one combat after she mistakes me for her ex.

ISABELLA: That sounds dangerous.

LEOPOLD: You get used to it. If you want, I can take you out sometime?

ISABELLA: That's OK.

LEOPOLD: Well anyway, I hoped I wouldn't leave empty-handed.

ISABELLA: If you want we have these Hummel figurines? I know they're not dolls but maybe your girlfriend—

LEOPOLD: —I tell you what—I don't usually do this...

Carbon Pages

ISABELLA: What?

      Leopold whipped out a cocktail napkin from an inner pocket.

LEOPOLD: Before I do this, I want you to feel it. Go on, go on, take it.

      Isabella took the napkin in her hands awkwardly.

ISABELLA: It's a napkin.

LEOPOLD: I've had issues with fans thinking it's a reprint. See? Now. Watch — I'll only do this once.

      He unsheathed a bic and scribbled a simple cartoon, next to which he signed his name.

LEOPOLD: Now, I'm a fairly renowned musician. Especially back home in Nevada — that is, one of the United States of America. With that said, any such renown does not preclude me from the eventual INFAMY one of my standing will accrue over the course of a lifetime. I wish there was something I could do about that — I value my privacy — but fame has its own mind, its own pulse, understand?
I've already had to renounce most of my possessions to loansharks for this reason. But this I make especially for you. Take a look. The cartoon is incidental really. It's the signature that gives it value. The real deal.

ISABELLA: You're selling this to me?

LEOPOLD: Its value is mooning as we speak. I'd hold onto it. For a few decades at least.

      Silence...

ISABELLA: How much?

LEOPOLD: Seven hundred.

      Silence...

Boring and Broke in Buenos Aries

ISABELLA: Ok...seven hundred.

>They shook on it.

ISABELLA: Just sign these...Señor, estaré con usted en un momento.

>Arturo was gleaming at them, kind of distant, anxious about his own problems.

LEOPOLD: Artie!

ARTURO: Hm? Leopold.

LEOPOLD: Have you been to your butcheries already?

ARTURO: This is one.

LEOPOLD: (*signing*) No kidding. You know I'm prowling the 69 and the Kika for preorders for your book.

ARTURO: What are those?

LEOPOLD: Untz untz type beats. You meet degenerates, but rich degenerates.

ARTURO: Gee, thanks.

LEOPOLD: (*leaving*) They're all waiting on you!

>Artie and the shopkeeper were alone.

ARTURO: You know, you're meant to do a haggle with these guys.

ISABELLA: What do you mean?

ARTURO: You know... he says two-thousand, you say one, he goes one-seventy-five.

ISABELLA: Oh well, I'm sure it's worth what he says it is. He's a famous musician.

ARTURO: Musician?

ISABELLA: He rapped for me. It was very good.

ARTURO: If you say so.

Carbon Pages

ISABELLA: Plus he seemed in a rush — it's rude to quibble.

ARTURO: Hm. Can I see the owner?

ISABELLA: I am the owner.

ARTURO: Really?

ISABELLA: We talked before.

ARTURO: I'm sure I'd remember. I thought a viejo worked here.

ISABELLA: That was my padre. He owned the store before he passed.

ARTURO: Oh, sorry…
I have a magazine you're selling. For every item sold you offer an issue, see. Then you get a share of the profit—

ISABELLA: Yes, I know. I've sold a few of them actually. A good few.

ARTURO: Am I being rude?

ISABELLA: No!

ARTURO: How many customers does a pawn shop get per day?

ISABELLA: Twenty? No. Thirty — maybe. It's a lot of work, actually. I—I get rough types. And, I have to do everything by myself. The books — it's a lot. On top of everything I've to take care of my madre. She gets migraines.

ARTURO: My name is Arturo.

ISABELLA: I know. We talked…
I'm Isabella.

>   Arturo took his phone and jotted down some words.

ARTURO: "Arturo and Isabella".

ISABELLA: So you know that man?

ARTURO: Who?

ISABELLA: Leopold in the white hat.

Boring and Broke in Buenos Aries

ARTURO: (*absently*) Oh sure, every day at Café Dorrego. I can't tell when he's telling the truth anymore. You go Dorrego?

ISABELLA: No, it's...a lot of digital nomads. Do you like them?

ARTURO: They can be fun.

ISABELLA: Is it true Frank Johnston goes there?

ARTURO: Sure, I know him.

ISABELLA: Maybe you could introduce us?

> In reality of course, Isabella no longer had any interest in anyOne or anyThing but the attention of the young intellectual in front of her.

ARTURO: (*staccato*) Well you know — *I'm* writing a book too.

ISABELLA: What's it about?

ARTURO: A fisherman and his wife.

ISABELLA: That sounds interesting!

ARTURO: No, it doesn't.

ISABELLA: No.

ARTURO: It's sad. Though it's not so sad at the moment. The way it's going. It's a disaster... I mean — PREORDERS? I haven't worked it for weeks.

(hopeless)
What are they preordering, Isabella?

ISABELLA: I read your magazine, you know. I really — I mean — you probably get it a lot — but — I really enjoyed it. I took it home — actually — and read it. I'm sure your novel will be even better.

ARTURO: It's more of a prosimetrum. You know, I've read two books in my life — *The Bible* and *Don Quixote*. This one... I'm not sure I even want to finish it.

ISABELLA: Why not? You've done so well with your magazine.

Carbon Pages

ARTURO: Zine I printed myself. Anyone can do that. I've been thinking. I print the book myself and it ends up same dumpster truck as *all* those books. It doesn't deserve that. I wish I could get a real publisher.

ISABELLA: Why don't you?

ARTURO: No agent will look at it. It's not "socially relevant". Not that I can afford any of that.
It's just not in my blood, the hustle. Johnston, Leopold — they could make money in a dentist waiting room. But all that stuff that comes with publishing a book makes me gouge my eyes out.

ISABELLA: I think something that's beautiful will always be noticed.

ARTURO: I can't even use a printer. If only I could find someone willing to take care of all this stuff. I had one girl type the manuscript, but a week in she threw the pages out her window and disappeared. (*remorsefully*) If she had at least given me her number I could pay her—

ISABELLA: —I'll do it!

ARTURO: What?

ISABELLA: I mean why not? Why doesn't the shop publish ... what's it called again?

ARTURO: Mendiga de Plata.

ISABELLA: Mendiga de Plata. Published by Empeños Dorado.

ARTURO: Don't joke with me please.
(*clutching heart*)
I have this condition—

ISABELLA: I'm not joking! You're acting like I don't know a printer for Penguin in Charrua.

ARTURO: You do?

ISABELLA: And like he's not a gambler. Who pawns his wife's jewelry every week.

ARTURO: He does?

Boring and Broke in Buenos Aries

ISABELLA: He does!

ARTURO: (*overjoyed*) I can't believe what I'm hearing...You'll really publish my prosimetrum?

ISABELLA: You won't have to worry about a thing.

ARTURO: You make me so happy.

> Isabella blushed.

ARTURO: I'll be here tomorrow with the first chapter. After lunch. No — before.

ISABELLA: I'll be waiting!

ARTURO: (*can't wait*) We'll decide on the colours. I'll finish that chapter today. And then once we're together — don't start without me! — We'll —

ISABELLA: Everyone will hear of it!

ARTURO: (*rapturous*) Just don't start without me!

> History of a publication as told by a charlatan.

PARKER: ...It must've been Hirschfelder. Or maybe Tan. Remember Tan? At El Limon?

MARQUIS: Oh yes. With the corduroy pants.

PARKER: The one who learnt Mandarin so he could be more efficiently racist.

MARQUIS: That's right.

PARKER: He has it for certain. I'm never getting it back. There's this great passage. It's mostly rambling — most of the book he's being this pretentious kind of shit on the wall, um, but he mentions this movie. It's an 80s highschool movie — High Times at Ridgemond High or one of those. There's this scene. The main guy has a crush on Jennifer Connolly he does, prime Jennifer Connolly, and he sees her bathing in her bikini from his bathroom window with a pirate costume around his ankles. And she's so sexy, she's at the pool, and he starts wanking to her and then *he turns around and wanks with his eyes shut.*

Carbon Pages

MARQUIS: What's so weird about this?

PARKER: Why wouldn't he keep staring at her if he's wanking?

MARQUIS: This character is in a bathroom?

PARKER: Yes

MARQUIS: Looking through a window at Jennifer Connolly?

PARKER: Naked.

MARQUIS: Maybe he doesn't want to get caught.

PARKER: No the window is tiny.

MARQUIS: (*as if answering a hypothetical*) Then I would keep staring at her.

PARKER: What kind of imagination does that bloke have that overpowers prime Jennifer Connolly in a bikini, I want to know.

MARQUIS: And I suppose it's not some quirk of the, how you say, parent's guide?

PARKER: The ratings and all that? No, no. I think this is just how people were back then. Our generation still has some semblance of normality. But the kids growing up now. Arturo, say. To them that scene is totally nonsensical. Like it was made by an alien. No one would ever *turn away* from the source of their horniness.

MARQUIS: We are the last sane generation.

PARKER: I mean, when was the last time you even closed your eyes? Imagination is so outdated it's deviant. You can meet a hobo masturbating on the metro. Or you can meet a hobo masturbating with his eyes shut. But only one of them is a psycho.
This way, I think.

MARQUIS: You should come to Caballo after this. I'm free all day.

PARKER: Eh I don't know.

MARQUIS: Walking with your girlfriend?

PARKER: I don't have a girlfriend.

Boring and Broke in Buenos Aries

MARQUIS: Arturo said you were with a woman at Guebara. Argentinian woman.

PARKER: I don't know...

MARQUIS: Beginning with H.

PARKER: (*seeing the cover is blown*) Helena. I didn't even think of her immediately.

MARQUIS: Days of being a bachelor are over, hm?

PARKER: Please, it's nothing serious...Who told you? Arturo? Hm.

MARQUIS: Well bonne chance.

PARKER: It's not so cracked up. Barely got in there and I'm already being treated like a son-in-law. Just this morning: I'm about to go down on her and her mother calls me to fetch constipation pills...
I was planning on writing that morning. I didn't even want to "do anything" with her, Helena! I'm ignoring her all morning, staring at this blank screen but she's a certifiable succubus and I capitulate. Total loss of dignity by the way! And then I don't even get the satisfaction of what I sold out for.

MARQUIS: What are you writing?

PARKER: A Noir. It's set in the future, in this cyberpunk city. And we follow a hardboiled cop who's down on his luck until he's arrested and brought to his old drinking buddy who's now this mega-corpo with his own police force. Anyway, he says to him he won't put him away as long as he finds this hacker who's been messing with the corpo's plans. The only problem is this hacker has facial oscillation tech, are you with me, tech which allows him to change appearance instantly. Our hero is caught up in a mystery which takes him to the grimy depths of society and upends his whole worldview it does.

MARQUIS: You know, I very enjoyed parts of *STARSHIP: Genesis*.

PARKER: That's not what you said when you read it.

MARQUIS: I've been working on a play myself.

> He was tall as a twig. Invariably, Marquis dressed up — when Parker put on clothes. Pinstripe pants and sweater vest and brogues in a style pretty close to that whole Dark Academia

thing. Those Victorian glasses on his eagled nose. He had neatly combed hair, and ratlike features, or maybe catlike. Depends who you ask.

The name Marquis when misspoken with a "kiss" conjured in certain people a connection to the noise a cat makes which, rather than pskpsk, is closer to "ksskss" in other languages which altered the man's physiognomy significantly. In any case, it was easy to imagine the Frenchman sprouting whiskers, were he not to shave which he did. Always. Clean like a baby.

PARKER: What's the premise?

MARQUIS: I don't believe in premises.

PARKER: But what's the plot.

MARQUIS: There is no plot.

PARKER: Alright.

MARQUIS: It's an elaboration on Orientalist prose. Byron has a handhold in many ways but his skill is unrefined in aspects I hope to perfect.

PARKER: Mhm.

MARQUIS: Okay the "*premise*" is...It is a dialogue...

PARKER: And where does it take place?

MARQUIS: in the Rub 'Al Kali desert... between a masked traveler and his subordinate guide. I aim to depict his slow realization, that is the subordinate's realization, that his master is in love with God for demonic, indulgent reasons.

PARKER: I'd go see it.

MARQUIS: It's almost finished. Safely locked up. No one will rob it.

PARKER: Under the mattress.

MARQUIS: In my head. Haven't written a word, see?

PARKER: You know Humphrey's convinced that Moby Dick was a psyop?

MARQUIS: Who is this?

Boring and Broke in Buenos Aries

PARKER: He's the professor.

MARQUIS: Oh I dislike him.

PARKER: He hangs about.

MARQUIS: Only time he says anything is to get on my nerves.

PARKER: He spits when he talks. He should keep his jaw shut. Washed up prick.

MARQUIS: I suspect he has his university friends.

PARKER: I suspect, Marquis, he has his university students. He can't be bothered to bang any of them so he takes it out on us.

MARQUIS: One time he calls an Uber for Melman so he can get out of his sight.

PARKER: Melman's a real prick too.

MARQUIS: He looks like a weasel.

PARKER: Ha! Those eyebrows...

MARQUIS: So wait what does Humphrey say about Moby Dick?

PARKER: So, you know, in the cold war you had this big no-no on everything Russian right. McCarthyism it was. But then you have all these American intellectuals reading Dosto and Tolstoy cause they think it's great literature. So the CIA decides to pull out of their ass some obscure tome. Some obscure tome no one's heard of before. No one's heard of it before the 60s. So they parade it around the bloc trying to make it the American answer to War and Peace. And it worked. Pretty sure Moby Dick is still required reading in Russia. Or something.

MARQUIS: He's a prick.

PARKER: Yep.

MARQUIS: He says he'll quit.

PARKER: He'll quit?

MARQUIS: After he writes his saga.

PARKER: Haha yeah he'll write a saga, right after you bench three-fifty.

MARQUIS: (*distracted by passerby*) Of course two-fifty eight is my limit on most days.

Carbon Pages

PARKER: (*unbelieving*) Really?

MARQUIS: Yes.

PARKER: Two-fifty eight. My max is two-thirty.

MARQUIS: I'm very agile. I limbo to eight inches. Et toi?

PARKER: I've never seen you limbo. I've never seen you do anything.

MARQUIS: Come to Jamaicana night at Limon. I'm well known.

PARKER: How're your football skills?

MARQUIS: (*staccato, gotten himself into a hole*) Exceptional — Adorno — do you know Adorno. No? He was a retired traineur who lived in my apartment block as a child. He played with Marradona in the yards as an enfant. In the summer we'd run on the grass, he was a good friend of my mother's and he instilled in me a love for the ball.

PARKER: Oh well you should come round by mine. I toss the ball with the Argie kids. I'd love to see your prowess.

MARQUIS: (*clawing out*) I'm a bit rusty now.

PARKER: Now anyone who benches two forty can't be *that* rusty. They're out there every evening. Today. After we find this thing let's go play.

MARQUIS: I'll have to see — maybe later in the week.

PARKER: Tsk tsk you said you've no plans all day.

MARQUIS: It just doesn't interest me anymore, to tell the truth.

PARKER: What?

MARQUIS: Football — at some point one realizes they achieve such a level that it only serves to humiliate others to play. I love humanity. I'm a humanist first and foremost, that's why I'm a maoist. So it doesn't interest me — to play football.

PARKER: I like it when you talk. (*smugly*)

MARQUIS: And it's undignified, anyway—

Boring and Broke in Buenos Aries

PARKER: (*sarcastic*) Oh I hear you, absolutely. Let's cut through here. I can't see those bakeries.

MARQUIS: —because it's wishy-washy. First you're this then you're that. I could not be like this. If you believe you have a fate you must clench it in your jaw grip it like a woodwork vice.

PARKER: What are you on about?

MARQUIS: I wouldn't say anything but clearly all this time with me you've been so adamant that I'm a writer I'm a writer capital W I'm a struggling artist the world is not ready for me.

PARKER: I never know what you're saying. (laughing) What, because I write I also can't play football with some kids?
Oh er, I think we got turned around hm.

MARQUIS: Personally, when I was in your shoes if I'm a writer I write write. I hole up and I don't come out. I emerge with a beard I'm unrecognizable.

PARKER: You're baiting me.

MARQUIS: Can a man not express his opinion?

PARKER: What appears on the page—word document—is the fruit of the process of living. No one has ever written without *living*...

MARQUIS: Please, Parker you write *science fiction stories*. If they're the fruit then you should be reading boat manuals. I don't know—

PARKER: ...Character. Emotion.

MARQUIS: —quantum studies.

PARKER: Everything I—the football—I go into this world dry and I return with a full tank because the meat of everything that I write makes its way bleeds into the page it's a reflection of me. If I do *nothing*—if I "hole up"—then my *story* will be *nothing*.

MARQUIS: No, and I will tell you why No:
The football kids, it's the same to you as Helena, and that Guebara brawl or whatever. It's the *affect* you really care about. "I was in a drunken brawl and I woke up with a black eye so had a *whiskey* at my *typewriter*".

Carbon Pages

PARKER: Oh *I'M* an affect — look at you — YOU'RE the affect. Why do you dress like this huh huh? You look like you're from nineteen-fifty.

MARQUIS: I understand why you're angry but don't try to insult me it's a duck in water.

PARKER: As if you "hole up", too. Where — at the nail salon?

MARQUIS: I have no friends. I don't smoke. I just read, read, read. That's all I do is read and write.

PARKER: Then it must be shit.

MARQUIS: Shit is the theater you look it is a congerie of uh autofiction, and er suicide warnings. "I'm so interesting I killed myself or was a bullfighter I want to tell everyone".

PARKER: To write about life you must first live it.

MARQUIS: Shakespeare wrote The Tempest he never saw the sea...

This moment even, I am not here I am at home transcribing this into a dialogue. The secretary is here. You're talking to my secretary. When I get home I will nail you like a butterfly to my board.

PARKER: ...

MARQUIS: ...

PARKER: Christ, I know you're gay but must you be such a fag?

MARQUIS: It's my vocation. I haven't had sex in years, I have *canal carpien*, I don't go outside I speak to the shopclerk in a sweat I can't make eye contact.

PARKER: (*well good for you then*) Well I couldn't do that.

MARQUIS: Because this isn't life this is an edifice, reality is what I put on the page because that's Eternal, that's immortality if you want to live forever.

PARKER: Well I care too much about life to live forever.

MARQUIS: That's your choice!

PARKER: Yes, I'm a son, a brother, uh, a boyfriend.

Boring and Broke in Buenos Aries

I don't write for anything like what you mention, but rather because I can't do anything else it's like breathing for me.

MARQUIS: So you're not a writer.

PARKER: (*Tesly*) I'm not a writer.

MARQUIS: And that's wonderful, my Parker, an adventurer is born, you have a word for that. Keep a diary.
Oh it says Britanico is this way.

    And they entered where it was cool.

    Britanico was a lunch-time cafe. Cool, clean, well lit. They put up the glass after that young Venezuelan drove his bike through the fileteado. It was local and small and expats didn't go there, and because expats didn't go there you heard mostly Spanish as working and middle class porteños chatted, wooed, kvetched, cajoled, and drank doppios with medialunas. Some drank an early aperitif.

PARKER: They don't even speak English here. Did you say he checked this place?

MARQUIS: He was here. But Kley doesn't speak Spanish really and he thinks the waiter doesn't like him.

PARKER: He's so paranoid. It's all that medication.

MARQUIS: How a man like that can be a security guard...beyond me.

MARQUIS: (*to the waiter*) *Hola señor...* [My name is Marquis and this is my companion Parker. I would like to inquire if you or any of your colleagues on this fine sailing ship have happened upon a most valuable possession of one of our mutual friends. This friend has lost a collection of papers which are of utmost sentimental value. It is an oeuvre of supreme importance, the gem of his nascent artistic catalog. So please do tell, have you seen it? And if you have could you lay these pages in my hands so I can bequeath them to their noble progenitor?]

    The barista boy wrinkled his nose and spoke:

BARISTA: [I have it.]

Carbon Pages

The barista disappeared out back.

PARKER: (*to Marquis*) What did he say?

MARQUIS: He says he has it.

PARKER: What did you say?

MARQUIS: I asked politely if he had seen my friend's oeuvre which he's very keen on. Waiters like anyone must be treated with respect. Then comes what you want.

PARKER: Well good. Maybe I'll get back in time to put some words down.

MARQUIS: Let's have a fainá.

PARKER: Not hungry yet.

MARQUIS: And by the way yes I agree to read your piece and give you feedback.

PARKER: Oh yeah?

MARQUIS: Yes. You would like this, yes?

> Before Parker could reply the waiter stormed out with a shut briefcase from which white pages peeked.

WAITER: [Now, you have your trash. Now out. Now.]

> The waiter was pissed.

PARKER: Do you know him or something?

MARQUIS: No. [Waiter what is your issue?]

WAITER: Out please!

> Then the portly manager of the cafe burst out from the back, went around the bar and pulled the duo by the scruff and threw them on the street. He yelled in Spanish so that the whole cafe heard and looked at the commotion.

Boring and Broke in Buenos Aries

MANAGER: [And don't come back here again, you sleazy American faggots! If I see you again I will rip your head off and shove it so far up your ass you'll have toes for teeth!]

MARQUIS: Hey! (*brushing himself off*) I am not American! (*to Parker*) What was that?!

PARKER: Long as we got Kley's papers.

MARQUIS: Did you see that there? Do you think he heard me?

PARKER: Who knows *what* goes through their head.

MARQUIS: What is his problem... the nerve of some people! And you know I knew it the moment I walked in. He was scowling at me — when I walked in — before I said a word. Maybe there's something to what Melman says...judging a book by its cover...you know, I never met a person who didn't act exactly like I expected them to.

PARKER: You are a very wet man.

MARQUIS: (*annoyed*) What?

PARKER: With the...clammy hands. Forehead. I bet you get a runny nose when it's cold.

MARQUIS: Now you are trying to make me angry.

PARKER: ...And you forget to pack tissues

MARQUIS: Do you think he misunderstood?

PARKER: ...so you wipe your sleeve when no one's looking.

MARQUIS: I should have *ordered* something first!

PARKER: I'll find Kley.

MARQUIS: Wait, don't forget to send me your book oui?

PARKER: Let me tell you something—

> The briefcase fell open, and the papers scattered over the pavement.

Carbon Pages

MARQUIS: That's the trouble with paper.

PARKER: (*picking up*) Bloody thing... Hold on.

MARQUIS: What?

PARKER: Look at this. These aren't Kley's. They're drawings.

MARQUIS: With the video game...maybe drawings are part of it.

PARKER: (*showing page*) Look at that. LS. Who does this remind you of?

MARQUIS: Leopold?

PARKER: Tosser.

MARQUIS: So...

PARKER: So Kley's papers are still out there.

MARQUIS: It's only...almost four.

PARKER: What now...

MARQUIS: Let's keep looking. I should have taken a fainá. You think Kley goes to Napoles?

PARKER: Napoles? Maybe. Bloody Leopold...

Back at the pawn shop...

ARTURO: (*entering*) Sorry. I wasn't ignoring you.

ISABELLA: (*at counter*) It's okay.

ARTURO: I was so locked in.

ISABELLA: Me too. I tried messaging you but I've been busy too. I've been learning so much about book publishing. We've been getting so many pre-orders like you wouldn't BELIEVE and all night I—

ARTURO: —I have a good idea for what the cover should be. Look at this. I drew it myself. What do you think?

ISABELLA: Wow — you drew this yourself?

Boring and Broke in Buenos Aries

ARTURO: Wait, you tried to message me? What about?

ISABELLA: Well, the launch? That book launch. It's a sure thing, and I'm even working on getting someone from the Herald invited.

ARTURO: The Herald? What's that?

ISABELLA: It's the city newspaper.

ARTURO: Newspaper. You know I don't want you working so hard. I don't want you working yourself this hard.

ISABELLA: Oh it's nothing. It's actually—

ARTURO: I feel bad. You know? You're doing all this work I feel I should be paying you or something.

ISABELLA: You know — it's — hm — exhilarating. I'm exhilarated! All the negotiating—

ARTURO: —Now look. Look at this I think this one we'll use for the cover. And…this one for illustrations inside. I figure we'll have an illustration top of each canto. And one big one at the copyright page. Do we get a copyright page?

ISABELLA: Do we need copyright?

ARTURO: I don't know. No I don't think we need copyright.

ISABELLA: I think we need copyright. If it's a professional release it must have copyright.

ARTURO: Now look at this drawing here. Fug I should've scanned these. I have to get the bus in ten minutes, now I can only scan it over the weekend. You know what I'll just take a picture.

ISABELLA: My madre can scan it.

ARTURO: Your mother? She's helping too? Look at this version. It's cleaner.

ISABELLA: She's typing up the book into a word doc. Since you only write on your phone it has to be retyped before I find someone to format it.

ARTURO: Do you think it's too late to make some changes to canto three?

ISABELLA: Well — it's already typed, but I suppose—

Carbon Pages

ARTURO: I think we can copy this, or maybe I'll sketch it.

ISABELLA: She's made a lot of progress. She's up to the spider carcass decaying in the chamber of the young King.

ARTURO: It reminds me of the Paradise Lost engravings.

Boring and Broke in Buenos Aries

ISABELLA: She's so efficient, I think, because she doesn't speak English, my madre.

ARTURO: Uh-huh.

ISABELLA: My mother would really like to meet you.

ARTURO: Yeah, yeah. I had this thought the way over: what if instead of having just one possum transformation, I double it into two?

ISABELLA: She could have you over for dinner — maybe Friday? Are you allergic to anything?

ARTURO: Not allergic, but I once threw up after eating too many pistachios. How much for this little box?

ISABELLA: Sorry?

ARTURO: This little box—

ISABELLA: That's a snuff box. I think it's — I can check — let me check —

ARTURO: My grandfather came back with one of these after he served.

ISABELLA: It's probably 35 thousand. Give or take.

ARTURO: He ended up gifting his box to a bricklayer who frequented this bodega.

ISABELLA: You want it—?

ARTURO: —When I was very young I took note of him. Each time the bricklayer spoke his tongue made a clicking sound at interspersed 's' sounds. Cuz of a childhood inflammation from which he never recovered. To this day, when I hear the consonant I think of him.

ISABELLA: I noticed it in your writing.

ARTURO: ...Did you?

ISABELLA: Yes.

ARTURO: (*worried*) ...How so?

Carbon Pages

ISABELLA: Well each time the vassus talks he omits words that would usually have that s sound. Like, instead of "shrouded in darkness" he says — you write — shrouded in cthonia.

ARTURO: Oh yes. That reminds me...never mind, I lost my train of—

ISABELLA: Does it take long to think of these things?

ARTURO: (*shy*) Oh — uh — ...sometimes.

ISABELLA: I think *all* of the dialogue is quite brilliant, and my favorite is canto thirteen. It's like poetry, I find it really beautiful, don't you?

ARTURO: It depends.

ISABELLA: My favorite line is *"And faces of adobe and slate— lick their fingers, bite their nails the seven phalanxes they shred their thighs"*. Phalanxes. Did you read that somewhere?

ARTURO: I don't remember.

ISABELLA: I wish I knew more about writing and books and such, too much of it goes over my head, and, and canto thirteen is my favorite, my mother added some breaks between sentences, and also—

ARTURO: —What??

ISABELLA: What?

ARTURO: What do you mean breaks?

ISABELLA: Oh no, it's nothing. It's just some sentences were going for so long that she threw in a comma here, a semi-colon there.

ARTURO: Threw in? Who did?

ISABELLA: My mother.

ARTURO: Why did she do that?

ISABELLA: To make it easier to type. And I think it flows more smoothl—

ARTURO: How — but that's not what I wrote—

ISABELLA: —Yes but—

ARTURO: —Is she typing right now?

Boring and Broke in Buenos Aries

ISABELLA: My mother?

ARTURO: Yes! Your mother!

ISABELLA: Well it's after her nap. So I suppose so.

ARTURO: I gotta see her!

ISABELLA: Right now?

ARTURO: Yes, right now! I can't have her salt and peppering semi-colons higgldy piggldy. It's — I mean — Lord help me — it's a Violation!

ISABELLA: (*deathstruck*) I didn't know it was so bad.

ARTURO: It's not your fault — *Dios mio* — if I wanted to write shorter sentences I would write shorter sentences. Please take me, I have to see your mother, open that door, I'm sorry Isabella but take me to her I feel sick right now I feel sick.

> Inside Napoles one felt almost at home when the waiter spoke to you English with a smile and the interiors felt like you were in a French brasserie. It was a rich place with good food which came on white plates dressed in stripes of black, black balsamic.
>
> The seats were ribbed leather and the walls were lacquered with inlays all around which reflected the lustre light in the way table no. 12's candle flames might reflect in gooey lava cake. Table twelve! Table twelve? You dumb veneca bitch why would you change their order half way through?! Good lighting. Rather than aspirants Napoles kept a diet of entrepreneurs, businessmen and foreign spendthrifts. Meal of the day was some sort of fish.

PARKER: (*looking at menus*) Look at this — they don't even write the prices anymore.

MARQUIS: Changes every day.

PARKER: Are you eating?

MARQUIS: If you want I can pay for your meal.

PARKER: That's not what I was asking.

Carbon Pages

...Have you heard that beetles make up 85 percent of all animals on earth?

MARQUIS: Some time I really did not eat for 4 months. I was in school. It goes away the hunger because you start eating yourself. Then it comes back when there's nothing left. I was very hungry — it was painful. I lie awake and think of McDonalds. So my mother cooks a massive meal and I decide to break my fast. So she lays in front of me a plate — and I'm starving. The smell — just the smell — of peels in the trash — smells so good it gives me a headache. On my plate is fish and aubergine. The fish is cooked safely. There's no chance of worms. It's *crowded* together with the vegetables. When no one's looking I throw it in the trash and that night I gorge on stale Tuc crackers until I am full...
It would have been very passable...

PARKER: (*looking distantly*) Oh no...

MARQUIS: What?

PARKER: Look. Look behind you.

> Marquis looked. A ragged hobo had made his way inside and from a young couple's table he snatched a drink and, quite naturally, downed it without thought before returning it.

PARKER: Actually don't look.

MARQUIS: You know him?

PARKER: I do actually. That's Boris.

> The hobo at the bar was reamed in dirt, blots on his knees, dust up to his brows, and stinking of stewed sweat.

PARKER: Russian. Barmy, totally gone. (laughing) He threw a bottle of urine at me.

MARQUIS: Lots of Russians in this city.

PARKER: Not like him. Back home he was on Forbes top one hundred. Something to do with nickel — I guess there's money in nickel. He had a "European maschina" airlifted in his penthouse. As an icebreaker, mind you.

MARQUIS: What's a maschina?

Boring and Broke in Buenos Aries

PARKER: Like a Ferrari...

So Ukraine kicks off. He says something stupid about the war. I think his mistress had just swallowed a bottle of pills or some such. So he makes a blab. Putin doesn't like it. Suddenly he's under investigation for some hookers he buggered in 2004 and his company's shares are sold to the government for a "mutually equitable sum".

MARQUIS: That's HIM? I swear I passed him before...

PARKER: (chuckling) The Kremlin's leading crackhead-in-exile — I MEAN — critic in exile.

MARQUIS: This is the issue with you. You have no empathy for people. Me, I'm sure I've given him money.

PARKER: Maybe.

    Boris approached. Marquis buried his face in the menu.

MARQUIS: Where's the waiter?

PARKER: The world needs more maniacs. What's the matter, Marquis? You look nervous.

MARQUIS: (*to Parker*) Don't stare. It's none of our business.

PARKER: (*greeting*) Boris.

BORIS: Parkin.

PARKER: (*excited*) Parker, actually.

BORIS: You're American?

PARKER: From the UK.

BORIS: Ah. I...*love*...ze English. Sherlock Holmes. Robin Hood, eh? Shakira.

PARKER: Shakira isn't English.

BORIS: I know. Listen, Park—

MARQUIS: (*Spanish*) —[Good evening. Excuse me for not being in a talkative mood. Unfortunately my English is very poor and—]

Carbon Pages

PARKER: Have a seat, Boris.

Boris sat.

PARKER: This is my friend. He's an autistic savant. He won Mongolia's national maths tournament last year, but was disqualified after having sex with his dog. *Ponjatna?* They don't take kindly to faggots... They're just not as tolerant as we are. Eh, that's not to demean *Russia* by any means! I'm sure YOU'RE satisfied with the current political situation over there right Boris? Right?

BORIS: (*sigh*) It's depressing topic...

PARKER: My friend says he gets his skills from watching those sex island shows on Netflix. He doesn't really understand the words but he likes the titties.

BORIS: My friends. I want to apologize for in any way making you feel uncomfortable or otherwise unsafe in my presence. If ever I take money from you, I must pay back you. My condition necessitated this be that as it may but there is no excuse for miserliness.

PARKER: No, please it's alright—

BORIS: And too I need get hold of a phone.

PARKER: Oh — I left mine—

BORIS: I will not impose on you!

(to himself)
Oh I must make calls. There's a girl I know in Sochi. She finishes ski lessons around this time and I should make call.

PARKER: Well, if you *really* need it I have roaming—

BORIS: Oh but what am I saying skiing lessons — that was who knows how long ago. I need to shave this godemn beard.

PARKER: Who's this girl, Boris?

BORIS: She's a friend of mine, poor woman, I pay for rhinoplasty. Maybe she help *me*. I hope it won't be too forward. I need to ask her for a loan. Small loan. Few thousand. We kept in touch for a bit but — ah — I stink like a bomzh.

Boring and Broke in Buenos Aries

Marquis ate scallops on a plate.

PARKER: Oh, Boris, look! You like scallops don't you? Try some!

Marquis deathstruck.

BORIS: No thanks. They give me indigestion.

Silence...silence...

PARKER: Boris, tell me something. Have you been taking something? Seeing someone?

BORIS: What mean?

PARKER: Nothing — just that you seem to be in a better way since I last saw you.

BORIS: Really?

PARKER: You look good. You're very lucid.

BORIS: I don't feel — *lucid.* I feel like I have *shit* under *fingernails.*

PARKER: Time was you thought fingernails were a FSB psyop.

BORIS: Now that you mention to me, it feel like I've been in coma for eight months and I finally wake up and someone dressed me in this silly rags and let my nails grow.

MARQUIS: (*to Boris*) What changed?

BORIS: I thought you were a Spaniard?

PARKER: He's a frog.

BORIS: What changed. I don't know. I was going about day. I sell flowers. I feed pigeons (TVOO — TVARI!). I take shovel and dig deep hole.

Parker chuckled and Marquis found himself joining.

BORIS: Tvoo, I don't wish to talk of it. I seem like clown.

MARQUIS: Maybe it was the digging.

Carbon Pages

PARKER: Sure — it triggered something.

BORIS: Vwat-evar.

PARKER: Whatever it was, it worked like a charm.

MARQUIS: We have a confused friend. He lost his manuscript and we're finding it for him. Have you seen it?

BORIS: No.

PARKER: You need to retrace your steps.

BORIS: What is manuscript?

MARQUIS: He develops video games in his spare time. He writes everything out on paper.

BORIS: Ah — No I haven't seen. I'm sorry for your friend. I hate losing things.

MARQUIS: I'd never write anything on paper. It's self-indulgent.

BORIS: You are a writer?

MARQUIS: I'm a playwright. But my new work is safely locked up. (*taps head*)

PARKER: Very good.

BORIS: (*discovering thousand peso note*) I think I *will* have a meal actually. Waiter, please.

PARKER: You have to be louder. Waiter!

MARQUIS: (*on Parker*) It's this one I'm worried about.

PARKER: Yes, yes.

MARQUIS: It's true. You have remarkable potential, and you're wasting it.

BORIS: Interesting.

MARQUIS: Take *Dynasty Overdrive* for example, it reads like a banal movie written in a day.

BORIS: Really? Parker you never strike me as the banal sort.

MARQUIS: Very unfortunate.

BORIS: Vwy is it like this?

Boring and Broke in Buenos Aries

PARKER: Oh bloody hell.

MARQUIS: Parker dreams of being so famous that he doesn't need to write anymore. It's the mindset of a repair man, don't you think? His writing is rapidly degrading so he publishes a dozen books a year like he's playing scratch cards what do you make of that?

BORIS: Parker is that true?

PARKER: I—

BORIS: (*to Marquis*) It's been so long since I've read a GOOD BOOK.

MARQUIS: You're a big reader?

BORIS: Yes I like...Emily Henry. Happy Place.

PARKER: Marquis, I didn't ask for your advice.

MARQUIS: I think you should listen to those with more experience than you is all. So withdrawn.

BORIS: (*distracted*) Exactly; each man can stand to be more humble. Ah yes — (*to waiter*) — I have cream cappellacci, and lemon bavaroise. And the Milanesa de bif de chorizo and very well done. Please — no spices. And please a glass of tereré to wash this down.

WAITER: Mint or mango?

BORIS: Mint.

MARQUIS: Can you believe it, first time I met him, Parker swore his life goal was to win a Nebula.

BORIS: Really? Oh my God! I just remember Zagarov owes me that favour. What is your name?

MARQUIS: Marquis.

BORIS: Marquis, I'm a new man. You know, first thing I do once get out of here is have relaxing sauna and exfoliation.

PARKER: I can't believe I — I shouldn't even be here.

Carbon Pages

MARQUIS: He's angry because I'm right! Before it's too late return to your craft its eros. We are living in a post-movie world. One cannot write movies. it's TikTok world. I'm trying to save you before you end up writing tiktoks!

PARKER: (*standing up*) I'm leaving.

MARQUIS: So you don't care about your art? You simply want to sell books? Not even for money but for prestige. Of whom? And you look at me and think "he's content with perfecting his form and having his circle read it. That's enough for him. He's crazy."

PARKER: So I want to sell. So I want people to know about my work. What of it? You don't want to be big because you have nothing to say! You think you do — but you have nothing to say — If you did, you'd want Everyone to know. You'd yell it from the rooftops, from the balcony. You'd tell anyone who'd listen, you'd make connections to get it out there, you'd spend your days with idiots and bellends. *You don't even write.* There isn't a single person who's buying what you're selling.

MARQUIS: Calm down.

PARKER: (*yelling*) No one in this bloody damn city actually writes. All they do is suck down lattes and fernets and roasts and whatever else. All they do is talk and talk about what great ideas they have and all the things they'll do once they make it now let's go whoring Parker. Just once — just ONCE — I'd like to spend a quiet evening at home — in a LIVING ROOM if I had one. All I have is an old bitch calling the gorra at the slightest. All I have. That's all I own except that one bloody damn seat at Guebara. And even THEN someone's taken it.

The good ones don't stay here. Say, I don't know, look at Arturo — *he's* not gonna stick around here long. The ones worth a damn leave.

BORIS: My friend please — people are staring.

MARQUIS: Sit down.

PARKER: Well you've dragged me down enough. I'm leaving. This is the last time I want to see you two.

And Parker was gone.

Boring and Broke in Buenos Aries

MARQUIS: (*to Boris*) So. He is pissed off and he takes it out on us.

BORIS: A fiery man!

MARQUIS: He should go see his girl.

BORIS: Yes.

MARQUIS: But don't take it out on me.

BORIS: I agree.

MARQUIS: This reminds me of Leopold — I see him at Dorrego — he's a copywriter. One time, so he tells, he comes to a girl and says I am a male prostitute. You pay 100 dollars. American. The prostitute says to him no I charge 80. Okay, says Leopold, in that case you only pay 20.

BORIS: Oh haha, yes, well. Good play.

MARQUIS: Yes...

BORIS: I had some crazy nights like this.

MARQUIS: I bet they would let you get away with murder, no?

BORIS: ...I don't understand? I have massive respect for sex workers...

MARQUIS: I didn't mean by this—

BORIS: —And there is much misinformation out there on this topic. It's a multi-faceted issue. It important to remember to stop spread of misinformation.

MARQUIS: Hm...Boris — something odd that has been happening to me. Recently, each time I get into a taxi late in the evening, or in fact any time I am speaking to a stranger, be it to the grocer or Caballo barman. I say to them lies. At first I only sprinkled them in here and there, like I change my name from Marquis to Marquez or say I live in Palermo instead of San Telmo. Then they start growing and growing — like plants — I start watering them, no? I am Heraldo from Xianping, China or Alfonso the crypto millionaire from Bermuda who owns a private submarine company. I'm a new man.
Suddenly I exit a taxi, and I am a total fabrication.

BORIS: I don't understand.

Carbon Pages

MARQUIS: It's good exercise. In the end everyone wears a mask. And the thing that encouraged me most is no one ever catches on that I'm lying. Now, sometimes I call an Uber simply because I feel the urge to be someone else. It is an inexorable addiction.

BORIS: I do not follow.

MARQUIS: It's an addiction.

BORIS: (*not really getting it*) Oh. That's funny.
...But you know you shouldn't do stuff like this. It hurt people's feelings if they ever find out. It could be disorder. I do not think there is anything wrong with this — but just so you know.

MARQUIS: Alright... (*about Parker*) I'm glad he's gone. What a midwit.

BORIS: Here's what I don't understand. And I have seen only you together for a little bit, but you and Parker are friends?

MARQUIS: When he's not so stubborn.

BORIS: That brings me to next point. You seem to despise each other. You seem like you cannot *stand* each other.

MARQUIS: Yes?

BORIS: I mean, you are gay and he calls you a faggot — how can you stand such a person?

MARQUIS: We see the same people.

BORIS: It sounds like they are all like this!

MARQUIS: You can't get away from someone. A city is a hundred little villages.

BORIS: I would get NEW friends.

MARQUIS: He does grind my gears.

BORIS: What?

MARQUIS: It's an expression — to grind gears.

BORIS: Zer you go.

MARQUIS: You know what I do?

Boring and Broke in Buenos Aries

BORIS: What?

MARQUIS: For work — do you know what I do?

BORIS: What do you do, my friend?

MARQUIS: I resolve queries. I used to tutor English a little on the side but now with the apps — not anymore. My manager doesn't care where I am, as long as I put the hours in. (*seeing Boris's confusion,*)
(*miming*) With the — calling — yes — ok...
It drains me. I *despise* the people I talk to. I hate them...And it's mutual I am sure! If eve—

BORIS: —Striking a balance between responsibilities and mental health is crucial for long-term well-being.

MARQUIS: ...Anyway...what was I saying...Anyway the people — with the killing time — like Parker.
(*searching for words*)
Half of them are fascists or just deplorable or have a widely incorrect interpretation of Dasein or something...
(*searching for drift*)
But at least they *know* what Dasein is.
...Oui?

BORIS: I suppose. Still at some point, you must love yourself.

MARQUIS: Oui.

> Now Marquis was regretting the whole moment, as well as his startup capital in it.

MARQUIS: (*bored*) Shall we get some fernets?

BORIS: Let's get vwild! Well actually...hm — no, no. I not wanting to risk a headache. Just a nice terare for me. Not too sweet. Let's wait for my food to be ready.

MARQUIS: Okay. (*checks phone*)

> A man trapped.

Carbon Pages

Into Isabella's Pawn Shop entered Isabella and Arturo.

ARTURO: ...So he turns to the cow and says... "Madame!".

ISABELLA: (*giggling*) Ha...and the cow...

Arturo leaned over the counter on the interior side.

ISABELLA: It's so nice to spend some time, yknow, not thinking about Business with a capital B.

ARTURO: (*from behind counter*) POV: you're you.

ISABELLA: You know it'll be three months tomorrow since we started working the book?

ARTURO: I didn't realize.

Isabella picked up an envelope by the door, read it and crumpled it discreetly.

ARTURO: What's that?

ISABELLA: It's nothing.

ARTURO: Before I forget; I have to tell you this. A Spanish-English side-by-side. It's already translated from the Spanish in the first place so it's no sweat. A side-by-side type of thing on the one page. What's it called, like they do in the Bible?

ISABELLA: Double columning?

ARTURO: Yes! Double columning!

ISABELLA: Artie—

ARTURO: I'm shaking just thinking of it. It'll be gorgeous, I mean really gorgeous.

But Isabella was despondent.

ARTURO: What's the matter, it means we'll get double the clientele won't it? That's a good thing ain't it? Is it the letter? Isabella?

Boring and Broke in Buenos Aries

Swapping counter positions.

ISABELLA: It's just — the whole thing — the shop. It's so much.

ARTURO: What is it?

ISABELLA: A man defaulted his DeWalt saw. A year he's been paying vig on it. Now it's come off and we own it.

ARTURO: What's that mean?

ISABELLA: It means the shop was getting fifty thousand pesos a week. We lost that and I'm stuck owning a saw!

ARTURO: So? Isn't that a good thing? Now you can sell it. That's how business works, my dear Izzy.

ISABELLA: Except I can't. Apparently this whole time it didn't have a guard or something and I'm not allowed to sell it. *Regulaciones de seguridad* — they're really strict on this stuff!

ARTURO: It's OK…

ISABELLA: What am I going to — between this — and keeping the lights on — and the rent — and the advertisements — and that typist. I mean I know we had to hire her.

ARTURO: It's alright…Izzy..

ISABELLA: I *know* we had to hire her. But did you *have* to be so rash with that whole thing with my mother? Couldn't you have given her another chance?

ARTURO: But you volunteered… I thought—

ISABELLA: I *know*. I mean — I don't know — you're right — I don't know *what* I'm complaining about. It's not *your* fault. Why couldn't he have just — gotten things in order.

ARTURO: Who—

ISABELLA: Papa. Why did he have to — just hoist all of this on me. If he had just — taken the time to get his affairs in order. *I* didn't ask for all this.

ARTURO: Isabella.

Carbon Pages

ISABELLA: All his baggage? Now I'm the one stuck with it because he had to go and...

ARTURO: Izzy — Isabella — if you can't afford the typist — then — you know what — I say — let her go. Let her go. I can finish it myself. I'll have to learn some...and I'll finish the interior. I did the artwork didn't I?

ISABELLA: I don't — we can't let her go now.

ARTURO: And the double columning. I can do the double columning myself too. Of course I'll need to use your computer—

ISABELLA: (*tearing up*) Double columning?

ARTURO: Yes, the Spanish-English side-by-side. Also, I was thinking of maybe changing the colour of the binding to a darker green. I know you said it's set in stone but if we make it more shamrock and less viridian then it evokes the quality of a maize stalk and makes the whole thing prettier. Listen, Isabella. You're brilliant. I won't let you be down. Being with you — it's like — ever since I met you you're a magnet for ideas. Being in this state — it's like a cracked dry clay tablet with notched panels for each thought and concept and now whenever I think of one of these symbols it's like it gets lushed and watered and though it takes a while piece by piece the entire mosaic is dark and wet and alive at duress only by the time takes me to cognize it.

ISABELLA: Really?

ARTURO: EVERYONE knows I'd be NOWHERE without you. I've been recommending you left right and center!

ISABELLA: You... what?

ARTURO: You're gonna be a massive publishing house. My friend Melman. Humphrey? Parker?? I'm just a puny button in your cap. You're gunna have *so much* business like you wouldn't *dream*. You'll publish LIBRARIES of authors.

ISABELLA: Libraries...

Yes, my dear Isabella; Arturo is in love with his book.

Boring and Broke in Buenos Aries

ARTURO: Now stand up...stand up. I'll start work tonight. Just tell me what to do.

ISABELLA: Start work?

ARTURO: Yes.

ISABELLA: Artie...

She composed herself.

ISABELLA: A Spanish translation will double the manuscript's word count.

ARTURO: It's oka—

ISABELLA: Double the word count means I'll have to shrink the text by at least half to compensate and that means for my part a total reworking of the margins and gutter size for the text to not be buried in the crease.

ARTURO: What about the binding? I still think the binding should be darker—

ISABELLA: Altering the binding means AT LEAST a week of back and forth with manufacturing which means calling Elaine and delaying the launch—

ARTURO: —I don't care about the launch. I just want the binding changed. Viridian is ugly as—

ISABELLA: —As your editor, as your publisher and finally as your accountant I'm telling you; You can't afford shamrock binding. You can't afford ANY thread sewn binding. MAYBE I won't go as far as glue—

ARTURO: —Glue is cheaper?

ISABELLA: ...IN EXCHANGE for taking out that bloody dithering illustration on page seventeen AND changing the paper from cream to eggshell.

ARTURO: Isabella...I can't remove the Beelzebub illustration...

ISABELLA: Then no cigar.

ARTURO: Fine, make it black and white.

ISABELLA: Sorry. Best I can do.

Carbon Pages

ARTURO: Wait, OK. Wait. Fine — Ok. Count out the illustration, and the cream, but change that font to Garamond.

ISABELLA: To Dante, AND you do that podcast.

ARTURO: ...

ISABELLA: ...

ARTURO: Fine. Ok.

ISABELLA: Deal.

> Then there was the smell of hot metal when the ingénue stepped into the evening orange. And he stood for a while looking at the clouds and eventually he thought there must be things in this world greater than him which were a mystery and will be mysterious forever. And then

BORIS: Little boy! Boy, over here!

ARTURO: Me?

BORIS: Yes come here.

ARTURO: The Russian. I thought you were better. I'm sorry — I've no change.

BORIS: I am better.

ARTURO: Then why are you digging a hole in the street?

BORIS: Come here. Listen to me. (*stops digging. Then immediately starts again.*) I need you to fetch me a coke.

ARTURO: Digging's got you thirsty, huh.

BORIS: Have money in back pocket. Reach in and grab. Like Freddy Mercury. Can't stop.

ARTURO: I thought your head was all fixed. Someone said you're all better.

BORIS: I am.

ARTURO: But—

BORIS: I got better once I start digging hole. God help me why. But the moment I leave, I feel my mind go muddy, go back to how I was.

Boring and Broke in Buenos Aries

ARTURO: That's very odd, chamo.

BORIS: I *refuse* to lose myself again!

ARTURO: So...

BORIS: So I have to keep digging.

ARTURO: *How long* will you keep digging this hole?

BORIS: (in existential terror) I... don't know!

ARTURO: Alright (*backing away*) Well—

BORIS: Wait.

ARTURO: I'm meant to be somewhere.

BORIS: Come back!

ARTURO: I'm already late (*far away*)

> Boris dropped his shovel and chased the boy for a second, before remembering his situation and surrendering to the hole promptly.

BORIS: I'm...so afraid.

> At El Caballo, nomads mingled with porteños. The wealthy brushed shoulders with scalpers, aspirants, sexpats. Deep into the night when all were drunk no one would have any idea who they were talking to or which table was theirs. Depraved little hole. The hookers in the corner scanning for prey. Management with the blind eye to smoking. Whole place had the aroma of cigarettes.

> The night was moloda but on the down and Marquis sat at a table with Agnes who drank white wine, and with Melman who drank a kiwi cocktail. A glass of sauvignon cost $1.45 but I pay for the atmosphere you know it's like I pay for the atmosphere. Agnes liked strawberries with wine, but they did not serve strawberries at Caballo, not even frozen ones.

Carbon Pages

    Kley the rim of his fifth glass of vodka did finger at the lonely bar. This is the scene as it did materialize.

MELMAN: I got this idea for a universe. It's half medieval and half— hell what am I explaining this for? I'm drunk.

MARQUIS: You want to publish this?

MELMAN: Publish? I got better things to do.

MARQUIS: For yourself then?

    He did that hand swipe thing that Livia Soprano would do.

MELMAN: Use your brain, man. Why would I write it if no one's gonna see it? It's lore, man. No one's gonna pick that up.

MARQUIS: Well when you *write* it, I will read it. I will give you my thoughts.

MELMAN: (*smiling*) Your thoughts. (*loses it*) Who knows what you'll do to it, man. Who knows. Agnes, say I come to you and tell you I'll give feedback on your "*stuff*". Would you take that offer?

AGNES: I don't write, but no I would not.

MELMAN: Why not?

AGNES: (*coyly*) Because you might steal it.

MELMAN: See? And what is it you do again?

AGNES: I draw.

MARQUIS: She draws.

MELMAN: What do you draw?

AGNES: Oh don't get me started.

MARQUIS: Don't get her started, Melman.

MELMAN: What? C'mon whaddaya draw?

AGNES: Landscapes. For money: porn.

MELMAN: Porn?

Boring and Broke in Buenos Aries

AGNES: (*inhaling smoke*) Furry porn.

MELMAN: People pay money for that?

AGNES: (*exhaling*) Commissions. Lots. It's just for a short while. I'm saving. Another month or two and I'm done with all that. I'm saving.

MELMAN: Fuckin gyp. See what I mean?

> The longer Marquis looked at Melman the more he seemed like a police sketch. Wiry ungroomed eyebrows on the kind of man David Letterman once described as the type you'd see sleeping on a bus. Bags under the eyes. Short and recessed in every way a man *can* be recessed. New fat on old muscles on a small frame.

> At this moment Arturo met the table.

MARQUIS: Good evening Artie.

ARTURO: Sup.

> Artie sat next to Agnes...

AGNES: Hey Artie.

> ...who ruffled his hair.

MELMAN: The age of the Kali Yuga is upon us.

> That perpetual hoarseness — Melman always spoke like he had thirty years of dust bunnies built up in his throat.

MELMAN: Artist, writer. It's all pointless. There's nothing to write about no more. Everyone has the same boring life, man. The same blue screen childhood followed by 8 hours of school. That's your early twenties right there. Then wageslave till you die leap frogging from Netflix show to videogame.

MARQUIS: And I agree with you.

MELMAN: Just use your head. Before World War 2 there were young men writing everywhere all the time and people were reading them.

Carbon Pages

MARQUIS: It was better then.

MELMAN: But now everything is solved. There's no reason to read. Nothing happens.

Not that you can earn a cent. Back in the day you could live in a loft cranking out shit. If you were poor you could be notorious. Or at least you'd have some rich layabout to patronize you. Who's gonna patronize me, man? We got all these billionaires and they only care about their bottom line. That's it, just money. *The billionaires care about their money. The writers care about nothing. And the publishers are sodomite negrophiles.* Biedermeier Two. What the hell is even a short story anymore? The written word is dead. This gay world killed it and then invented AIDs to kill the audience and then sent in the termites. Everyone's gotta be the same now. Everyone's gotta have the same shitty education where you read 2-bit niggers and women. We used to have mentors, man. Now — you know I can't stand Pound. I loathe Pound but uh...what was I saying...but Pound was mentored by Yeats and then Pound took under his wing some other canaanite. I mean uh what the hell. Everyone's too busy stacking shelves to take anyone under their wing now. That's it. A thousand year chain has been severed. Damn I'm drunk.

AGNES: Have you tried smiling more?

MELMAN: I'll smile when I got something to smile about, man. The Greeks never laughed. There's no record of it before around 1700. I can tell exactly which of you are morons just by lookin atcha cause you smile *too much*. You can tell a whole lot about a person just by looking at them. (*drunk*) I'm so sick— makes me wanna puke this crap about don't judge a book by its cover.

MARQUIS: You've said this before.

MELMAN: I say judge EVERYONE *only* by their cover. Good looking people own this world for a reason. As they should.

AGNES: Melman, if we're judging people by their appearance I'd hate to know what that says about you.

MELMAN: I — are you kidding — Look at me. I'm nowhere, I'm in the dogs. Use your brain; Ugly people — uh — are *skunks*!

Carbon Pages

At this Melman's interlocutors had a good laugh.

MELMAN: Yeah.
...Yeah...

MARQUIS: (*to Arturo*) So, what have you been up to?

ARTURO: Nothing really.

MARQUIS: Mhm.

ARTURO: You?

MARQUIS: This and that.

A moment.

MARQUIS: Let's go to Guebara. They're just getting started and I believe we should go to Guebara.

ARTURO: I just sat down.

AGNES: Artie's right Guebara is a walk. Now that's a walk.

ARTURO: Guebara's winding down.

MARQUIS: No, Guebara's beginning!

ARTURO: What time is it?

AGNES: Ten to twelve.

ARTURO: I don't like Guebara it's a walk.

AGNES: How about Derillo?

MARQUIS: Derillo disagrees.

ARTURO: What's wrong with this place?

AGNES: Let's get food.

MARQUIS: It's a snooze.

ARTURO: We'll never find a table. Why do we have to go somewhere?

AGNES: Maybe Rom is at Guebara.

Boring and Broke in Buenos Aries

ARTURO: Rom don't come out.

MARQUIS: The night is young.

ARTURO: We could try Derillo.

MARQUIS: I don't like Derillo.

> Of well-renowned Argentinian meat the chain of supply is massive and, says a recent evaluation, is comparable to the scale of the 13th century's Dvaraka–Kamboja road. When Marquis eats, he raises his hand. When Arturo eats, he lowers his head.

AGNES: Actually, boys — I should head home. I'm pooped. I'm worried my roaches are missing me.

> And she did.
>
> Three blind mice were left at the table.

MARQUIS: (*to Arturo*) Did you know molluscs compose 85 percent of all organisms on Earth?

ARTURO: ...No.

MELMAN: What time is it?

MARQUIS: It's—

ARTURO: —Look it's Parker.

> True enough, the stubborn Parker approached the bar, not seeing Melman, Arturo, or Marquis.

PARKER: Kley. Hey Kley. Hey.

KLEY: Huh?

PARKER: It's me.

KLEY: Leave me alone.

PARKER: How are you? I've a gift.

Carbon Pages

Parker looked at Kley, and then down to what he was holding. Then Kley — he looked at Parker and then down at what he was holding. For the gargantuan security guard all time stopped. He sobered, and then the evening's drink hit all at once.

KLEY: Where?

PARKER: I popped by the chemists', uh, the pharmacy. Man there said someone left it on the zinc rack.

Kley took the thick pink ring binder from Parker's hands. From the table one felt a strange sense that he could just as soon wring his neck.

KLEY: (*embracing Parker*) I'll never take it out my sight.
I'll never take it out my sight. Never, ever, ever. I'll buy you a drink. I don't like to drink, it's bad for the liver. It's bad for the pores, but let me buy you a drink.

PARKER: Buy me a drink, and I'll buy you a drink.

The table was staring so Parker approached.

PARKER: Melman. Artie. Marquis.

From name to name there was no change of tone which struck the *coup de crayon* as odd. The cumbia now was loud as hell.

MARQUIS: Seat?

PARKER: Okay.

MARQUIS: I thought you said you never would see us again.

PARKER: Yes, well. I went home. I went home and I put some words down. For a few hours I wrote and they were fairly not bad. Then I went to get some...equipment...at the chemist. And that paragraph's as good as it's gonna get, until tomorrow. So until tomorrow... Anyway, what happened while I was gone?

ARTURO: Not much.

MELMAN: Thinking where we should go after this.

Boring and Broke in Buenos Aries

MARQUIS: More drinks por favor.

> Generate for me a triptych, gesso, of four foreigners at a San Telmo table. One biting his nails maybe, or thinking how to relieve a toe rash...

MELMAN: Parker, avoid Leopold. He's scalping people.

PARKER: I know — He got me this morning.

MARQUIS: Un relleno, por favor!

> ...Around them a school of raconteurs here and there in a series of walls now yelling, now drinking, leg on chair, arm on shoulder...

PARKER: What about Derillo?

> ...The smell of thunder gathering or maybe it'll pass and an old landlady in the mid of night pulling in the laundry from the balcony, and a girl on the barrio footpath in plastic chair with the sense that life will never recover, and a cat in the tiled antespace tween iron bars and door. Hot ventilation streaming out into the cool night. Bums bouling on the Plata. Generate Diodati on the rocks. The hashish club as streetsweeper. The feeling of cold drinks. Of pulling a rug under your knees. The smell of emulsified tallow on a butcher's knife. Ships hauling forth. There's a dirty official around here somewhere, and as he's waiting for his coffee he's calculating how best to rename his town rococo so it sounds more Second Empire and then his coffee is brought by a girl in a tanktop. At the Grand Splendid a million eradicants, humanity exterminated a thousand times down. Adendum Operandi: Portrait of a city en tango.

The End.

Daniel Gavilovski

Carbon Pages

Daniel Gavilovski is a Russian-Irish playwright and author. He currently resides in Daugavpils, Latvia. You can contact him at danielgavilovski@gmail.com.

theunrealpress.com

www.ingramcontent.com/pod-product-compliance
Lightning Source LLC
LaVergne TN
LVHW091547070526
838199LV00024B/568/J